TEN BLOCKS FROM THE WHITE HOUSE

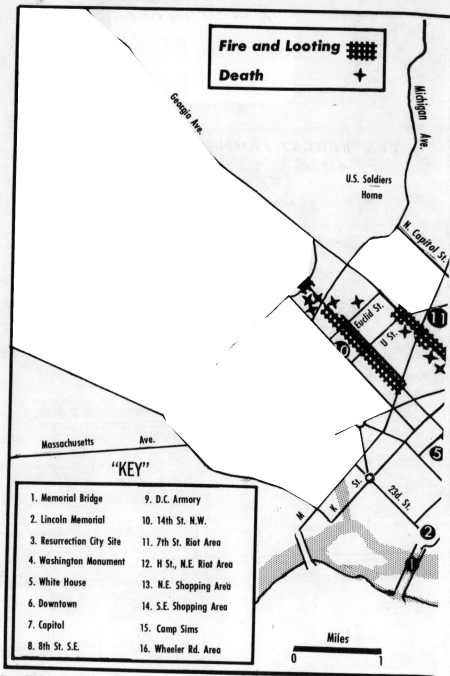

Fire and Looting

Death

Georgia Ave.

Michigan Ave.

U.S. Soldiers Home

N. Capitol St.

Euclid St.

U St.

Massachusetts Ave.

"KEY"

1. Memorial Bridge	9. D.C. Armory
2. Lincoln Memorial	10. 14th St. N.W.
3. Resurrection City Site	11. 7th St. Riot Area
4. Washington Monument	12. H St., N.E. Riot Area
5. White House	13. N.E. Shopping Area
6. Downtown	14. S.E. Shopping Area
7. Capitol	15. Camp Sims
8. 8th St. S.E.	16. Wheeler Rd. Area

M St.

K St.

23d. St.

Miles

0   1

Detailed maps of riot areas and police precincts follow Page 44.

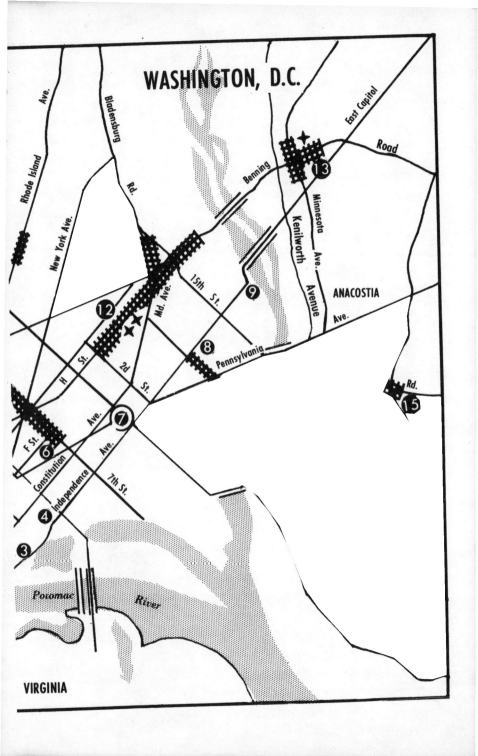

Ten Blocks from the White House

Anatomy of the Washington Riots of 1968

Ben W. Gilbert
AND THE STAFF OF
The Washington Post

FREDERICK A. PRAEGER, *Publishers*
New York • Washington • London

FREDERICK A. PRAEGER, PUBLISHERS
111 Fourth Avenue, New York, N.Y. 10003, U.S.A.
5, Cromwell Place, London S.W.7, England
Published in the United States of America in 1968
by Frederick A. Praeger, Inc., Publishers

Library of Congress Catalog Card Number: 68–8903

Printed in the United States of America

To two newspapermen
EUGENE MEYER, 1875–1959
PHILIP L. GRAHAM, 1915–1963

Foreword

"All we wants is that we get our story told, and get it told right! What we do last night, maybe it wasn't right. But ain't nobody come down here and listen to us before."—FROM *Rivers of Blood, Years of Darkness*, BY ROBERT CONOT.

Federal Communications Commissioner Nicholas Johnson has suggested that a riot is a form of communication.

"A riot is somebody talking," Commissioner Johnson has said. "A riot is a man crying out, 'Listen to me mister. There's something I've been trying to tell you and you're not listening.' "

What were the Washington rioters in April, 1968, trying to say? Were they simply angered by the untimely death of Dr. Martin Luther King, Jr., apparently at the hands of a white assassin? Or did they have something else to say to the city of Washington and the world at large?

How did they deliver the message, and how was it received? In fact, was it received?

And what was the reply? Was it the beginning of a dialogue or the end of a conversation that never really started?

What did the rioting—and its various patterns—mean? Why were particular areas burned down and not others? What about "the fire next time"?

This book does not attempt to provide complete answers to all these questions. It does endeavor to put together events, to seek patterns of action, and to reconstruct the background of the rioting to aid in an eventual assessment. The principal record it uses is the extensive reporting and photography by the staff of *The Washington Post* during the riot period and the weeks following.

More than 100 newsmen—reporters, photographers, and editors —participated in that coverage. Among them were veterans who had covered every major civil disorder in the United States since the Little Rock affair in 1957 and newsmen, familiar with the byways of the capital city, who had concentrated on reporting local problems. The group included fourteen Negro reporters and photographers, who helped correct the kinds of misjudgment that coverage of the black community by whites and for whites sometimes produces.

Two dozen reporters and one dozen photographers had roving assignments to stay with the action on the streets. They kept in touch with the newsroom from nine cruising, radio-equipped cars. Other newsmen covered key officials and their command centers.

Weeks after the events of those traumatic days in April, this entire staff went back to the officials, the eyewitnesses, and the participants to examine again, in depth, all aspects of the riot and to prepare this report. Documents from the newspaper's own reporting files, including a foot-thick pile of memos dictated by reporters from the radio cars, were checked against the records of the extensive hearings held by Congressional committees and the Washington City Council. Research, made available after the riot, on preriot attitudes of blacks and whites toward each other and toward rioting in Washington and other cities was analyzed. *The Washington Post* also prepared a computerized study of more than 850 persons arrested for serious offenses in the rioting to provide background information on typical participants. In August, a startling interview with three self-styled arsonists was obtained and added to the record.

In a few cases, the accounts turned in by *The Washington Post*'s newsmen differed in some significant respects from other journalistic accounts and official records. Because *The Washington Post* had covered the story in substantial strength, staffers were able to check and cross-check each other's notes. *The Washington Post* believes this account comes as close to the whole truth as is now possible.

In February, 1968, the National Advisory Commission on Civil Disorders, headed by the then Governor of Illinois Otto Kerner, suggested that the way riot news was selected and displayed might distort the nation's image of the disorders. Editors around the nation, the Kerner Commission said, "appear to have given more headline attention to riots occurring elsewhere than to those at home during the time of trouble in their own cities." The editors of *The Washington Post* share the Commission's belief that:

> It would be imprudent and even dangerous to downplay coverage in the hope that censored reporting of inflammatory incidents somehow will diminish violence. Once a disturbance occurs, the word will spread independently of newspapers and television. To attempt to ignore these events or portray them as something other than they are can only diminish confidence in the media and increase the effectiveness of those who monger rumors and the fears of those who listen.

The disturbances in Washington began shortly after 7 P.M., April 4, 1968, the time that the first reports of the shooting of Dr. King in Memphis were received on the wireroom teletypes of *The Washington Post.*

The first word was received from the United Press International in this form:

```
MEMPHIS, TENN. (UPI)--DR. MARTIN LUTHER KING JR.
WAS SHOT OUTSIDE A MEMPHIS HOTEL THURSDAY
AFTERNOON.  HIS CONDITION WAS NOT IMMEDIATELY
KNOWN.
```

Subsequently, Dr. King's death was announced in dispatches such as this one:

```
MEMPHIS, TENN. (UPI)--DR. MARTIN LUTHER KING JR.
WAS SHOT AND KILLED LATE THURSDAY AS HE STOOD
ALONE ON THE BALCONY OF HIS HOTEL.
```

In the newsroom of *The Washington Post,* the first bulletin produced an immediate reaction. An interracial team of reporters was dispatched to Memphis to cover the story. Simultaneously, reporter-photographer teams were sent into the streets of Washington to observe, at first hand, the city's reaction to the news from Tennessee.

The first bulletins left open the possibility that Dr. King's wounds could be superficial. The second report destroyed that hope and raised the question of the event's impact on America's fragile racial peace. For Washington, the question was quickly answered.

That night, there were these two eight-column headlines:

King Assassinated in Memphis
Shouting Crowds Smash Stores in District

14th Street Sealed Off; Fires Set

Tennessee Guard Ordered Into City; Sniper Is Hunted

MEMPHIS, April 4—The Rev. Dr. Martin Luther King Jr., a man who lived by nonviolence, was shot and killed tonight by a sniper as he stood alone on the balcony of a motel in Memphis.

Two white men were taken into custody, then released. Four others were sought.

President Johnson said on television that he was shocked and saddened by Dr. King's death. He appealed to the Nation to forgo further violence.

But there were a few scattered violence in Harlem and Negro sections of Washington, Boston, Birmingham, Ala., Jackson, Miss., Raleigh, N.C., and other cities.

In Memphis, authorities said rioting had broken out. Two policemen were injured and looting was "rampant," they said.

Gov. Buford Ellington immediately ordered 4000 National Guard troops back into Memphis, and by midnight the city was reported quiet.

Dr. King died in an act of senseless violence — victim of an assassin's bullet—as he prepared for the biggest test of his philosophy of nonviolence later this month.

The 39-year-old civil rights leader and Nobel Peace Prize winner was to lead a Poor People's Cam-

For the next three days, the local story occupied the lead position unchallenged:

6000 Troops Move Into District;
4 Dead in Day of Looting, Arson

Johnson Cancels His Trip

950 Are Arrested; Over 350 Injured; Curfew Imposed

91st Year · · · No. 124 · · · SUNDAY, APRIL 7, 1968 · · · Phone 223-6000 · · · 25c

11,600 Troops Enforce Curfew; Arrests Total 3263; Six Dead

**City Cracks Down
To Curb Disorder;
Fires Mount to 595**

91st Year · · · No. 125 · · · MONDAY, APRIL 8, 1968 · · · Phone 223-6000 · · · 10c

Calm Returning to Scarred City

**U.S. Troops Called
To Baltimore as
Fires, Looting Rise**

**Fires Dying Out,
Looting Declines,
Curfew Continues**

On the fifth day, the Washington story shared first position with nearby Baltimore, where violence had flared while the capital was quieting:

91st Year · · · No. 126 · · · TUESDAY, APRIL 9, 1968 · · · Phone 223-6000 · · · 10c

D.C. Quiet; Baltimore Looting Spreads
U.S. Receives Formal Hanoi Reply on Talks

**LBJ Acts
To Fix Site** **City Turns
To Relief**  **Sniping Reported
As Tension Grows**

For three days, as the city coped with serious rioting, and for the dozen days of its occupation by federal troops, reporters, photographers, and editors provided the newspaper's readers with the most complete, accurate, and meaningful account possible of the city's agony. During the first week after the death of Dr. King, *The Washington Post* published more than 170,000 words and more than 180 photographs on the civil disorders, with the greater part devoted to Washington events.

The story did not vanish from the columns of *The Washington Post* with the end of the rioting and the disappearance of the troops. The reporting and photography teams were kept intact to cover the aftermath, as well as Dr. King's legacy, the Poor People's Campaign, which preoccupied the capital during much of May and June. There were two climaxes—the gathering of 50,000 persons at the Lincoln Memorial for "Solidarity Day," a dramatic and orderly occasion, and the dismantling of the Mall shantytown, "Resurrection City," which gave impetus to a brief renewal of rioting.

This second riot was contained quickly. It appeared that some lessons had been learned in early April.

That rioting started up again suggested that constructive communication between the races was still to be achieved. But at least, in midsummer, 1968, the issues raised by the riot were being discussed openly. Blacks and whites were both starting to talk about the kind of city they wanted, even though the conversation was heated and sometimes hostile.

The Kerner Commission, in an effort to shock the United States into a realization of the magnitude of its racial problems, had starkly said:

"Our nation is moving toward two societies, one black and one white—separate and unequal."

But, "The movement apart can be reversed," the Commission also said. "Choice is still possible. . . . The alternative is not blind repression or capitulation to lawlessness. It is the realization of common opportunities for all within a single society."

It is the hope of those who prepared this book that it will foster increased understanding of why men riot and, in so doing, contribute to the reversal of that movement apart.

BEN W. GILBERT

Washington, D.C.
August, 1968

Acknowledgments

This book is a collaboration—a product of the newsgathering staff of *The Washington Post*. A great debt is owed to the dozens of reporters, photographers, and other staff members whose work went into it.

Two writers stand out because their contribution to the work was so large that, in fairness, their names should have been listed with mine on the cover. They are Leonard Downie, Jr., and Jesse W. Lewis, Jr. Downie tackled the formidable job of sorting out conflicting reports and putting events into their moment-by-moment relationships. In addition, soon after the occupation of Washington was over, he talked to military officers and men of all ranks back at their bases while their experience was still fresh. His interviews highlighted the role of the military during the riots. Lewis, a native Washingtonian, brought to the book invaluable insights and background on the city and its residents and provided illuminating accounts of the behavior of the rioters and their impact on the community. Particularly noteworthy is the tape recording he obtained on which Chapter X is based.

Many other staffers of *The Washington Post* helped to shape the book through their initial reporting and the research they did after the events of April. Outstanding in this group are: Robert C. Maynard, Hollie I. West, Jim Hoagland, and Paul W. Valentine. Other reporters and writers who made important contributions are: James Clayton, Carl Sims, Leon Dash, Peter Milius, Robert G. Kaiser, and Ivan C. Brandon. Also, William

xv

J. Raspberry, Glegg Watson, Elsie Carper, Robert Asher, Alfred E. Lewis, David A. Jewell, Carol Honsa, Jack Eisen, Bernadette Carey, Robert F. Levey, Willard Clopton, Jr., Jack White, Jr., Claudia Levy, Paul G. Edwards, Ronald Smothers, Susan Jacoby, Carl Bernstein, Stuart Auerbach, William Shumann, Claude Koprowski, Tom Jones, and Carolyn Lewis.

The significant roles of the following should be noted: Richard J. Darcey, director of photography, who selected the illustrations and made the layouts; Bill Williams, chief of data processing for the newspaper, who prepared the special study of the rioters; artists Joseph Mastrangelo and Kenneth Burgess, who were responsible for the maps and charts; and secretaries Eileen Peterson and Pamela Whitehead, who typed the manuscript.

The pictures in the book were selected from the 2,000 taken by *The Washington Post*'s photographers during the riot and its aftermath. Their names are listed in the picture credits below.

Numerous officials who agreed to interviews in depth and made their riot-period records available have my warm thanks for their cooperation. Among them are Mayor Walter E. Washington and his top staff, the ranking officials of the police and fire departments, Director of Public Safety Patrick V. Murphy, the members of the City Council, the activist leaders of the black community, some of the city's leading businessmen, David Ginsburg, Executive Director, National Advisory Commission on Civil Disorders, and Senator Robert C. Byrd of West Virginia, whose extensive files of the closed hearings he conducted were very useful.

I have a particular debt to two editors: Stephen Isaacs, city editor of *The Washington Post,* who mobilized his reporting staff to meet sometimes seemingly unreasonable demands to report and re-report the events of the riot, and Lois Decker O'Neill, Washington editor of Frederick A. Praeger, Publishers, Inc., who successfully kept her sights on the whole book as it was produced and set in type. I would also like to thank the newspaper deskmen who carefully edited the initial riot reports for *The Washington Post* and the Praeger copy editors who toiled over the finished manuscript—both unsung heroes of the publishing business. I know there are others who deserve mention. I hope they will forgive me when they do not find their names here. Their efforts are indeed appreciated.

Although the list of those who made important contributions to the book is long, the list of those responsible for its shortcomings is brief. It contains one name—mine.

B. W. G.

Picture Credits

Listed below are the staff photographers of *The Washington Post* whose photographs appear in this volume. The photographs are identified by the number accompanying each picture.

Robert Burchette—52, 53, 54, 55, 58, 63.

Victor Casamento—57, 60, 72.

Douglas Chevalier—29, 30, 32, 35.

Ellsworth Davis—10, 14.

Arthur Ellis—73.

Ken Feil—3, 5, 11, 64, 65, 66, 67, 68, 70, 74.

Frank Hoy—25, 69, 86.

Matthew Lewis—2, 4, 6, 8, 24, 31, 34, 37, 39, 40, 42, 43, 81, 82, 84.

Jim McNamara—12, 13, 17, 18, 21, 23, 78, 80.

Wally McNamee—9, 33, 36, 46, 47, 56, 75, 79, 87.

Harry Naltchayan—38, 59, 76, 77, 85, 88.

Stephen Northup—1, 7, 15, 16, 19, 20, 22, 28, 44, 48, 49, 50, 51, 71, 83.

Steve Szabo—26, 27, 45, 61, 62, 89.

Margaret Thomas—41.

The color photograph, showing fire destroying the building on the northwest corner of 7th Street and Mount Vernon Place, N.W., is by Frank Hoy.

Contents

Prologue to April: The Riotproof City

To citizens of Washington, D.C., one of the great shocks of the rioting of April, 1968, was that it was allowed to happen.

For years, the comfortable citizens of the nation's capital, black and white, had told one another that their city was riotproof. The same expanding federal government that provided so many jobs and assured the city its outward prosperity had protected Washington from destructive racial clashes. This was not Los Angeles, Newark, or Detroit. In Washington, a great many blacks had secure, well-paying government jobs, with pensions at retirement. They would not riot, it was thought, because they had a real stake in the city. To protect this stake, they would discourage others from misbehaving—at least by example. And, if some Washingtonians were reckless enough to riot, one could count on decisive intervention by the federal government.

Only a few knowledgeable officials questioned the accepted notion that the city was riotproof. Some of these questioners held key posts, but so all-pervasive was the "it won't happen to us" psychology that nobody listened.

Negroes had made enormous progress in the capital. One out of every four federal employees in the Washington area was black—a total of 75,000. A Negro housing official, Robert C. Weaver, was in the Cabinet. Thurgood Marshall, who, as attorney for the National Association for the Advancement of Colored People, had argued a landmark 1954 school segregation case on behalf of Washington school children, was an Associate Justice of the Supreme Court. The Mayor was a Negro. There was a black majority on the new nine-man City Council and on the school board, and the Corporation Counsel was a Negro. Private industry, which generally had accepted the Southern segregationist practice of restricting Negro employment to menial

1

work, was following the government's lead and opening new doors to the city's blacks. If anything did happen to fracture the peace and domestic tranquillity, everybody knew that there were plenty of hand-picked troops, with special training in riot control, nearby: the elite 3d Infantry at Fort Myer, the versatile 91st Engineers at Fort Belvoir, the tough Marines at Quantico, and the crack 6th Cavalry at Fort Meade.

Troops had been called to the capital on three occasions in a half-century. In 1932, 800 Fort Myer cavalry troops, under General Douglas MacArthur, had forcibly evicted the remains of an "army" of bonus-seeking, unemployed war veterans from their Washington encampment. In October, 1967, 1,200 area troops and 500 military police from Fort Bragg, had been brought in to prevent Vietnam peace demonstrators from overrunning the Pentagon, just across the Potomac from Washington. But only once—in 1919—had troops been called to deal with racial strife. Then, a series of sex crimes, which, it was eventually established, were committed by one person, had "whipped the city into a fury of alarm and rage," according to historian Constance McLaughlin Green. Whites attacked Negroes, who fought back. It took five days for police, reinforced by 400 Fort Myer cavalrymen and 400 Marines from Quantico, to end the fighting.

Much of the world sees Washington, the seat of the U.S. government, as a tourist mecca of marble monuments and stately buildings. People from everywhere come to visit and photograph it. Each spring, hundreds of busloads of high school students descend on the city. They return home with souvenirs and thousands of rolls of exposed film. In the blossoming spring of 1968, the riot provided scenes no tourist had ever snapped for a photo album: ugly gray smoke, ballooning near the ice-white Capitol dome; Cherry Blossom Festival visitors departing as soldiers patrolled the wide avenues, laid out by Pierre L'Enfant; looting and burning not far from the well-kept, middle-class homes of black and white families, their yards proud with azaleas and dogwoods.

After a notorious slum within camera range of the Capitol building was razed in the 1950's, tourists rarely saw "the other Washington." For years, that other Washington, away from the monuments, had done a shockingly poor job of teaching its children, healing its sick, caring for its needy, finding jobs for its hard-core unemployed, and controlling crime.

Washington's rat-infested slums were off the main tourist paths, but many of them were astride commuter roads. Yet, before the riot, thousands of suburbanites, passing by on the way to air-conditioned downtown offices, had failed to notice that many dilapidated buildings were posted as condemned. Others should have been, but were not. Many, apparently structurally sound on the outside, gave no hint of their inside condition or of the intolerable overcrowding among their unlucky tenants.

Washington's school system was a classic of neglect. More than one-third of its 185 buildings were constructed before World War I. Only one of every three pupils who enrolled in the ninth grade managed to graduate from high school. Three out of every four students were reading at levels below national norms.

Only Mississippi exceeded the District of Columbia in infant mortality. The city-run hospital was often so crowded that sick persons were turned away. Washington's gonorrhea infection rate was higher than that of any other city in the nation; its syphilis rate, the second highest; its tuberculosis rate, the sixth highest.

The city's welfare caseload was heavy and increasing. Two out of every five children receiving welfare assistance were illegitimate. More than one out of every four families had an income below the poverty level.

Washington has had a Negro majority since 1957. In 1960, census-takers failed to tally thousands of slum-area Negroes, thereby substantially understating the city's population. In 1968, the total was informally revised upward, to 854,000, and the Negro proportion was estimated at 67 per cent, highest for any major American city. By then, the proportion of Negroes enrolled in the public schools exceeded 92 per cent.

Perhaps 25,000 persons were listed as unemployed, about 4 per cent of the whole work force. But this was a misleading statistic. Among the unemployed, a disproportionate number were Negroes, a disproportionate number were young, a disproportionate number had inferior education, lacked basic skills, or had criminal records. In the parts of the city torn by the April riot, the unemployment rate was more than two to three times greater than in the city as a whole. At the end of the line were those young Negro school dropouts with criminal records who lived in the slums. Officials acknowledged that they had lost all contact with thousands of such "hard-core" unemployed.

"Hard-core" unemployment was only part of the picture. Many thousands of Washington Negroes were "underemployed," working below their potential or on jobs that did not draw on all their skills. A study of "subemployment" had indicated that more than 120,000 Washingtonians could have been employed more profitably.

The city's banks and public utilities were beginning to give Negroes more than menial work, but further upgrading was unusual. Many private enterprises permitted blacks to move behind counters to wait on customers, but some continued to deny them access to the cash drawer to make change. Proportionately few skilled Negro mechanics held cards in the elite craft unions, although building construction was a major source of black employment.

Similarly, many of the so-called good jobs in the federal government were not that good. More than 20,000 of the 75,000 Civil Service blacks in the Washington area earned between $3,700 and $6,400 a year.

It is not possible to say how many of the city's unemployed and underemployed engaged in criminal activity before the riot. The city ranked seventh in the nation in the number of active narcotics addicts. In 1964, drug users accounted for more than half of all offenses related to prostitution and a quarter of all housebreakings. The city's serious crime rate was rising.

Washington in 1968 was a legally integrated city. Such enterprises as restaurants, barber shops, theaters, swimming pools, hotels, and bowling alleys were forbidden to discriminate. An open-housing ordinance applied, but, in practice, substantial housing segregation remained. Affluent whites lived in still largely segregated areas, while an increasing number of affluent Negroes moved into luxurious homes in previously all-white areas. There were also "gray" blocks, where both blacks and whites had lived side by side for years. Poorer Negroes were largely confined to virtually all-black areas, where high rents, congestion, and substandard conditions prevailed.

Money and credit continued to be a problem for Negroes. Even the simple act of cashing a check was often difficult and embarrassing. Because of their inability to secure bank loans and their unfamiliarity with department-store credit arrangements, Negro buyers often wound up in the hands of high-credit merchants.

Large sections of the city were without adequate bus transportation, precluding jobs in the thriving white suburbs. Such lack of transportation had been an important ingredient of the Watts riot in Los Angeles in 1965.

One measure of the intensity of a disorder is whether it is maintained at a high pitch for more than one day. Using this standard, the capital had forty-nine years of civil peace between the 1919 riots, which lasted five days, and the April, 1968, disorders, which peaked after three days.

The peace was deceptive. Tensions had developed out of official and unofficial moves to remove racial barriers and integrate public facilities. Generally, they were accomplished without disorder, but in the 1960's, as the fight for Negro rights took on increased militancy, public confrontations between the police and groups of blacks became more frequent and less orderly. Washington was becoming less riotproof.

Large gatherings began to be marked by trouble. The annual Thanksgiving Day high school football games ended in rioting, in 1962. The city closed a carnival in August, 1965, when a fracas produced a disorderly mob that police could not control. An overflow crowd turned Glen Echo Amusement Park into a shambles on Easter Monday, 1966, after a nervous management had decided to close it. A similar abrupt closing of a Washington Coliseum rock-and-roll concert in October, 1967, sent angry youths into the street to break store windows along H Street, N.E.

Committees of civic leaders looked into some of the more spectacular incidents. Their reports warned of unrest in the city. These were duly read, but produced no significant reaction.

Arrests, tinder of the riots in Los Angeles, Newark, and Detroit, more and more frequently were sparking public confrontations between police and citizens. Trouble was narrowly averted in September, 1965, after two white officers used questionable judgment and detained four boys, aged twelve to sixteen, for playing ball in an alley near 14th Street and Park Road, N.W. —a location that was prominent in the April, 1968, riot.

Rocks, bottles, and firecrackers were thrown around a police station house in southeast Washington in August, 1966, after a crowd gathered to protest an arrest it considered unjustified. In the following year, street disorders requiring police action became regular, almost weekly, occurrences.

A tense, nervous, and hot city came close to a full-scale riot during the early morning hours of August 1, 1967, after days filled with rumors that a riot was about to occur. Youths threw bottles and stones at firemen and policemen attempting to control an outbreak of fires, and smashed windows in an inner-city area between 7th and 14th streets, N.W. The disorder was quelled quickly.

By August, 1967, the message that the city could not count on being secure indefinitely had reached the White House. President Johnson had directed that the city government be reorganized to enable it to deal more effectively with its problems. That month, he sent to Congress a plan for the government of the District of Columbia, substituting an appointed mayor and a council for the ninety-three-year-old government under a three-man board of commissioners.

By a close vote, Congress permitted the reorganization plan to go through. The President then named as mayor a black man, Walter E. Washington, and gave the new council a Negro majority. Senate confirmation came speedily. Mayor Washington, a fifty-two-year-old public-housing executive and resident of the inner city since his student days at Howard University, took office on November 3, 1967, just five months before the assassination of Dr. Martin Luther King, Jr.

A year earlier, the President had considered making Walter Washington one of the three commissioners, but abandoned the idea when it became evident that some congressmen and senators objected to a black man's taking command of the police department. Washington then resigned as head of the city's National Capital Housing Authority (NCHA), which he had served for twenty-five years, to become head of New York City's public-housing agency.

In 1967, control of the police department continued to be a sensitive issue. The question no longer was whether the final orders would be given by a black man or a white man but the more sophisticated one of the relationship to be maintained between the police force and those policed.

Mayor Washington had a charge from the President to reduce tensions and improve relationships between the police and the citizenry. But he also had a charge to do something about the rising crime rate—to show that his administration was not going to be "soft" on crime, which was, in Washington as in other cities, a product of poverty, with Negroes the principal offenders and victims.

During the 1964 campaign, Lyndon B. Johnson had learned the hard way that the President could be made accountable for "law and order" in Washington, D.C. Had Barry Goldwater been a more effective opponent, he might have seriously troubled the Administration with this issue. Richard M. Nixon and his running mate, Spiro T. Agnew, made the crime rate in Washington an issue early in the 1968 campaign.

Mayor Washington inherited a police department regarded as racist by many Negroes. To them, it was a white man's department, responding more rapidly to the notions of conservative Southern congressmen than to the voteless citizens of Washington. Four out of five policemen were white, in a city where two out of three citizens were black.

A Presidential crime commission took a hard look at the police department in 1966 and called for many changes to modernize it and make it more responsive to the community. The commission saw the need for measures to reduce the "tension, anger, and fear" that affected the relationships between police and the city's black citizens.

Chief of Police John B. Layton, fifty-five-year-old head of a

3,100-man department, realized that an ill-considered action by one officer could ignite a spark that might burn the city down. But Layton, a cautious and aloof man, also worried that rapid changes might hurt the morale of his force and draw fire from Capitol Hill. His department did not change very rapidly.

With the encouragement of the Justice Department and the White House, the Mayor brought in forty-seven-year-old Patrick V. Murphy, former police chief of Syracuse, New York, and placed him in a new post of Director of Public Safety, over Layton and the heads of the city's fire and civil defense departments. Murphy, who is white, had worked on the crime commission report as deputy director of the Justice Department Office of Law Enforcement Assistance. He regarded establishment of good relations between the police department and the city's blacks as urgent and immediately promoted Negroes to higher ranks and stepped up recruiting to persuade more Negroes to enroll on the force. As part of his effort to improve police relations with the city's black residents, he himself appeared at many neighborhood meetings.

At first, it was believed that Layton would quit, but the two men worked out an accommodation. Murphy, rather than Layton, became the man on the spot—the lightning rod drawing the wrath of those conservative congressmen who feared that the new city government would not give the police support in their day-to-day street encounters. One uneasy congressman introduced legislation to take the police force away from the city and have Congress run it.

Relations with Congress were crucial for the new Mayor and his Director of Public Safety. Each year, the city of Washington must go to Congress for its money—even though the bulk of it is provided by local taxpayers. Southern-dominated committees have refused to yield to pressure to allow the city to govern itself or determine how its own tax money should be spent. (As a concession, to stave off self-government, the Congress authorized the election of a local school board in November, 1968.) Some congressmen, at heart really aldermen, are delighted to give more attention to municipal requests than to those of the

Department of Defense. For years, they have been not only responsive to the views of local businessmen with conservative notions about law enforcement and fiscal policy near their own but also have encouraged rank-and-file policemen to bring their grievances to Capitol Hill. This tradition served as a brake on change in the police department and in the whole municipal government. Congress looked to the new mayor and his team to keep it informed about the condition of the city.

At NCHA, Mayor Washington had built up a unique network of civic and public contacts. He had also discovered that he sometimes could get more accurate information about what was happening in the city by keeping in touch with its tenants. On his return from New York City after an absence of ten months, he took soundings in Washington that told him the city was in serious trouble. He was particularly alarmed to learn that the signals of unrest were slow to get through to city officials.

A splintering of Negro civic leadership was making it difficult for these officials to know where to turn for information and guidance. Some of the older, more familiar figures were fading into the background, and newer, more militant personalities were occupying the center of the stage. Older leaders tended to regard the newcomers as little more than transients, stopping in Washington because it was the capital and hoping to make a score. The younger and more flamboyant types felt that the older, established community organizations had lost touch with their constituents, the city's blacks. Periodically, efforts were made to draw all Negro rights organizations under one tent to present the city with at least the appearance of unity.

Washington, D.C., had a special status not enjoyed by such cities as Cleveland, Chicago, or San Francisco with similar social problems. As the capital, it was the "target city" for any group of demonstrators desiring to impress Congress and the White House with the merits of their cause by exercising the constitutional right of freedom of petition and assembly.

Early in December, about a month after Mayor Washington took office, Martin Luther King reaffirmed his intention to hold his Poor People's Campaign in Washington in the spring. He had participated in the famous March on Washington of the summer of 1963, which had brought more than 200,000 persons, black and white, to the Lincoln Memorial's reflecting pool.

"I have a dream," Dr. King had said then, "that one day this nation will rise up and live out the true meaning of its creed: 'We hold these truths to be self-evident; that all men are created equal.'"

This time, Dr. King would be the leader. But this march would be no one-day stand. Demonstrators, he said, would camp in the capital until the government moved against poverty. Nonviolence would escalate into civil disobedience, with efforts made to disrupt the government by blocking the entrances to federal buildings, including the Capitol itself. Dr. King said he was prepared to face jail or forceful oppression.

"I imagine the Army may try to run us out," he predicted.

President Johnson expressed the hope that the energies of the civil-rights movement could be used in "a more productive and a more effective manner," but Dr. King rejected this appeal, commenting that nothing had been achieved for civil rights "without putting real pressure on."

Mayor Washington suggested publicly, on March 2, that "The community and its government should be concerned, but should not overreact in terms of being fearful."

Bayard Rustin, who had coordinated the 1963 march, tried to persuade Dr. King to abandon the planned demonstration, and Roy Wilkins, Executive Secretary of the National Association for the Advancement of Colored People, said there was a "real danger" that Dr. King would be unable to control all participants.

Wilkins did not name any "mavericks" who might pose a threat of violence, but many people thought of such militants as Stokely Carmichael, a spokesman for the Student Nonviolent Coordinating Committee (SNCC), who had coined the controversial "Black Power" phrase in Mississippi, in 1966. Carmichael had moved to Washington in 1967.

Speaking for worried merchants, Andrew Parker, president of Woodward and Lothrop, the city's largest department store, acknowledged:

"We all look to the future with some apprehension. Dr. King has demonstrated in the past that his marches have been basically peaceful, but there are some elements that might be brought into play on the part of men like Stokely Carmichael, who are more militant."

Originally, the campaign had been scheduled to start in early April, during the height of the Cherry Blossom Festival. Later, Dr. King had fixed April 22 for the starting date—a change that did not, as things turned out, save the Festival.

Mayor Washington had felt that the months ahead, in the summer of 1968, would test the ability of the city to avoid a major riot, but he had not expected to face one as early as April 4. He was concentrated on improving community relations and developing constructive programs for the "long, hot summer." But, with the added risk that the Poor People's Campaign would stir a response in the ghettos and embroil the city, the police and the military were perfecting standby, riot-control plans, and the Justice Department was working with them under the watchful eye of the White House.

The military had speeded up development of a special riot-control plan for Washington, called "Cabin Guard." The plan would apply lessons learned when troops were sent into Newark and Detroit in 1967. The District of Columbia, it was agreed, would be controlled from a joint command center at police headquarters. But, in April, there were still numerous details to work out. For instance, simplified arrest forms, which the Pentagon demonstration had shown were needed, had been designed but not printed.

On March 31, Dr. King, although insisting that the campaign would go on to its climax, endeavored to reassure the uneasy city. Speaking to 4,000 persons in the National Cathedral, he said:

"We are not coming to Washington to engage in any historic action, nor are we coming to tear up Washington. I don't like to predict violence, but if nothing is done between now and June to raise ghetto hope, I feel this summer will not only be as bad, but worse than last year."

Four days and four hours later, Dr. King was dead, shot by an assassin in Memphis, Tennessee, where he was working on plans for his campaign.

Alerts were flashed at the White House, the Pentagon, the Justice Department, and City Hall. The first cautious moves to protect the city were taken. No one wanted to provoke trouble by overreacting. Nor could the event be ignored.

The feared response was not long in coming. It began at the intersection of 14th and U streets, N.W.—a bus transfer hub, one of Washington's most congested inner-city intersections, a place notorious for tension and trouble.

I

Thursday Night: First Sparks of Anger

The intersection of 14th and U streets, N.W., was filling up with its customary nighttime crowd. It was a balmy Washington spring evening, but tension was in the air. The transistor radios many youths carried in their hands had announced at 7:16 P.M. that in Memphis, Tennessee, an assassin had shot the Reverend Dr. Martin Luther King, Jr., director of the Southern Christian Leadership Conference (SCLC) and America's most respected civil rights leader.

Homeward-bound black workers were thronging the 14th and U intersection, changing buses or stopping to shop in the drug and liquor stores, before moving on. Transients and other newcomers to Washington's "Harlem" often wound up here looking for action. This was a spot to pick up a woman, purchase narcotics, make a deal. It was also the unofficial nerve center of active black leadership groups—the place to go with a grievance.

Dr. King's SCLC Washington headquarters was on the northwest corner in an old, high-ceilinged converted bank building. Both the Student Nonviolent Coordinating Committee and the National Association for the Advancement of Colored People had offices not too far away.

Police considered this intersection the most volatile in the city's crowded Negro sections. Angry people had gathered here often in the past. Only two nights before, a crowd of several hundred youngsters and young adults had tossed bottles and stones at white policemen responding to a trouble call at the Peoples Drug Store outlet next to the SCLC office. Stokely

Carmichael, former national chairman of the Student Non-violent Coordinating Committee (SNCC), had told that crowd to "go home." Lieutenant Joseph Frye, a resourceful white plain-clothesman who was on the scene, sensing that the presence of uniformed policemen was provocative, had sent them away. He had stayed alone to listen to the complaints of the crowd. Eventually, it dispersed. A fireman, using a hand hose to put out a small fire lit with lighter fluid in a nearby tree, was told, prophetically, by one of the youths:

"Don't worry, motherfucker. We'll just light it again."

By 8:00 P.M. on Thursday, April 4, prostitutes, pimps, and female impersonators were lining the fronts of buildings between T and U streets, and the cafes had their doors open. Youths in their teens and twenties loitered in small groups on the corners, with the sidewalk in front of the SCLC office drawing the largest congregation.

At 8:19 P.M. came the news bulletin everyone had feared. Martin Luther King, the thirty-nine-year-old Nobel Peace Prize winner and apostle of nonviolent protest against poverty and racial discrimination, had died fourteen minutes earlier. Memphis police flashed a bulletin for a white man seen darting out of a flophouse near Dr. King's motel.

Hollie I. West, a reporter for *The Washington Post,* arrived at the 14th and U intersection just after word came that Dr. King was dead. The crowd was unusually large, even for this normally busy place; the atmosphere, unusually tense.

Betty Wolden, a reporter for NBC News, who appeared to be the only white woman in the predominantly black crowd, said to the black newsman that the sudden quiet in the area just then struck her as "ominous—like before a hurricane strikes."

She told West she thought she should leave the area. He agreed.

As Miss Wolden sought a taxicab, an elderly Negro woman said to her, "I hope no one picks you up."

The news of Dr. King's death spread rapidly along the 14th Street shopping strip and its narrow tributary streets. As minutes passed and the gathering crowd in the intersection of 14th and

U swelled, expressions of shock at the tragedy in Memphis began to turn to hot words of anger.

"They did the wrong thing this time," was one comment.

West went inside the Peoples Drug Store, the third busiest in the prosperous area-wide chain, where a dozen persons were huddled around a transistor radio on the camera counter in the rear. They were listening to the muted voice of President Johnson speaking from the White House:

"America is shocked and saddened by the brutal slaying tonight of Dr. Martin Luther King. I ask every citizen to reject the blind violence that has struck Dr. King, who lived by nonviolence."

On receiving the report of the events in Memphis, the President had canceled a scheduled appearance at a Democratic Party fund-raising dinner and postponed a trip to Honolulu, where he was to confer on Vietnam. His concern was evident in the tone of his words.

"I know every American of good will joins me in mourning the death of this outstanding leader and in praying for peace and understanding throughout this land," he said.

"We can achieve nothing by lawlessness and divisiveness among the American people," he went on. "Only by joining together and only by working together can we continue to move toward equality and fulfillment for all of our people."

The President's cautious phrases seemed to anger his listeners around the crowded counter.

"Honkie," said one.

"He's a murderer himself."

"This will mean one thousand Detroits."

Alive, Dr. King had been unable to avoid the eruption of violence in Memphis, where a protest march of garbage workers on March 28 had ended in looting and window-breaking and the fatal shooting by police of a sixteen-year-old looting suspect. A curfew had been imposed, and 4,000 National Guardsmen were summoned to restore order.

It was almost too much to hope that violence could be avoided after his death. Waves of disorder were to spread that night and during the weekend through the Negro sections of more than 120 American cities. And damage was to be heaviest in Washington.

At 14th and U that first night, the President's statement was still coming over the radio in the back of the Peoples Drug Store when a group of about thirty youths burst inside.

"Martin Luther King is dead," they shouted. "Close the store!"

In the group was a tall, silm twenty-six-year-old, with a startlingly handsome face—Stokely Carmichael, Trinidad-born, acknowledged revolutionary, and black activist, who had put together a "Black United Front" of Washington Negro organizations to provide a sounding board for black leadership. He sought out the manager.

"It's closed; it's closed," Carmichael excitedly told the white manager G. N. Simirtzakis. As soon as he understood what was happening, Simirtzakis agreed.

Youths roaming store aisles told customers, "It's closed now, you can go," and steered them to the door. The fluorescent lights began to flicker off as Carmichael and his group left.

On the sidewalk outside, they joined more people, mostly young men in their twenties, and the growing crowd rushed diagonally across the busy intersection to Carter's liquor store, which had been about to shut, anyway, because the 9 P.M. usual closing hour was nearing. The crowd then began moving farther south on 14th Street.

When Carmichael first heard of the shooting of Dr. King, he had gone at once to the SCLC headquarters. There, sitting between two desks, with one foot on each, he had started making telephone calls to Memphis to find out what happened.

"Well," he was heard to state over the telephone, "if we must die, we better die fighting back."

Older men and women stepped inside the SCLC office to ask over and over again, "Is it true? Is it true?"

Off the telephone, Carmichael muttered:

"Now that they've taken Dr. King off, it's time to end this nonviolence bullshit. We gotta get together."

He then went two blocks north to the 14th Street storefront

Washington office of SNCC. In an inner office, Carmichael conferred with Lester McKinnie, Washington head of SNCC, and C. Sumner Stone, former editor of the *Washington Afro-American* newspaper and one-time aide to ousted New York Congressman Adam Clayton Powell. Eleven other men and four women, mainly SNCC members, were in an outer room, where a radio was tuned to Station WOL, popular "soul" outlet in Washington.

Bearded disk jockey Bob Terry, who usually works in an undershirt and sunglasses, tapping his feet and bobbing his head to the big beat and shouting, was talking calmly and quietly. There was organ music in the background.

"This is no time to hate," Terry was saying. "Hate won't get you anywhere."

"And let me tell you something, too, white man," he continued. "Tomorrow, before you get back in that car and go out to the suburban house, you better say something nice to that black man on the job beside you. You'd better stop hating, too."

McKinnie came out of the inner office to tell the others that he and Carmichael and Stone had considered calling a black strike and asking stores to close in tribute to Dr. King, but that he felt it might be better "if we took some time to react to this great tragedy."

But at that moment, Carmichael, wearing his familiar green fatigue jacket, burst out of the inner room, with Stone at his heels. Waving his hands, Carmichael shouted:

"They took our leader off, so, out of respect, we're gonna ask all these stores to close down until Martin Luther King is laid to rest. If Kennedy had been killed, they'd have done it."

And then demanding, "So why not for Dr. King," he bolted out the front door. All but McKinnie and Stone followed him. By now, it was 8:45 P.M.

Heading south for the intersection, the group stopped first at Eaton's Barber Shop, where Johnny Jones, the only barber and a Negro, readily agreed. "The black man has just been pushed around too much," he later remembered thinking.

Next was the YanKee Restaurant, owned by How K. Chen. Chen nodded his head in acquiescence. "Solid," said Carmichael, and left.

Like a Pied Piper, Carmichael made his way toward the Peoples Drug Store at 14th and U, collecting a crowd as he went.

"Stokely, you're the one," a youth told him.

"Now that Dr. King's dead, we ain't got no way but Stokely's way," another said.

Mostly young men fell in with Carmichael. Many wore light jackets over flashy sports shirts or turtlenecks and slacks. Some had put on raincoats against the on-and-off-again drizzle that had begun. Others were in workclothes or blue-collar uniforms. Although it was dark, some did not remove their sunglasses. Many of the men wore their hair in natural Afro style and had goateed beards. Dotted through the growing crowd walking with Stokely were past and present students of nearby Howard University. Tension rose as the crowds were swelled by more and more teen-aged youths and adults under thirty.

A short while earlier, the Reverend Walter Fauntroy, vice chairman of the Washington City Council and an official of Dr. King's Southern Christian Leadership Conference, had come to the SCLC Poor People's Campaign office immediately adjacent to the drugstore in response to a call that an angry crowd was gathering.

He found only a few persons outside the office when he arrived and went upstairs to meet with some of the SCLC staff. Looking out a window, he spotted Carmichael and his following, moving diagonally across the intersection from the drugstore. Fearing trouble, Fauntroy hurried downstairs and outside.

Carmichael and the crowd around him headed south on 14th Street for a time, crisscrossing the street, stopping at open stores, and asking them to close. (Berkeley Chaney, night manager of the Wings 'N' Things chicken carryout, remembered that the group was polite when it asked him to close, about 9:10 P.M.)

Catching up with Carmichael a block south of U Street and grabbing his arms, Fauntroy said,

"This is not the way to do it, Stokely. Let's not get anyone hurt. Let's cool it."

Carmichael, a foot taller than Fauntroy, continued to walk, rocking back and forth to free himself.

"All we're asking them to do is close the stores," Carmichael said. "They killed Dr. King."

Convinced that Carmichael was finding a "useful channel of frustration," Fauntroy returned to the SCLC office, stopping to tell a plainclothesman in an unmarked car that he thought everything was going to be all right. He advised against bringing many uniformed policemen into the area, fearing such action might be provocative. By now, it was 9:25 P.M.

When Fauntroy again reached the second floor of the SCLC office, he heard glass breaking in the Peoples Drug Store window next door. It was the start.

Corners such as 14th and U streets in Washington's northwest Negro community exist in most large- and medium-sized cities in the nation. New Yorkers would recognize it as 125th Street and Lenox Avenue; Chicagoans would call it 63rd Street and Cottage Grove; San Franciscans, Fillmore and Ellis; Atlantans, Ashby and Hunter. In Cleveland, 55th and Hough or 105th and Euclid; in Memphis, Third and McLemore; in Minneapolis, Plymouth Avenue and Broadway; in Pittsburgh, Center and DeVilliers.

The report of the President's Commission on Civil Disorders says that such intersections, with a "relatively high concentration of pedestrian and automobile traffic," are places where riots are likely to start.

The 14th and U Street intersection is on the southern end of a twenty-block shopping strip bordering a congested and deteriorated area.

Among the more than 300 businesses on the twenty-block stretch of 14th Street and some of its side streets are clothing, specialty, five and dime, hardware, appliance, pawn, dry cleaning, and other shops that bring daytime crowds to the street. Some are branches of stores and national chains found in middle-class Negro and white neighborhoods; others are ghetto-oriented businesses selling on credit at high interest.

At night, this stretch of 14th Street turns on in neon. There are movie houses, bars, rock-and-roll palaces, other night spots, the rooming houses where the prostitutes take their clients, as well as the after-hours joints that open up after everything else but the carryout stores close down.

The crowd with Carmichael had come back to 14th and U and turned east onto U Street, moving along the north sidewalk and passing the Jumbo Nut Shop, where Katina Mandes, a white woman and a co-owner of the shop, was working that night. She did not close when first asked. But, when the crowd passed her a second time a few minutes later, she was told this time that she had five minutes. She closed the store and hurried home.

As the crowd passed the Republic Theater, a block farther west on U Street, a stocky fifteen-year-old boy, wearing dungarees, a tan sweatshirt, and a sailor cap, suddenly punched his fist into one of the movie theater's glass doors. The glass shattered, and a younger boy slipped through the door frame into the theater and came back with a large bag of popcorn. The fifteen-year-old stood by the door, rubbing his fist, which was not cut, and smiled broadly.

"Way to go, kid," somebody called to him.

But Carmichael came up to the teenager and pulled him away from the front of the theater. "This is not the way," he shouted, so that others could hear him. Some SNCC members rushed over to the broken glass and told other youths in the crowd to stay out of the theater. The swirling crowd had grown large by now, and, on its eastern fringes, farther down U Street, a few twenty-year-olds went into the Lincoln Theater and told the manager and the customers that it was closed. They shouted at the people sitting in the dark theater, ordering them out onto the street. By now, it was 9:45 P.M.

Carmichael grew more and more concerned about what was happening. He turned around and headed back to 14th Street. Most of the crowd followed him. Reaching 14th and U, Carmichael turned north on 14th Street, walking along the sidewalk on the east side, across from the Peoples Drug Store.

After stopping at the Zanzibar Restaurant and asking owner Moy Hon Toon to close (he did), the crowd crossed to the west side of 14th Street, still heading north. The mob was so large now that it covered the entire block from U Street north to V

Street. Those at the rear, in front of the Peoples Drug Store, began kicking in the rest of its broken plate-glass window. Some knocked over display cases before SNCC workers could get back to the store to stop them.

A middle-aged man walked up to the shattered drugstore window and aimed his foot at a piece of the glass that remained in place. There were tears in his eyes, and he was angry. He began shouting about the white man's evil. He picked up a city trash can off the sidewalk and threw it through the drugstore window. Still screaming, he went across the street and threw a bottle from the street gutter through the window of the National Liquor Store.

The mood of the entire crowd grew uglier.

"This is it baby," someone said, "The shit is going to hit the fan now. . . . We oughta burn this place down right now. . . . Let's get some white motherfuckers. . . . Let's kill them all."

The cries became so loud that Carmichael stopped the crowd again and began arguing with a young man who had been among those suggesting that they should act to avenge Dr. King's death.

"You really ready to go out and kill?" Carmichael asked at the top of his voice. "How you gonna win? What you got? They've got guns . . . tanks. What you got? If you don't have your gun, go home. We're not ready. Let's wait until tomorrow. Just cool it. Go home, go home, go home."

There were echoes of his words in the crowd, probably repeated by SNCC workers.

"We're not ready," they said. "We'll be back. This ain't the way." Carmichael began telling the people to go home.

"Get off the streets. This is not the time, brothers," he shouted.

And Carmichael began walking north on 14th Street fast, the crowd still following him.

As they walked up the steep 14th Street hill, some of the teenagers began chanting: "Beep, beep, black power. Beep, beep, black power."

On a fringe of the crowd, a man ran into the street, went up to a D.C. Transit bus, and put his fist through the small window next to the driver. Others in the crowd ran out to grab him and pulled him away, as blood ran out of cuts in his hand.

From the SCLC office, Fauntroy could hear and see the trouble growing on 14th Street. With two of his nine brothers, Billy and Raymond, he drove to radio station WOL to broadcast an appeal for order. He was speaking as a SCLC leader and as vice chairman of the City Council. Then he got a police escort and rushed to all four major television stations and made brief appearances on the air, with the same plea for order. At each stop, there were tears in his eyes, sorrow in his voice.

Carmichael and the crowd passed the SNCC office on 14th Street and continued north. When they reached the corner of 14th and Belmont streets, five blocks north of 14th and U, a heavy-set woman in her thirties, wearing a raincoat, leaned against the window of the Belmont TV and Appliance Store and started bumping it with her broad backside. The window cracked and then fell in. The woman stepped away, smiling as the fifteen-year-old had smiled at the Republic Theater. A few young men in the vanguard of the crowd, mostly SNCC workers, rushed to the shattered window and stood in the way of anyone who might want to take the television sets that were left exposed, an arm's reach inside.

Carmichael, hearing the breaking of glass, ran over and grabbed a youth who was trying to get past the SNCC workers and through the broken window. He took the teenager by the shoulder and shook him. Then, Carmichael produced a large, black revolver.

"If you mean business," he told the boy, "you should have a gun. You're not ready for the 'thing.' Go home. Go home."

The mob had turned south and was heading back toward 14th and U. Its size had shrunk and it seemed to be out of steam. As it passed the SNCC office, more people dropped off, some going inside SNCC, some appearing to start home. A light rain was falling steadily now.

But Carmichael could see that crowds were gathering again down the hill at 14th and U. He continued walking south, and some of the people around him followed. No uniformed policemen could be seen on 14th Street yet, although there were plainclothesmen in the milling crowd.

Just as Carmichael reached 14th and U, he heard what sounded like gunshots a block away. It was 10:24 P.M. At police headquarters, the sounds produced the first two trouble calls from 14th Street—windows breaking at Sam's Pawnbrokers and the Rhodes Five and Ten store, both a block south of U on 14th Street. This time, youths in the crowd made it to the stores before SNCC workers could intervene and began pouring through the display windows to grab watches, jewelry, radios, and television sets.

As Carmichael heard the two loud sounds, he saw a man in his twenties in the crowd brandishing a gun. Carmichael wrested it away from him, ending another argument about whether the crowd should act to avenge the assassination.

"Go home, go home, go home," Carmichael shouted. "None of this," he cried, waving the man's gun in the air. "None of this, we're not ready."

"But we've got no leader," a voice in the crowd called out. "We lost our leader. They killed him."

Carmichael answered: "You won't get one like this. You'll just get shot. Go home, go home."

Down the street, two SNCC workers, one a high-school youth who was wearing a Carmichael-style, green field jacket and had two binoculars around his neck, began pulling looters out of stores and display windows and telling them to "go home." The pair soon became discouraged. As soon as they cleared one store, rioters hopped into another to grab what they could.

A girl in her twenties, who had been in the SNCC office earlier, reached through one of the store windows. She came out with several transistor radios cradled in her right arm and a large cooking pot, which she rhythmically hit against her left hip.

"Got me something; got me something," she shouted to the thumping beat.

Youths with television sets, electrical appliances, clothing, shoes, and other items began streaming past Carmichael at 14th and U. Slipping away, he ducked into the doorway of the SCLC office, stood for a moment, and then dashed across 14th Street to get in a waiting Mustang and speed away. It was 10:40 P.M.

Carmichael knew his actions were being watched closely by federal authorities. He has since said he was determined to give them no cause to arrest him. Clearly, his decision to close the stores was an important factor in collecting the crowd. But he and his aides made strenuous efforts to check the mob when it grew unruly. He took his exit at the precise point of no return— as the memorial street demonstration exploded into riot.

By 11 P.M., windows were breaking on all sides of the intersection. Display dummies from the Federated Five and Dime on 14th Street were stripped and tossed on the sidewalk. Persons went by carrying suits on display hangers, cases of liquor, and expensive appliances. A man in a heavy jacket, work pants, and work shoes paused on the sidewalk to get a better grip on the portable television and three-piece portable stereo he was carrying.

"They got London, they got London," shouted excited teen-agers, as they ran down the street.

Looters were coming out of the London Custom Shop just down U Street with shirts, slacks, suits, and hats. Trails of clothes were left behind. (Later that night, nineteen-year-old Carl McKinley Harris was arrested in front of London, carrying seven new hats. Just three hours earlier, at his grandmother's house a few blocks away, he had seen the television bulletin about Dr. King's shooting and he decided to go out to see "what would happen." He was charged with attempted burglary and released on $500 bail pending trial.)

The evening had started with a hostile, antiwhite tone. Now some of the hostility seemed to be forgotten in the carnival excitement produced by the looting.

The crowds continued to grow, as more and more persons poured out of the tenements on either side of the 14th Street strip to join the activity. They gathered along the twenty-block area in clusters.

Looting on 14th Street consisted mainly of hit and run attacks on display windows, the looters hurrying off to elude the police, who began to appear in force. By midnight, the police had effectively sealed off and occupied the 14th and U area. But farther north, where there was a concentration of larger clothing and specialty stores, more widespread looting occurred.

Six blocks above U Street, at the intersection with Clifton, youths stood in the middle of the street and tossed rocks and bottles at passing cars and busses. A teenager threw a bottle through the windshield of one of the first police cars on the scene, hitting the driver on the shoulder.

As police strength increased, the officers began arresting any looters they could pull away from the crowds. One of the first to be put in a paddy wagon was thirty-one-year-old Charles Herman, who was standing in front of the Belmont TV and Appliance store, where the plate glass had been broken ninety minutes earlier by the heavy-set woman in the raincoat. Herman, who lived nearby on Belmont Street, was carrying a brand-new portable phonograph. He was charged with burglary and jailed to await action of the U.S. Grand Jury.

Shortly after 11:30 P.M., the evening's intermittent light rain suddenly erupted into a heavy downpour. For a time, the rain helped break up bands of looters along the strip, but it ended only a few minutes after it began.

Up the 14th Street hill, a dozen blocks north of 14th and U, a crowd of about 100 youths grew quickly to 300, and then 500, as the rain ended. Singly and in groups of 6 to 20, they spread over a six-block area, between Girard Street and Park Road, smashing windows and looting dozens of the clothing and specialty shops there. The stores were in low structures built on what had been the lawns of six- and eight-story apartment buildings and old mansions, now overcrowded with large families. These buildings had been occupied by whites, mostly Irish and Italian Catholics, in the 1920's, when the first commercial incursions of the lawns began. Just before World War II, Negroes began pushing into the area from the 7th Street and Georgia Avenue neighborhoods to the east. Only a handful of white families remained immediately east of 14th Street.

The police were still badly outnumbered on upper 14th

Street. They rushed at the massed crowds of looters, flailing nightsticks to break them into small groups that could then be isolated and arrested or chased away.

A group of touring city officials, including Mayor Washington, drove north on 14th Street from U just before midnight and saw the shadows of looters darting in and out of darkened storefronts. Police cars raced by, heading for the more serious trouble farther north. As the official party proceeded up the hill, looters were seen coming out of hardware stores, clothing shops, milk and ice cream stores, and package liquor stores, with loaded arms.

"Look at that stuff, will you," the Mayor commented as the car passed two teen-aged girls carrying dozens of dresses, coats, and skirts.

At 14th and Kenyon, the street was filled with frenzied blacks. An occasional rock or bottle sailed through the air. A policeman who stopped the car and recognized the Mayor advised, "You better get out of here."

The official party, which included Corporation Counsel Charles Duncan and Julian Dugas, Director of Licenses and Inspections, went on to the Thirteenth Precinct House near 16th and V streets, where a temporary command post had been set up.

Police later were told about another automobile that was being driven frantically through Northwest Washington. Three young white men, in a late model Chevrolet, reported they were carrying a dying companion to the hospital. According to their uncorroborated account, they (four men in their twenties, all from distant suburbs in Virginia) had stopped on 14th Street, above U Street for gasoline. At the filling station, they later told police, they had gotten into an argument with about eight Negro youths, who attacked them with sticks and knives. They said their companion had been hit hard and stabbed in the head. So they took off wildly, searching for a hospital.

They insisted they knew nothing about Dr. King's death or any trouble in the city. They had decided to "ride around" Washington after having had dinner and "a few drinks" at a party in nearby Alexandria. Words were exchanged, they said, and the Negro youths demanded an apology.

"For what?" one of the white men demanded, and the Negroes attacked, according to the survivors.

They said they became lost on unfamiliar Washington side streets, but eventually found their way across the river to Fairfax County Hospital, where their companion was pronounced dead of his injuries.

It was the first death listed in the rioting and the only one to occur Thursday night. The victim was George Fletcher, a twenty-eight-year-old electrical worker and father of three, who lived in Woodbridge, Virginia.

The place where Fletcher received his fatal injuries is unknown and is likely to remain so. Police later took Fletcher's three friends up and down 14th Street, but they have not been able to identify the gasoline station where, according to their account, the attack took place. Officially, doubt remains about the connection of this death to the rioting.

It was now past midnight and more than 500 policemen were on 14th Street, many on foot, equipped with tear gas and gas masks. They continued to try to break up the crowds. It became a game of hare and hounds. Youths would dart out from alleys and hit a store, to loot its merchandise or try to start a fire inside it, and then run when chased by police.

By 12:30 A.M., the mobs succeeded in starting the first full-scale fires of the riot in two neighborhood food markets on opposite corners of 14th and Fairmont Streets. The first fire call actually had been received more than a hour and a half earlier, four blocks south at Belmont Street. Two Ford vehicles, a 1966 sedan and a light truck, had been set ablaze on the Barry-Pate and Addison used-car lot. These blazes were quickly extinguished, but they served to alert fire-alarm headquarters to the trouble ahead. At that time, Fire Chief Henry Galotta rushed to headquarters and put into effect an emergency plan doubling the men on duty at each firehouse during the next four hours.

At 14th and Fairmont, firemen were called to a blaze at the Central Market on the southeast corner. Five minutes later, flames broke out in the Pleasant Hill Market on the northwest corner behind them. This fire quickly spread to the adjacent

Steelman's liquor store and threatened a four-story apartment building next to the liquor store. A small fire had already been started earlier downstairs in this building, in Judd's Pharmacy, by a man in his thirties who set burning newspapers inside the front door. But the rain had extinguished it.

When the firemen first arrived at 14th and Fairmont, a mixed crowd of youths and adults poured out of the apartments and the side streets to surround the firemen and pelt them with stones, bottles, and cans. Several dozen policemen converged on the intersection, and policemen and firemen donned gas masks. The police rolled and tossed more than 100 baseball-sized tear-gas canisters at the crowd—many from the windows and back door of a patrol wagon that was driven repeatedly into the midst of the crowd in an attempt to split it up. It was the first large-scale use of gas in the riot.

The smothering, eye-burning vapor drove the crowd back a block in all directions. Some people went home, but many continued to throw stones and bottles from a distance. As the firemen doused the flames at 14th and Fairmont, police answered the rock throwers with grenade launchers that sent gas shells in hissing arcs 20 and 30 feet into the air toward rioters as far as two blocks away.

At one point, a bottle, dropped from the roof of an apartment building, smashed to the street with a loud report that sounded like a gunshot. *Washington Post* reporter Robert Maynard had parked his radio car right by the spot where it fell. He radioed to the newspaper's city desk:

"There are four policemen ducking for cover right beside my car. . . . They are down on one knee behind the hood and the trunk . . . with their guns drawn and cocked . . . aiming over the car at the roof above us.

"I'm now getting onto the floor under the dashboard as fast as I can. . . . Over and out."

Another policeman shouted that it was just a bottle. A tear-gas grenade was lofted onto the roof of the apartment building. The policemen holstered their guns. No shots had been fired, nor were there any other guns reported drawn by police that night. It was now nearly 2 A.M.

A group of youths, scattered by the tear-gas barrage, re-formed a block away, at Euclid, to attack another food store, the Empire Market. When they could not kick in the heavy front door, a short, husky youth wrenched a "No Parking" signpost out of the dirt. Half running, half dancing, he rammed it against the door, which gave way, and the youths rushed in.

In a fury of activity, the youths began pulling down lights, displays, and shelves and tossing foodstuffs at the windows, walls, and ceiling. When a group of twenty-five policemen arrived on the double, running downhill from Fairmont Street, the youths dived through windows and escaped to a parking lot across the street. A policeman fired a tear-gas grenade at them, but one boy picked it up and quickly tossed it back toward the police, who had taken off their gas masks. It exploded at their feet.

For forty-five minutes, the police jousted with the youths, who kept coming back determinedly to the store, trying to set it afire with matches and burning newspapers. Finally, a big fire was started and flames shot out the window openings and through the roof.

When the firemen arrived, the youths began to stone them. Police moved in quickly with more tear gas. This time, the gas dispersed the dwindling band of youths, and the firemen doused the flames. By now, it was 3:00 A.M., Friday, April 5, and the last large-scale confrontation on 14th Street had ended.

In about six hours, more than 200 stores had had windows broken; 150 of them had been looted. There had been 7 fires. More than 150 adults and nearly 50 juveniles had been arrested. There were 30 injured, including 5 policemen and 1 fireman. No one had been seriously hurt except Fletcher, the electrician from Virginia, who by this time was dead.

Most of the damage was on 14th Street, but stores at about a half-dozen locations outside the 14th Street police perimeter suffered broken windows and minor looting from roving bands of youths driving automobiles. The Hecht Company's main downtown department store, at 7th and F streets, N.W., had some windows broken. Also hit was D. J. Kaufman's, at 1005 Pennsylvania Avenue, N.W., an expensive, high-fashion men's shop, heavily patronized by blacks.

The downtown store was less than ten blocks from the White House and about the same distance from the Capitol along the historic Presidential inaugural route. Although the damage was not serious—a few pairs of shoes and some items of clothing were taken—the looting of Kaufman's suggested that the contagion could easily spread beyond the area the police had sealed off. Some of the looting occurred while employees, who had responded to the burglar alarm, were engaged in clearing the broken windows of merchandise.

At dawn Friday, with hundreds of policemen still lining the sidewalks, 14th Street was quiet. The rays of the rising sun glinted on those store windows that still contained unbroken glass. White foam, sprayed by street-cleaning crews, ran down the steep hill, carrying broken glass and debris along with it. Mayor Washington had ordered the crews out early and in force. Failure to clean the streets, it had been learned from the 1967 riots, invited more damage the next day.

Eye-stinging tear gas still hung in the air. Burglar alarms continued to jangle in an unsettling chorus. An early riser, viewing a ransacked clothing store for the first time, turned away, shaking his head.

"Oh, my God," was his only comment.

hursday night, stunned Democrats are led in prayer after learning that Dr. King is dead.

1

Word that Martin Luther King is dead travels swiftly —to the Washington Hilton Hotel, where it shocks 3,000 Democrats at a fund-raising banquet *(above)*; and to 14th Street, where, by 10:24 P.M., the window of Brookland Hardware, near 14th and U, gives way *(left)* as the looting begins.

2

The first extensive looting begins south of 14th and U.

Looters carry clothing yanked off racks—hangers and all. They walk by a looted hardware store.

4

National Liquors, at 14th and U streets, N.W., is an early victim of looters.

5

By midnight, shelves are bare in liquor store off 14th Street, N.W.

Despite the smashed window glass *(above)*,
a woman grasps for items from the showcase
of Federated Five and Dime at 14th and U.

The weight of heavy appliances catches up
with this man, who pauses to readjust his
burden of television and stereo *(right)*.

After midnight, Civil Disturbance Unit police shoot volleys of tear gas at youths setting a fire near 14th and Fairmont streets, N.W.

The looted Pleasant Hill Market on 14th near Fairmont is set on fire; flames spread to liquor store and threaten apartment building.

II

Thursday Night and Friday Morning: The Police Problem

"We're surrounded by a mob of fifty people at 14th and Irving. What do we do?"

"They're looting Irving's Record Shop. . . . Do we arrest them, or do we leave?"

"We're being stoned in the 2600 block of 14th Street. What the hell do we do?"

The cries of policemen in trouble crackled over the police radio, at 10:45 P.M., on Thursday, April 4. Earlier that evening, the 14th Street crowd had been content to persuade storekeepers to close their shops in memory of Dr. King. Now the police radio reported that the crowd had become a window-breaking, looting mob.

More than an hour earlier, a decision had been made to keep large numbers of police out of sight to avoid provocation. But, starting about 10:30 P.M., uniformed policemen were being introduced in force at the lower end of the affected area, at the intersection of 14th and U.

A police officer later told Senator Robert C. Byrd of West Virginia, in an unusual series of closed, nighttime interviews, what it was like when he first came upon the looters:

"The policemen in the precinct, we all got on the scene. We were outnumbered; it must have been hundreds to one, children of all ages, woman, everybody, just like a holiday.

"They thought everything was for free down there. They were

running and grabbing, holding up dresses to see if they fitted them.

"The officers there in the area, they started to arrest the subject, but, what officers that there were, they weren't sufficient. There wasn't near enough officers to control the situation. They had some tear gas. They used that. But some of the officers didn't have gas masks; so we were hurting the officers by the use of tear gas when it was used."

That was the beginning of police involvement in the Washington riots of April, 1968. What happened on 14th Street that Thursday night stunned Washington. But it was only the prelude to the frenzy that was to grip a large section of the city, starting at about noon Friday. By that time, civil, police, and military authorities had braced themselves, seeking to put into practice whatever lessons they had learned—sometimes well, sometimes vaguely—from other civil disorders of the recent past.

In the end, the vandalism, looting, and setting of 1,000 fires caused more destruction than any recent big-city riot in the United States, except those that hit Los Angeles (Watts), in 1965, and Detroit, in 1967. The total number arrested (7,600) and the total number of regular Army, Marine, and District of Columbia National Guard troops called into Washington (13,600) exceeded the totals for any other of the big-city riots of recent times.

Yet, only twelve persons died during Washington's riot, compared to the thirty-four killed in Watts, the forty-three who died in Detroit, and the twenty-three who perished in Newark's less massive riot in 1967. A total of six policemen, firemen, and soldiers lost their lives in the three cities.

Just two of the twelve deaths in Washington were caused by police bullets. No one was shot by a soldier. No policeman, fireman, or soldier was killed. Most of the victims died trapped in fires.

In Watts, Detroit, and Newark, according to the report of the National Advisory Commission on Civil Disorders, city and state police and guardsmen were responsible for the vast majority of deaths. Some innocent persons were struck down by wild-shooting policemen and guardsmen during those riots, and buildings were riddled by rifle, shotgun, machine gun, and tank fire. In Newark, 13,326 rounds of ammunition were expended by state police and the New Jersey National Guard, according to the Commission's report. In Detroit, a cigarette, lit near a window of an upper-floor apartment, brought .50 caliber machine-gun fire from a National Guard tank, which killed a four-year-old girl and nearly tore off her mother's arm. Persons sitting on their porches, sleeping in their beds, and riding innocently in their cars were wounded or killed by police or National Guard bullets. Great bitterness remained afterward over the role of authorities in these three cities.

Federal officials learned these bloody lessons from the report of the riot commission and from the observations of Cyrus Vance, special Pentagon representative in Detroit during the riot there. Vance performed the same role in Washington, starting Friday night.

Moving to apply the lessons, the military acted to shape up poorly disciplined and badly trained National Guard units. Hurriedly revised riot training was given to the Guard and the regular Army. Guardsmen were placed under the supervision of regular Army commanders, versed in Pentagon contingency planning for the "long, hot summer" of 1968.

The new training emphasized the use of "minimum necessary force" to get the job done "in a professional manner." Troops were told that indiscriminate use of force and wild gunfire had aggravated rioting in the past and that they were to carry empty guns on the street and load them only on the specific order of an officer, in situations where life was threatened. In place of gunfire, extensive use would be made of tear gas. Early and stringent curfews would be imposed. Sheer numbers of troops and police would be used for their psychological effect and to provide the ability to split up large mobs, protect storefronts, and seal off affected areas.

On the inside cover of the new training manual for the crack 82d Airborne Division, which was called to Washington for the

April rioting, was this quotation from Greek military historian Thucydides: "Of all the manifestations of power, restraint impresses men most."

The Justice Department had launched a program similar to the military's for big-city policemen, including members of the Washington police force. With the help of the International Association of Chiefs of Police, seminars with federal experts were held for local police and public officials. Special training was given to ranking officers in many local police departments at the Army's busy riot-control center at Fort Gordon, Georgia. Two dozen precinct captains and other high-ranking officers from Washington had attended. Before he became Washington's Public Safety Director, in December, 1967, Pat Murphy had had a special role in these training efforts, as a Justice Department aide. For several years, Washington's police, under Chief John B. Layton, had been governed by policies emphasizing the restrained use of force in daily police work. Written departmental policies, based on an Act of Congress for the city, directed policemen to use guns only in defense of their own lives or someone else's life, to shoot a dangerous animal, or to apprehend a felon when *all* other means had been exhausted.

These Washington police regulations paralleled the recommendations of the Federal Bureau of Investigation:

> The decision to resort to firearms is indeed a grave one. Among the important considerations, of course, are the protection of the officer's own life, as well as the lives of fellow officers, and the protection of innocent citizens. A basic rule in firearms training is that a firearm is used only in self-defense or to protect the lives of others.

More than a year before the outbreak, Layton, at the urging of federal officials, had decided that a riot in Washington would be combated by large numbers of policemen, rather than fewer officers using guns. Unless looters somehow threatened the lives of policemen or other citizens, they would not be shot, Layton made clear in a recorded staff conference. And Murphy, after taking over as Public Safety Director, reiterated this policy in his contacts with ranking police officials.

"The law does not allow you to walk up to a group of people engaged in unlawful activity and start blazing away with guns," Layton was to explain later to a reporter.

But Layton, inclined to avoid public fanfare and controversy about his activities, characteristically had failed to circulate his views beyond his top officers, leaving it up to them to carry out the program with their individual commands. And, although Chief Layton did nothing to encourage it, some members of the policemen's lobby and their Congressional friends were spoiling for a chance to challenge Murphy, who was altering fundamentally the promotion and decision-making processes in the police department. Thus, Washington's April riot was to become a twofold test: of Murphy's ability to control his men and of the restrained tactics that D.C. civilians had sold to the military and the police.

On Thursday night, Murphy got the news of the shooting of Dr. King while he was at home watching television. He immediately called for his white, unmarked police-cruiser so that he could see how the city was reacting. He also alerted Assistant Chief Jerry Wilson, his choice to be the department's director of operations. Wilson quickly went to police headquarters.

Meanwhile, at the Pentagon, the Army Operations Center went into action after receiving news of the assassination. Its first concern was to check on conditions in Memphis and then to look at other cities, including Washington. Under Secretary of the Army David E. McGiffert, a tall, lanky, spectacled man, with a quiet, cool manner, was in charge of supplying troops to any city unable to handle disorders. Army General Counsel Robert Jordan was on hand to help coordinate the move, should a Presidential executive order calling for troops be required.

At the Justice Department, Attorney General Ramsey Clark was meeting routinely with top Justice Department officials when a telephone call informed him of the Memphis shooting. Later, at the President's request, Clark flew to Memphis to supervise personally the hunt for Dr. King's slayer. The task of watching the mood of the nation's cities and evaluating any requests for troops before presenting them to the President—the Department's historic role in such situations—thus fell to Deputy Attorney General Warren Christopher.

Murphy drove in his white cruiser along 14th Street and saw the crowds building up. He conferred with plainclothes Lieutenant Joseph Frye, who, two nights before, had called for the withdrawal of uniformed policemen from 14th and U streets and had worked alone to help quiet a hostile crowd gathered in front of the Peoples Drug Store. Frye told Murphy of the Reverend Walter Fauntroy's request that uniformed policemen be kept out of sight this night. Since there were no visible signs of the crowd going out of control, the two men agreed that it would be a good idea to wait to see what would happen.

Murphy's next stop was the Washington Hilton Hotel, six blocks northwest on Connecticut Avenue, where a ninety-man Special Operations Division detail was on duty, awaiting the arrival of President Johnson, who was scheduled to speak at a Democratic fund-raising dinner. When Dr. King was shot, the President canceled his appearance, and Vice President Hubert Humphrey was to substitute for him.

A reporter outside the hotel asked Murphy about the tense crowds on 14th Street.

"We're giving it the light touch," Murphy said. "There are no great numbers of men visible."

The Special Operations Division (SOD) forms the nucleus of an emergency, 400-man Civil Disturbance Unit (CDU), which can be formed on short notice in the various precincts. This unit has intensive riot-control training. Deputy Police Chief Raymond Pyles, who was in charge of the SOD, received a radio report that a crowd was marching toward Mayor Washington's home at 4th and T streets, eleven blocks from 14th and U, in the heart of the inner city. Not knowing what to expect, Murphy and an SOD detail of ten men hurried to the Mayor's house.

This was a diversion of police manpower and attention that cost him a vital thirty minutes, Murphy later admitted. At the Mayor's house, Murphy found Sammie Abbott, a white public relations man from Maryland, who, together with a small group of black pickets, had opposed the construction of freeways in the city of Washington. Abbott's group had decided that the death of Dr. King was an appropriate occasion to push the antifreeway campaign. It was now 9:45 P.M.

Back in his car, ready to return to the Hilton, Murphy heard the police radio report window-breaking at 14th and U. Pyles, who heard it too, transferred forty men from the SOD detail to the Thirteenth Precinct station house for possible use on 14th Street. He wanted to send more of his men, but the Vice President was still at the Hilton and the remaining men were required to protect him.

Minutes later, back at the Hilton, a quick strategy huddle was held by Murphy, Pyles, and Jerry Wilson, who had come up from headquarters. They decided to send uniformed men into the 14th Street area to see if they could contain the crowd while more policemen were rounded up. Headquarters was told to hold the 4 P.M.-to-midnight shift on overtime and bring the midnight-to-8 A.M. shift on duty immediately—moves that increased police manpower, on and off the street, from about 500 to 1,000 men.

Pyles, by now, had alerted Chief Layton, who was at Fort Myer, Arlington, Virginia, attending a Cherry Blossom week military program. Layton was in a special box with Colonel Joseph Conmy, commander of the 3d Infantry's "Old Guard" battalion, who in less than a day would take his men into Washington for riot duty. Layton immediately returned to Washington and went, at Murphy's request, to the Thirteenth Precinct station house to set up a temporary command post.

At 10:24 P.M., the calls came, telling of the window-breaking and looting at Sam's Pawnbrokers and the Rhodes Five and Ten, just south of 14th and U streets.

Uniformed policemen began moving into the area. Murphy passed a few officers wading into a large crowd at 14th and U. Farther up the street, Murphy and Pyles saw a liquor store being looted. They left the car and chased the looters themselves, but without success. When they returned, the car radio was reporting that the policemen back at 14th and U were being stoned by the crowds.

"Pull those men out of there and keep them back until we

get help," Murphy directed Lieutenant Frye, who relayed the order.

Each time another frantic call came in, the dispatcher reached Murphy's car and relayed the message.

"Do whatever you think you should," Murphy would answer in his soft voice, emphasizing, however, that the policemen should retreat if in danger, until more men could be brought up.

A month later, Murphy was to tell the House District Committee, which had a generally critical, conservative majority, about his basic approach in such situations:

"We police most of our cities and most of our counties in this nation with a relatively small number of police officers, and it is sometimes difficult for them to deal with a situation that gets out of hand suddenly involving large numbers of people. When that occurs, our officers must be concerned about their own personal safety. But just as soon as it is reasonably possible, our officers have made arrests and will continue to make arrests."

Thirty police cars were rushed to police headquarters, along with a busload of SOD officers from the Thirteenth Precinct station house. Uniformed officers and detectives, selected for Civil Disturbance Unit duty, were given riot helmets, tear-gas canisters, gas masks, and long white billy clubs, and were put into prowl cars in groups of four.

The process was clumsier and more time-consuming than was expected. Men being brought from other parts of the city and from homes in the suburbs took time to get there. The official who had the key to the Civil Disturbance Unit supply room was not called right away. At one point, a tear-gas canister was accidentally detonated in the supply room, filling it and the entire main floor of headquarters with choking fumes.

By 11 P.M., a little more than half an hour after the looting began in earnest at Sam's Pawnbrokers and the Rhodes Five and Ten, Inspector Mahlon Pitts at police headquarters radioed to Murphy and Pyles:

"Cruiser 24 to Cruiser 10, I have eight cars ready to leave."

Followed by seven paddy wagons, the cars sped through the downtown area and around Thomas Circle to 14th Street, six blocks south of U Street. Pyles broadcast to the policemen in other patrol cars near 14th Street:

"Okay, we've got eight cars ready now. Let's go."

At 11:16 P.M., a busload of CDU men, fully equipped, went to 14th and Swann streets, and then walked to 14th and U. Lining up shoulder to shoulder in a wedge, the forty policemen sealed off car- and foot-traffic in all directions.

Now the cars and paddy wagons sweeping up 14th Street turned around and headed back toward the blockade of men at 14th and U. This time, they began stopping and making arrests.

The policemen on foot, who had been withdrawn by Murphy for their safety, were returned to help stop the looting and make arrests. They used their nightsticks as flails to help break up the crowds and facilitate making arrests.

Q. T. Jackson, a leader of a student takeover of the Howard University administration building a few weeks before, was one of those who was clubbed by a night stick on the head. As the police put him in the paddy wagon, he insisted that he had done nothing.

"They hit Q. T. for nothing," Anthony Gittens, editor of the Howard student newspaper, shouted from the sidewalk.

"What's the matter with you cops?" he called to a policeman sitting in a scout car nearby. "Don't you know that's the kind of stuff that makes people want to kill you? Do you want us to get guns? Do you want a bloodbath?"

The policeman protested: "It wasn't me. I didn't do it. Don't blame me."

The tempo of activity on 14th Street was continuing to increase, and the area of the shopping strip affected by looting was growing.

A call went out for all off-duty policemen to report immediately. Eventually, this brought into action 2,500 of the 3,000 men on the force. As policemen arrived from home, more four-men teams were sent in patrol cars to 14th Street. The area around 14th and U was already beginning to quiet down rapidly, but the police were still outnumbered several blocks farther north.

At 11:49 P.M., Deputy Chief Pyles radioed to all men in the area:

"Enforce the law vigorously for any violation and make arrests."

Mayor Washington, who had finished his tour of 14th Street at about that time, went to the Thirteenth Precinct station house. On his way to the temporary command post in the captain's office, he passed a hall filled with open green lockers containing tear-gas grenades and launchers.

Outside the captain's small office, the station house bustled as never before. Policemen from the street, with buttons and badges ripped off and uniforms rumpled and torn, were rushing in and out, picking up tear gas and masks or bringing in prisoners.

Some of the officers stood next to the police radio for a moment, listening to the reports of looting, vandalism, and stoning of policemen, and shook their heads. Policemen behind the counter were unusually courteous to prisoners, curious citizens, and reporters. The prisoners, themselves, were quietly cooperative, as they went through the involved process of being booked.

One prisoner wore a new pair of pants, two or three sizes too big for him, the cuffs dragging on the floor. Two young girls were brought in, giggling nervously and carrying a pile of clothes as tall as they were. A white man, in a gray three-piece suit, was brought in complaining about the "nigger bastards trying to wreck my town." He was charged with public drunkenness.

Pat Murphy toured 14th Street again and concluded that, although things were still serious, it looked as though the police would be able to establish control. Already nearly 100 people had been arrested, and the crowds were somewhat smaller and more scattered along the street. Several entire blocks were now occupied mostly by police, with hit-and-run bands of young looters their primary adversaries.

It was past midnight, and, although the force was still outnumbered, Layton told the Mayor that he felt the police could restore order without help from the outside. Enough policemen were moving onto 14th Street to do the job, he believed. He made the same report to officials of the Army Operations Center at the Pentagon. At this point, there were nearly 500 police in the area, including a few cars sent to 7th Street, where window-breaking had been reported after midnight.

Only four hours had passed since Dr. King died, and two and a half hours since the first window had been broken. Although the disturbance had turned into a serious disorder, it now appeared that relief was in sight. The police department thought it could bring the situation under control.

Murphy had left earlier for police headquarters to move the command post there. Now, Layton and the Mayor and his aides joined him. (When the Mayor knocked on the door of the fourth-floor communications center, a security-minded policeman who did not recognize him at first refused to admit him.)

"Shortly after midnight," Murphy later explained on a television broadcast, "the difficulties which had been confined generally to 14th Street were under relatively effective control by the police department. As a matter of fact, by early Friday morning, before daybreak, we were down to below normal police activity, the number of calls, the number of crimes occurring. And we were hopeful that Friday would be a calm day."

The Mayor, Murphy, and Layton conferred about the day ahead. Any more trouble probably would come at night, they reasoned, particularly if the day proceeded normally, with schools and commercial enterprises in operation. As a precaution, the police force would be kept on overlapping twelve-hour shifts to double the number of men on the streets, and the Civil Disturbance Unit would be activated in force late Friday afternoon.

A riot commission study of twenty-four disorders had indicated that major violence in all those cases had occurred during the night hours, and that, as a general rule, violence at night was followed by lulls during the daytime. However, there had been a few notable exceptions to this pattern. Washington was to be another.

The question of troops for Friday night would be reviewed with the Army Operations Center. Murphy met at the Pentagon with the Center's officers at 3 A.M. There, too, it was agreed that the predawn quiet on the streets suggested that the next crisis probably would not develop before nightfall. The District of Columbia National Guard would be put into uniform and assembled at the city's armory, prepared to go onto the streets Friday night, if necessary.

Some critics of the Washington riot-control effort, notably local businessmen whose businesses were wiped out on Friday, have argued that troops should have been brought into Washington in force early that day on a purely preventive basis—a step the federal government, historically, has been most reluctant to take.

Attorney General Clark, following the Detroit riot, wrote a circular letter to all state governors about summoning federal troops to deal with "domestic violence." Although the procedures set out do not apply strictly to Washington, because its Mayor is not an elected official but a Presidential appointee, the basic principles are relevant.

Troops may be alerted on the oral request of a Governor. But, the Attorney General wrote: "Even such preliminary steps . . . represent a serious departure from our traditions of local responsibility for law enforcement."

The Attorney General emphasized that "the President, under the terms of the statute and the historic practice, must exercise his own judgment as to whether federal troops will be sent, and as to such questions as timing, the size of the force, and the federalization of the National Guard."

Clearly, at 3 A.M. on Friday, with a report that the city was "under relatively effective control," there was little precedent for summoning federal troops. Those in the area had already been placed on an emergency alert for possible duty in Washington. Troops could be on the streets within two to three hours after the decision to move them.

Weeks after the riot was over, Senator Byrd of West Virginia conducted his series of closed nighttime interviews with officers and merchants, many of whom were critical of the way the disturbance had been quelled. He made available the 1,418 pages of testimony, on the condition that the identity of the witnesses not be disclosed.

A number of the police officers who testified were opposed to

Murphy's policy, feeling that the restraint that they attributed to him (although publicly Layton also accepted responsibility for it) had tied their hands and forced them to stand by and watch looters pillage stores. This view was shared by some businessmen as well. Other police officers, however, told the Senator that they were simply outnumbered and could not do much until additional police and troops arrived to give them an umbrella under which to operate.

A member of the CDU told Senator Byrd that his Ninth Precinct group was advised at 10:30 P.M., Thursday, that it was department policy not to shoot looters.

Asked to explain the difference between shooting looters and other felons, he replied:

"Shooting of looters is liable to precipitate a situation that could be worse than the present one. When the determination is made to shoot looters, there is no return. Once the first action is taken, there is no backing from it. It must continue."

A thirty-three-year-old veteran of seven years on the force, who said he questioned Director Murphy's qualifications, disagreed:

"I was not very proud to be a policeman. Things happened in front of me, like looting, and I was on the end of a few coke bottles, house bricks, and what have you.

"I stand there as a police officer, and I am instructed by the department to maintain order as much as I can, but refrain in the use of my service revolver.

"I felt as though I had handcuffs on myself. I really couldn't do anything. I felt as though the department did not want me to do anything out there."

A Negro policeman said he had no instructions to avoid arresting looters or to refrain from using his gun.

"We felt that if we used our service revolvers, we could have injured some bystanders," he told the Senator. "We felt that we would not get proper backing if we did not use better judgment."

When the outnumbered policemen pulled back, they rode up and down 14th Street in their prowl cars or parked on side streets to await reinforcements.

"Everybody on the street was standing around and joining in

after they saw the police cars cruising up and down the street," a twenty-five-year-old Negro policeman from Alabama told Byrd. "We weren't making any effort to make arrests."

Another policeman told of his efforts to arrest as many violators as possible.

"There's 100 people and five policemen—what do you have?" he asked. "All I could grab is one or two people maybe at most."

He said he agreed with the idea that the police revolver should be used to stop escaping looters, but commented:

"You should, but you wouldn't."

And, after it was all over, one inner-city ghetto resident told Mayor Washington that it was lucky the police did not start shooting, "because we had them outgunned two to one and were prepared to fire back."

At 3:10 A.M., Friday morning, Mayor Washington and Chief Layton left the police command center to meet with waiting newsmen. There had been no police radio transmissions concerning the disturbance since 1:52 A.M.

"The crisis is not over yet," Mayor Washington cautioned. "It's still out there, but the police have it well in hand."

He then departed to tour 14th Street and 7th Street. Finding both streets quiet, he went to his home at 408 T Street, N.W., at about 4:30 A.M.

Layton told the reporters he saw no reason to cancel the rest of the Cherry Blossom Week festivities or the parade scheduled for Saturday.

The Civil Disturbance Unit was sent home at 5:30 A.M., with orders to report back at 5 P.M., Friday, with shaving gear and prepared for several days away from home, if necessary. Thursday's 4 P.M.-to-midnight shift of policemen was sent home at 8 A.M., as the next shift arrived for duty, prepared for a twelve-hour-tour and what Pat Murphy hoped would be "a calm day."

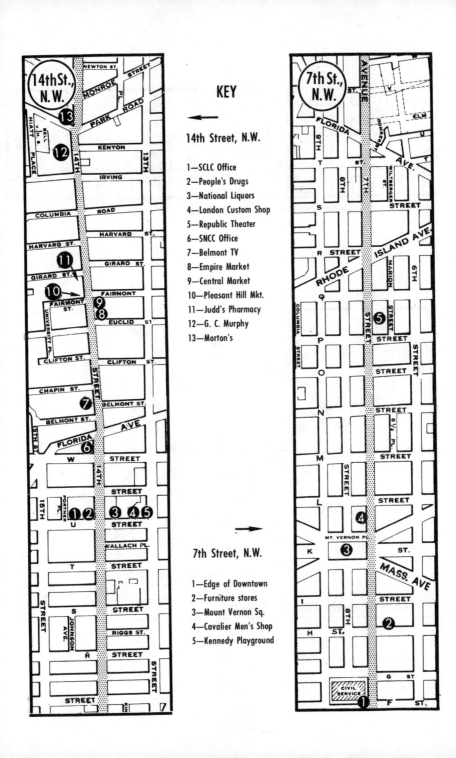

KEY

← **14th Street, N.W.**

1—SCLC Office
2—People's Drugs
3—National Liquors
4—London Custom Shop
5—Republic Theater
6—SNCC Office
7—Belmont TV
8—Empire Market
9—Central Market
10—Pleasant Hill Mkt.
11—Judd's Pharmacy
12—G. C. Murphy
13—Morton's

→ **7th Street, N.W.**

1—Edge of Downtown
2—Furniture stores
3—Mount Vernon Sq.
4—Cavalier Men's Shop
5—Kennedy Playground

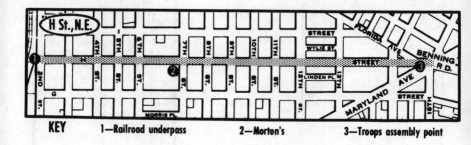

KEY   1—Railroad underpass   2—Morton's   3—Troops assembly point

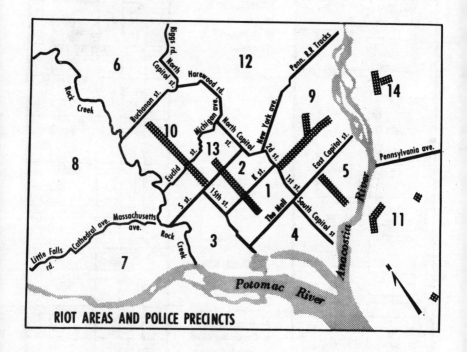

RIOT AREAS AND POLICE PRECINCTS

III

Friday: The Thin Line Vanishes

On the steps of the Jefferson Memorial, under clearing skies, a Hollywood production crew was filming George Peppard, Richard Kiley, and Paul McGrath in a scene for the motion picture *Pendulum*. Tourists were out early along the Tidal Basin, in the 60° weather, to photograph the pink blossoms of the famed cherry trees.

In the bumper-to-bumper mass of automobiles carrying commuters to their jobs downtown, car-pool conversation on Friday, April 5, was mostly about the rioting of the night before. But white Washington, noting that the night's trouble had been confined, clearly did not expect a new flare-up.

It was different in black Washington. There, the same ominous tension that had preceded Thursday night's inner-city outbreak was noticeable, not only on the riot-torn 14th Street shopping strip but also on 7th Street and in neighborhoods in the northeast and southeast sections of the city.

"It was terrifying, just terrifying last night," a black woman told a white neighbor in the integrated Capitol Hill area. "I hear that they are going to burn down the whole town this weekend."

She had been at her job in the Lincoln Theater Thursday night when the crowd demanded its closing in memory of Dr. King and forced the customers to leave.

Streets were picking up more than their usual crowds of idlers, as some working men decided to take the day off. On a side street near 14th and U, at about 8 A.M., three young Negroes were

45

standing on the curb when a garbage truck pulled up. The acrid aroma of tear gas still hung in the air.

"Get on," the Negro driver called out to one of them. "It's time to go to work."

"Not today, man," was the reply. "Not today. I'm not going to work today."

The driver pulled away.

Children, dressed for school, were standing on the street corners, telling friends that they were not going to classes, giving each other glamorized versions of Thursdays night's happenings.

The schools were regarded as a key to hopes for a peaceful Friday. If the city's 150,000 pupils could be kept in classes, the police felt they had a chance to maintain control.

At 1:30 A.M., School Superintendent William R. Manning had talked by telephone with Mayor Washington and Pat Murphy and agreed to keep the schools open. Manning, a newcomer to Washington from Lansing, Michigan, who had taken over as head of a much criticized school system only five months before, decided that special programs of tribute to Dr. King would be held. Students would be encouraged "to adhere to Dr. King's philosophy of nonviolence and to remain off the streets during the afternoon and evening."

But, from the first bell, the schools were under pressure to turn the children loose. Principals were aware of an unusual and alarming restlessness. William H. Simons, president of the Washington Teachers Union, wanted the schools closed so that teachers could attend memorial services. In an effort resembling Stokely Carmichael's action the night before in getting the 14th Street merchants to close their shops, William L. "Winky" Hall, Jr., a regional organizer for SNCC, demanded by telephone that the schools close in Dr. King's memory. Hall called Manning twice and also phoned the Reverend Everett A. Hewlet, president of the School Board, and the principals of the city's inner-city high schools.

"Close the schools within thirty minutes, or we will," he told Manning.

Worried parents began jamming the school's switchboards, asking that their children be sent home. Manning later reported that the flood of calls prevented his office from keeping in touch with the Mayor and with school principals.

By 10:30 A.M., growing crowds of Negro youths were appearing on 14th Street and elsewhere in the city. They ranged up and down the streets aimlessly, taunting white motorists. The Thirteenth Precinct requested neighborhood schools to keep their pupils in class, and Inspector Owen Davis, a ranking Negro officer, called Dr. Manning to stress the importance of such action.

During the morning, Assistant Superintendent of Schools George Rhodes used a regularly scheduled city-wide meeting with two dozen high school student leaders to urge students to stay in school, and principals at the high schools called special assemblies for the same purpose. Rhodes told a 12:30 P.M. School Board meeting that student leaders felt that "the people in the community had to say in no uncertain terms that looting is wrong," if violence was to be avoided.

"They found it quite understandable that students would react in a violent manner to what had happened," Rhodes said.

But, by noon, it was evident that the schools could not keep control. More than half of Cardozo High School's 1,700 students had departed, walking out during morning classes or at the lunch break. Students from McKinley High School, at 2d and T streets, N.E., and some other high schools, answered the summons of black militants and began marching to Howard University, where Stokely Carmichael was to appear at a campus rally. The School Board meeting authorized principals to dismiss schools on a staggered basis.

Sterling Tucker, who was then the executive director of the Washington Urban League and has since been appointed to head the organization's new "Urban Thrust" program, called Deputy Superintendent of Schools Benjamin Henley to caution him that "closing the schools is the worst thing that could happen."

"We can't hold these kids," Tucker quoted Henley as replying. "You don't know how they have been acting."

As more and more school youngsters appeared on the city streets, the pace of the disorder picked up and trouble spread. In some cases, boys and girls moved in groups toward the shopping areas, hitting them in force. By 2 P.M., reports of intense looting and heavy burning were being received from widely scattered points.

In other cities—particularly Chicago, Buffalo, Boston, Detroit, and San Francisco—school children were also reaching the streets that morning and early afternoon and joining in window breaking, looting, and burning.

This was a new experience for school authorities who had not given much attention to the problem of holding onto youngsters during a riot. Previously, riots in other cities had occurred during the summer or at night, when schools were closed. School staffs often had conveyed the attitude that their area of responsibility does not extend beyond the schoolhouse door.

Students, flocking to the 14th Street shopping strip from Cardozo High School and other schools in the area, could see the extent of Thursday night's damage—extensive window breakage, some stores looted clean, a handful burned out. But the shelves of most stores on the strip were still invitingly full.

A few store owners, frightened by Thursday night's events, did not reopen Friday morning. Metal grates protected some shop windows. As the crowds built up, other stores began to close, some in response to warnings to do so. Restless youths, milling on the sidewalk, teased and taunted white clerks in the stores that remained open.

The pattern on 14th Street was being repeated in other busy shopping areas, including the 7th Street strip, the H Street, N.E., strip, and parts of southeast and northeast Washington, across the Anacostia River. Rumors sped around the city, adding to the air of anxiety.

At the corner of 14th Street and Columbia Road, youths surrounded a white Mustang, which was stopped for a red light, and began rocking it, laughing at the driver before letting him pull away.

A block south, at 14th and Harvard, a mob of youths spilled onto the intersection. Motorists pressed their horns and zigzagged to get through. Cars that were stopped for red lights were rocked, and laughing threats were made to their drivers. A white youth was pulled out of a Volkswagen and beaten, until a neighborhood Catholic priest made his way into the crowd and intervened.

About forty teen-aged youths slipped into the charred hulk of the Pleasant Hill Market at 14th and Fairmont streets to drink canned beer found in the rubble.

There were few policemen on 14th Street at noon; the police department still did not have a full picture of the danger ahead. The Civil Disturbance Unit was not due back on duty until 5 P.M. Although the department was now on overlapping twelve-hour shifts, many men on the midnight shift had been sent home by 10 A.M., having been called to duty at 10 P.M. or earlier Thursday night. For a while, there were not many more men actually patrolling the 14th Street area than on a routine day. The next shift was not due on the job until 4 P.M.

"There is a dividing line, a thin line," Pat Murphy told a reporter later, "that keeps lots of people from breaking a window, or, once a store window has been broken, from taking what has been left exposed inside. Once that line is crossed, usually law-abiding people join in, and everything breaks out of control."

The "thin line," which up to then had protected the city from serious disorder, was about to vanish.

At noon, the sidewalks of 14th Street, from U Street, at the bottom of the hill, to Park Road, twenty blocks north at the top, were overflowing. The largest crowds, 100 or more people at each corner, were concentrated in the five blocks from Clifton Street north to Columbia Road, where the most serious trouble Thursday night had not been quelled by police until nearly 3 A.M.

The crowds on 14th Street and elsewhere generally were made up of bands of youths. Some were school children, younger than ten years old; some were teenagers and twenty-year-olds—many dropouts or unemployed. Curiosity-motivated adults, including some who had gone to the commercial area to shop, work, or eat, were on the fringes.

At 12:13 P.M., a fire broke out in the Safeway Supermarket a half-block south on 14th and U, N.W. The smoke could be seen and the wailing of fire engines was heard all up and down the 14th Street hill. The crowds grew.

At 12:17 P.M., a small fire started in a clothing store at 14th and Harvard, N.W. Like the Safeway store, it had been looted Thursday night. Firemen found the 14th and Harvard intersection choked by a swarming mob.

Suddenly, large numbers of youths began breaking windows and pouring into stores. Stones, bricks, and bottles, as well as debris from Thursday night, were used to smash windows and gain entrance to the stores. Liquor bottles, taken from the display windows of the first liquor stores hit, were used as missiles to break into other stores.

"It's lootin' time," was the signal phrase for those who bothered to voice the obvious.

"The death of Martin Luther King had nothing to do with what happened," a young black man, a roving leader in the city's recreation department, suggested later. "It was an excuse to be destructive or to clean up. Ever since the Watts riot, this has been picking up. Deep in your mind you have been preparing yourself for it."

Once the first break was made, one or two teen-aged youths kicked away the jagged glass and went inside. Others rushed in, followed by smaller children and, before long, by adults—in a few cases, their parents.

Stores that had been broken into and cleaned out Thursday night were set ablaze. Among them were the London Custom Shop at 14th and U, N.W., the Belmont TV and Appliance Store, and the Empire Supermarket at 14th and Euclid streets, N.W., already burned to a shell by the rioters who had clashed with police for an hour at 2 A.M.

On Thursday night, a man had tried to set Judd's Pharmacy at 14th and Girard streets on fire with burning newspapers but had been thwarted by the rain. Now, two teenagers spent several minutes yanking at the protective iron grating over the doors and windows of the drugstore. Finally, the two boys snapped the grating from the front door and kicked in the glass. With a dozen younger boys, they rushed inside and soon emerged with as much candy and merchandise as they could carry. One nine-year-old carried a dozen boxes of cough drops.

Outside, one of the older boys tore up a cardboard box, set

the pieces on fire, and placed them inside the front door. Flames spread quickly through the store and up into the four stories of apartments above it. Hours later, only a brick shell remained.

As firemen fought the blaze at Judd's Pharmacy, a looter emerged from Buddy's Beverage Store, a block away at 14th and Harvard streets. He set down two liquor bottles on the sidewalk, smashed a gasoline-filled soda bottle on the window ledge, and lit a match. The gasoline burst into flames, and firemen extinguished the fire with difficulty. Then they moved to the vicinity of 14th and Columbia Road, where another building was ablaze.

"The company took a hose line," a white fireman later told West Virginia's Senator Byrd, "and I was assisting the pumping man to make the connection. They were calling for water, when a gang of Negro males came across the street and pushed and shoved the pumper man and told him not to hook up the hose."

"We didn't build the goddamned fire for any white people to put out," one teenager shouted. "Don't worry, you will all be dead before the night is over."

The firemen ignored them and tried desperately to connect the hose, while their comrades at the other end of the hose called for water.

"Our main concern at the time was to get water in the hose so the men wouldn't burn up," the fireman recalled.

One of the youths grabbed the fireman by the coat and began pulling him away from the hose. "I'm talking to you, white motherfucker," the teenager said.

As the fireman pulled away, his coat ripped. The youth picked up a plastic store mannequin and threw it at him.

"Let the firemen alone; they aren't bothering you," a person in the crowd that formed around them called out. The firemen then connected the hose.

"But they didn't do anything to assist or help us to restrain him," the fireman told the Senator. "There were homes and apartment buildings on top of the store, and right behind it were heavy tenement sections, and the fires were raging out of control."

"We're being bricked," one officer called over the police radio near Harvard Street. "We can't get the fire trucks through," another officer called frantically over the radio.

Deputy Police Chief Raymond S. Pyles, who had returned to duty shortly after 11 A.M., answered, "Pull back until we can get more troops up there. Tell the firemen to pull back until we can get protection."

Tenth Precinct Captain Eugene D. Gooding led four patrol cars up 14th Street, clearing a temporary path through the crowd. The police stopped at 14th and Columbia, fired six canisters of tear gas into the crowd between Harvard Street and Columbia Road, and then blocked the intersection with their cars.

The roadblock was not maintained for long, because Captain Gooding and his four carloads of policemen were needed to protect firemen three blocks to the north, at Park Road, where a spectacular fire at the Worthmore Clothing Store drew a large crowd. As soon as the policemen left the Columbia Road area, the crowds surged northward and began looting the merchandise in the clothing and specialty shops between Columbia and Park roads.

Men, women, and children swarmed into Beyda's fashion shop, Kay Jewelers, Irving's Men's Shop, Mary Jane Shoes, the Lerner, Carousel, and Grayson dress shops, Howard Clothes, Cannon Shoes, Woolworth's, and the G. C. Murphy variety store. Most of these shops were white-owned, chain-store branches on the west side of 14th Street.

A couple in their forties, with two teen-aged children, emerged from Grayson's store with dozens of dresses and women's coats, still on display hangers and with plastic covers over them. Two women in their twenties carried a box piled high with yard goods. They set it down every few steps to secure a better grip on it. A young couple carried out of Beyda's double armloads of clothes in suit boxes.

Broken glass, stripped display mannequins, shoe boxes, and dropped clothes were trampled on the sidewalk. A few adults and school children walked by, stepping into the street to avoid the crowds.

In front of Hahn's Shoe Store, midway between Columbia and

Park roads, about three dozen school-age children cheered four older boys who smashed a big display window with bottles. The boys then climbed through the window and handed out shoes, hats, and other merchandise to the younger children. One ten-year-old boy ran off with a novelty hat.

After Hahn's was picked clean, an older boy placed a pile of boxes and paper in the display window and lit a match. The littered trash inside the store fed the flames, and the store began to burn. Across the street, Grayson's and Standard Drug burst into flames, and fire trucks and hoses were strewn suddenly all over the block, as firemen fought the blazes.

The men, women, and children, caught up in the carnival atmosphere of the looting, were oblivious of the fires and the equipment. As one store after another was set on fire, the looters barely kept ahead of the spreading flames and smoke.

A beer-bottle Molotov cocktail flew into Beyda's, while a dozen looters were inside. A policeman with a bullhorn shouted at the rioters to get out. The cloth stuffed into the end of the beer bottle burned down to the gasoline inside and, with a roar, sent flames shooting through the store. Those inside were able to make it to the street just in time.

A few minutes later, the nearby G. C. Murphy variety store began to burn. Two teen-aged boys were trapped inside. Police and firemen found their bodies in the remains of the burned out building at midnight Saturday. They were the second and third persons to die in the rioting and the first two of seven to perish in the fires.

Burned beyond recognition was the body of a boy slightly over 5 feet tall who had weighed about 120 pounds. The second victim of the rioting, he must be listed as unidentified, because no one has come forward to identify him. The coroner believes he was about fourteen years old. His body was found near the loading platform at the rear of the store.

George Neely was the third victim. An eighteen-year-old senior at Phelps Vocational School who had hoped to go to college on a football scholarship, George had left home Friday morning to register for the draft. That was the last his mother, who works days, saw of him. A sister said George returned briefly to their home and then departed before noon. His brother James, a college freshman, identified the body, which was found in a second-floor storage room. The Neely's home, at 1419 E Street, N.E., is about two miles from 14th Street, N.W.

As the fire in the spacious G. C. Murphy store burned out of control, a policeman warned looters to evacuate the Mary Jane shoe store, which was separated from Murphy's only by a narrow alley. The glass was gone from the still-locked front door, and the looters simply stepped through the empty frame, right past the policeman, and ran. A couple in their twenties made a hurried exit, loaded down with shoe boxes and purses. A woman and a young girl, possibly mother and daughter, carried out bags stuffed with shoes. Two well-dressed women in their twenties carried only two pair of shoes each, perhaps all they had time to try on before the alarm was sounded. A young man in shirtsleeves brought out a metal garbage can filled with loot.

As black smoke billowed out of more than half the buildings between Columbia and Park roads, the police tried to catch youths setting fires and to protect stores that had not been hit. But it became a game of tag, which the dozen policemen on foot kept losing. Youths, in packs ranging in number from six to twelve, darted back and forth across the street and behind stores to break in, loot, and then set the buildings afire.

Firemen continued to be targets, and the police had all they could do to protect them. Policemen rode on the fire trucks and grouped patrol cars around them up and down 14th Street. Here and there, policemen on foot in the midst of the crowds tried to shoo looters away from the stores, but they were generally ignored.

The police made arrests when they could, but they were more badly outnumbered than at the beginning of Thursday night. "We did not have the manpower to go into large groups of people and select persons out of the group to make arrests," one twenty-three-year-old officer from West Virginia later told Senator Byrd.

Two men, John H. Walker, a twenty-two-old machine operator, and Jessie J. Hinson, a twenty-three-old truck driver, were arrested about 1 P.M. in a clothing store near 14th and Harvard streets. Neither had had a previous brush with the law. They were on their lunch hour, watching the looting, when, as Hinson put it, they "fell in with the wrong crowd." They later pleaded guilty to misdemeanor charges and were put on probation.

Police Captain Tilmon O'Bryant, then the third-highest ranking Negro on the Washington force, stood in the middle of 14th Street and told *Washington Post* reporter Robert Maynard, "Look at this; just look at it. They don't know what they are doing, some of them. They are doing it just because everyone else is."

"Why are you taking those things?" O'Bryant asked a fifteen-year-old boy, clutching an armful of coats, blouses, and other women's clothes from Beyda's Petites Shop.

"I don't know, I just saw it laying there," the youth answered.

"Put it back," O'Bryant ordered.

The boy's face showed disappointment, but he went back to the curb, dropped the loot, and walked away.

Other Negro policemen tried to persuade people to drop what they were carrying and go home. Usually, the looters just ran away, confident that the police could not chase them.

Four Negro officers in a patrol car just north of Park Road were more successful in getting housewives to drop things they had taken from the Safeway store at 14th and Park.

Inside the store, cash registers were overturned and the contents of shelves pulled down into 3 inches of water on the floor. Mustard and catsup oozed past burst boxes of cake mix. A well-dressed, matronly-looking woman was one of several who assured newspaperman Maynard that they were not looting.

"Look," she said. "I come here to shop every Friday night. Where else am I to find food? All the stores are closed or looted. It's not that the food is free. It's just that there's not going to be much food around here for a long time."

The heavy looting and the string of fires began moving south on 14th Street.

"Where did you get the stuff from, Bonnie?" a man asked a woman friend he saw walking north across Euclid Street carrying two fancy new table lamps.

"Right down there," she said. "You better hurry up."

Martin Luther King and Stokely Carmichael, photographed together at a February, 1968, meeting, at which Dr. King told 100 black civil-rights activists about his Poor People's Campaign plans. This unusual picture was taken by a free lance photographer.

She pointed to the Hamilton and Jordan Fine Furniture Store, where men and women were carrying out sofas, assorted chairs, end tables, and lamps. Bystanders on the corner watched the spectacle and cheered the looters on.

"You got yourself something there," one youth shouted.

A man in his fifties, dressed in work clothes, recognized William Raspberry, a columnist for *The Washington Post*. He clasped his hand on Raspberry's shoulder.

"Soul brother," he said to the black reporter, "ask them to stop. Tell them they're doing the wrong thing. Plead with them. They won't listen to me."

There was less activity down the 14th Street hill toward U Street. The pickings were not as good, because there were fewer clothing and appliance stores. A number of stores at the bottom of the hill bore "Soul Brother" signs, scrawled in white paint or soap, on their still-unbroken windows.

It was 3 P.M., and fires were consuming whole blocks of buildings along 14th, above Euclid Street. Scattered fires burned as far south as U Street. Firemen, who had continued on doubled-up duty Friday morning, now stayed at each blaze just long enough to smother the flames. They rushed from one still-smoldering store to another, hoping that the fires would not rekindle. But they often did.

Billows of smoke began to appear in the sky above the parallel 7th Street, N.W., shopping strip, seven blocks to the east, and the H Street strip, located northeast of Capitol Hill. Marauding looters in cars and on foot were darting through the downtown shopping district and hitting stores just off fashionable Connecticut Avenue. A shopping row southeast of Capitol Hill, on 8th Street, S.E., was also mauled.

Later, it became clear that the riot that erupted with explosive force that Friday afternoon had been building up all morning, but the signals had not been recognized.

There was the early-morning tension and unrest—the men who refused to report to work, the school children who stayed on street corners, the students who left school to join them, the worried parents, the crowds gathering on the streets in different sections of the city, the youths taunting motorists and store clerks, the general feeling in the black areas that things were likely to blow up as the impact of the assassination sank in.

The ghetto telegraph apparently had a better early-warning system than the police department, which, by mid-morning, had released the exhausted men it had placed on extended duty. thereby reducing the force on the street to near-normal strength. Overnight, police reports of incidents had dropped sharply. Between 3 A.M. and noon, there were only about a half-dozen reports of lootings and fires at scattered locations. As late as 11 A.M., the police department was still reporting confidently that the situation was "not too bad." Police officials indicated more concern about a press conference and rally that Stokely Carmichael was about to hold than with the gathering storm on the streets.

The Mayor and Pat Murphy went to the White House shortly after 11 A.M., armed with the comparatively reassuring word from police headquarters. Murphy was going to nail down arrangements to have the D.C. National Guard available for night duty. The Mayor was answering a Presidential call to meet with civil-rights leaders, Cabinet members, Congressional leaders, and top-ranking Negro public officials to discuss ways of averting further violence in the nation.

But by 12:30 P.M., the police department had realized that things were coming apart in the streets. Suddenly, the volume of incident reports started to soar. It was evident that many areas besides 14th Street were affected, which ruled out using Thursday night's tactic of concentrating all available men in one area to bring it under control.

Assistant Chief Jerry Wilson, director of operations, ordered the 4 P.M. shift called in early and frantically went from office to office, sending all available officers onto the street. Chief Layton sent word to Murphy, who by this time had gone to the Pentagon, that he did not think the department could handle the situation much longer without outside help.

Members of Ujamma raise a black-nationalist flag. After the ceremony, the U.S. flag is restored to a half-staff position on the Howard University flagpole.

On the morning after the destruction of Thursday night, tension is in the air. On the streets, groups of teenagers march, shout, and start again to break windows. Authorities sense trouble ahead — sooner than they had expected.

Youths shout and wave along 14th Street, N.W.

As fires begin anew, police cars move north on 14th Street, **12**
N.W., from Columbia Road to Park Road, to protect firemen.

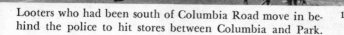

Looters who had been south of Columbia Road move in be- **13**   **14**
hind the police to hit stores between Columbia and Park.

Men, women, and little children join in sacking stores. They fill boxes and
other containers, pile hats on their heads, and hug bundles of clothes.

15   16

On 7th Street, just above the main downtown shopping area, police have closed off northbound traffic but are without the manpower to halt looting of the stores.

17   18

Inside the Safeway supermarket at 14th Street and Park Road, shopping carts become looting vehicles as men wade through food to make their selections.

21

22

20

Captain Tilmon O'Bryant scolds boy for looting and orders him to return the stolen goods, which he did.

Helmeted policemen join firemen on their
way past a row of liquor stores to a blaze
on 14th Street, N.W.

A lone policeman directs evacuation of
rioters from a 14th Street shoe store threatened by spreading fire.

23

A new store fire erupts.

24   Wholesale ransacking of liquor stores continues, at 13th and Florida, N.E.

25

It is 2:30 P.M., Friday, April 5, 1968. From the air, looking south, a pattern of heavy smoke becomes the trademark of devastated 14th Street.

26

27

28

At the top of the 14th Street hill, frustrated firemen are limited to a losing sidewalk battle against savage flames eating out the strip's most popular stores *(above, left)*. Where there is no fire, there is looting, while more and more hoses snake through the streets *(below, left)*. Inside the Murphy variety store *(above, right)*, two trapped youths are burned to death.

Policemen corner two suspects at 14th and G streets, N.W. Note dropped shoes.

At 14th and I, the fashionable D. J. Kaufman men's store is gutted by gasoline-fed flames after being looted.

31   32

Policemen downtown frisk a man over the hood of a car *(above)*.

In the late afternoon, H Street, N.E., goes up in flames *(left)*.

On 7th Street at 4 P.M. *(above)*, there are no police or firemen to respond right away to a huge fire because other blazes, looting, and traffic have delayed them.

Bewildered firemen *(below)* drag their hoses in a frantic search for hydrants to begin battling flames at Sears' garden shop in Northeast. 34

35   Friday afternoon, panicky workers leaving downtown create a huge traffic jam.

IV

Midday Friday: Hot Words

On Friday morning, April 5, the Washington, D.C., police department was concerned about what black activist Stokely Carmichael might do.

Although the city was tense, no looting or burning had occurred that morning, and the authorities had high hopes of keeping the lid on.

Police intelligence had learned that Carmichael would hold a news conference at the former headquarters of the New School for Afro-American Thought, at 2208 14th Street, N.W., which had been taken over by the Student Nonviolent Coordinating Committee. After that, he was expected to appear at an outdoor rally at Howard University.

The police felt they had cause to worry about Carmichael. On Thursday night, the tall, handsome, avowed black revolutionist had led a group of youths and young adults along 14th Street, ordering merchants to close their stores in Dr. King's memory. That night ended in looting and burning. Carmichael had tried to stem the violence, but, when it became clear that he was going to be unsuccessful, he had vanished into the night.

The volatile Carmichael had been in and out of Washington for several years, appearing and disappearing. For well over a year, however, he had made Washington his base, leaving only occasionally for such diverse places as Atlanta, Nashville, New York City, Havana, and Hanoi.

In 1966, he had excited Washingtonians' interest when he declared that his group would fight for local self-government in the capital "in the ways the boys in Vietnam are fighting for elections over there." He warned that, in the event of failure, "we're going to burn down the city."

Early in 1968, he had called together most of the city's Negro activists to form the "Black United Front" organization and had talked about the black community's "taking over" such local institutions as the police department and the schools.

To many whites, Carmichael was the personification of the "outside agitator" who moved from place to place creating trouble. Many were convinced that a cause-and-effect relationship existed between what he said and what happened subsequently in some of the nation's cities.

Carmichael and Dr. King had come to an ideological parting of the ways in 1966, during the Meredith march in Mississippi, when Carmichael coined the "black power" slogan as a rallying cry for a new antiwhite militancy that abandoned nonviolence as a way of effecting social change. Dr. King, by contrast, never accepted the concept of black separatism and shunned violence, but he fretted publicly that time was running out on nonviolence in America.

In spite of their differences, they had remained in relatively close touch, and appeared to have had a personal relationship almost akin to that of two brothers—including a certain amount of sibling rivalry. In February, 1968, when a photograph of Dr. King posing with Carmichael was published by *The Washington Post,* there was annoyance in Dr. King's camp that it had happened; but Dr. King, himself, just smiled.

"I don't know why he loves that little rascal so much," a ranking aide to Dr. King told an associate.

That the affection was reciprocated was revealed by Carmichael at his Friday morning news conference.

He described Dr. King as "the one man of our race that this country's older generations, the militants, the revolutionaries, and the masses of black people would still listen to. . . . He was the one man in our race who was trying to teach our people to have love and compassion and mercy for what white people have done."

It did not take Carmichael long to warn the white man that he faced retaliatory action.

"When white America killed Dr. King last night, she declared war on us," he said. "There will be no crying and there will be no funeral.

"The rebellions that have been occurring around these cities and this country is just light stuff to what is about to happen. We have to retaliate for the deaths of our leaders. The execution for those deaths will not be in the courtrooms. They're going to be in the streets of the United States of America.

"The kind of man that killed Dr. King last night made it a whole lot easier for a whole lot of black people today," Carmichael went on. "There no longer needs to be intellectual discussion. Black people know that they have to get guns. White America will live to cry since she killed Dr. King last night."

As he warmed up at the SNCC press conference, Carmichael became even more dramatic. Here are pertinent exchanges with the newsmen:

Q. Mr. Carmichael, are you declaring war on white America?
A. White America has declared war on black people. She did so when she stole the first black man from Africa. . . . And black people are going to have to find ways to survive. The only way to survive is to get some guns. Because that's the only way white America keeps us in check, because she's got the guns.
Q. Stokely, what do you see this ultimately leading to? A blood-bath in which nobody wins?
A. First, my name is Mr. Carmichael, and, secondly, black people will survive the bath. Last question.
Q. What accomplishments or objectives do you visualize from the encounter? What do you think you will accomplish?
A. The black man can't do nothing in this country. Then, we are going to stand up on our feet and die like men. If that's our only act of manhood, then goddammit, we're going to die. We're tired of living on our stomachs.
Q. One last question: Do you fear for your life?
A. The hell with my life. You should fear for yours. I know I'm going to die. I know I'm leaving.

At the news conference, Carmichael addressed himself primarily to "whitey." Immediately afterward, he went to Howard

University, where he was the featured speaker at an outdoor campus rally called by student militants at that predominantly black Washington institution.

The student-run rally competed for student attention with a University-sponsored memorial service, in Crampton Auditorium, which was much different in tone and content.

Relations between the University administration and the students had not been good. Only two weeks before, students had demanded a greater voice in the management of the University and had won some concessions, after occupying the institution's administration building for four days.

That morning, hundreds of students and faculty members quietly filled the auditorium. The University choir sang Brahm's "Requiem," "A Mighty Fortress Is Our God," and the hymn "Precious Lord," which Dr. King had requested shortly before he was shot in Memphis. There was a printed program. The men on the platform were mainly ministers, who appealed to God for strength and vision.

Speaking in the cadences of a minister, University President James M. Nabrit, Jr., said: "A shadow has fallen upon the land . . . the result of senseless violence, rampant racism . . . a blow to mankind and its hopes and strivings throughout the world. Howard University weeps for him. . . . His death shall not have been in vain if from his blood shall arise one thousand Martin Luther Kings. . . . He was a man, a Christian man, a man of love, a man of nonviolence, a black man."

A much younger man, Ewart Brown, Jr., president of the Student Assembly, struck a note of warning in his brief declamation: "The act which took the life of the Reverend Dr. Martin Luther King, Jr., serves as an indictment of white society. . . . It would be wise for white America to realize that she has erased a great portion of the buffer zone which has prevented daily conflict between white racists and the more aggressive elements of the black society."

The program ended at 11:45 A.M., with the singing of "We Shall Overcome" and the traditional joining of hands. A young black hesitated a moment before taking the hand of the white newsman, but then took it.

As the audience streamed out into the sunlight, the outdoor rally was already under way. A loudspeaker was set up on the steps of Frederick Douglass Hall, and a young woman was speaking vehemently into the microphone. Perhaps 600 of the 8,600 students enrolled at Howard were in the crowd.

If a black man went through a store window, the speaker said, she would go behind him with a first-aid kit, for, if he were shot, she would not want him bleeding on the doorstep of a white hospital.

"Martin Luther King compromised his life away," she said, "He had to avoid bloodshed. . . . If I'm nonviolent, I'll die. If I'm violent, I'll still die, but I'll take a honkie with me."

Speaker after speaker took the microphone to suggest that the white man was bent on exterminating the black man in America. The birth control program was cited as an attempt to drive down the black population.

A young man broke in breathlessly to take the microphone and shout that downtown Washington was burning and that the flames were reaching the white man's part of the city. There was a burst of cheering.

At one point, the American flag was lowered, and the red and black banner of Ujamma was raised on the campus quadrangle. (Ujamma is a campus-based, black-nationalist organization, which favors a separatist American black nation.) After a brief ceremony, the American flag was restored at half-staff, in honor of Dr. King.

At another point, six students, wearing black turtle-neck shirts, brought in a dummy that was wrapped in white cloth, stained with blood. They were carrying the dummy in the manner of pall bearers.

John Anderson, the education reporter of *The Washington Post* who covered the events at Howard, later commented: "The tenor of the speeches was vehemently antiwhite. I was standing there, very conspicuously white, and yet hardly anyone as much as glanced at me. I never had the sensation of being in danger. The hostility was directed at an abstraction that was white, and powerful, and downtown; it was not toward a specific white man standing in the crowd in the middle of the Howard campus."

Stokely Carmichael emerged from the back of the crowd and warned of violence ahead in Washington, even as smoke could be seen rising above 14th Street, ten blocks to the west.

"Stay off the streets, if you don't have a gun," Carmichael warned, "because there's going to be shooting."

He made the same statement several times, his voice growing louder and louder. He drew a pistol from his jacket and waved it over his head. He was duplicating his actions of the night before, when he had repeatedly urged individuals to go home because they did not have guns and were "not ready for the thing." After finishing his speech, Carmichael dropped from sight and was not seen in public again that day.

There appeared to be a contradiction between the basic violence of his "black power" rhetoric at the press conference, where he predicted that retaliatory action would occur to avenge Dr. King, and the restraint he urged with respect to the use of weapons by blacks on Thursday night and again at the Friday rally at Howard. His most menacing remarks were so phrased that they could be construed as forecasts, rather than calls to action. Nevertheless, the contradiction remained.

Carmichael told friends that he was determined to do nothing to court arrest. Perhaps he was remembering that H. Rap Brown, who had succeeded him as head of SNCC, faced trial in Maryland for incitement to arson and riot. Speaking to a group of blacks in Cambridge, Maryland, Brown had suggested that his audience burn down a decrepit and already fire-damaged elementary school. Within four hours thereafter, the school was burned down.

There was one close call for Carmichael. On Saturday, he and three friends were apprehended less than an hour after the curfew went into effect. As he was frisked, he shouted to the police, "Get your hands off me. If you're going to arrest me, arrest me, but keep your hands off me."

Asked if he knew there was a curfew, he said he thought it went into effect at a later time. The policemen, who recognized him, then allowed him and his companions to drive off in a late-model car. He was not seen again during the riot, although it was reported that he lost a new suit when a dry cleaning store was looted.

Agents of the Federal Bureau of Investigation later interviewed dozens of witnesses to the rioting to find out whether any connection existed between Carmichael and the disorders. An FBI source has stated that the Bureau has no evidence of the existence of any conspiracy in the nation or the city of Washington to cause the riots that occurred after Dr. King was killed. They felt that existing grievances—not a plot—were behind the disorders, and that the death of Dr. King, rather than a revolutionary conspiracy, plainly was the triggering incident. However, they carefully sifted everything that was printed and broadcast about Carmichael, including their own undercover reports, to reconstruct as best they could his activities during the riot. Their undercover men did not have much success keeping track of him. He was always suspicious of being followed and "made" (spotted) any surveillance almost immediately.

Although there was no plot—and the FBI's judgment on this point had not been disputed—there were some who saw the tragedy in Memphis as an opportunity to pursue their objectives. Among them were those who were committed to assaulting and overthrowing the system they considered to be racist.

By the time Carmichael held his Friday morning news conference—about 11 A.M.—there were already unmistakable signs of unrest in the inner city, although actual rioting had not started. It is doubtful that Carmichael had any better intelligence on that score than the police. Some rioters may have been moved to act when they learned what Carmichael had said, but the pattern of riot activity does not suggest that this happened in very many cases. But the comments Carmichael made at his news conference did contribute significantly to the uneasy atmosphere in the city, particularly among conservative white persons who reacted with indignation to Carmichael's violent tone. There were immediate demands on Capitol Hill that Carmichael be arrested and charged with inciting to riot. Soon after, Attorney General Ramsey Clark stated, "If we find evidence that meets the standards of criminal justice that Stokely Carmichael has committed a crime against the federal government, he will be prosecuted with all of the diligence and all of the energies at our command." By late summer, no indictment had been returned.

In an interview held after the riots, Carmichael would not discuss his activities during that troubled period, but he did acknowledge that he had accepted a telephone call from Havana, Cuba, on Friday. Columnists Drew Pearson and Jack Anderson somehow obtained a transcript of the conversation, which Carmichael authenticated.

The call was from Mike LaGuardia, a commentator for Radio Havana. Significant portions of the conversation follow:

LaGuardia: Say, Stokely.

Carmichael: Si.

LaGuardia: We would like to have a statement from you on Martin Luther King's assassination.

Carmichael: Right.

LaGuardia: And what has been the reaction of the Afro-Americans in the face of this crime?

Carmichael: Right, a white American has Rap Brown in jail right now. An American killed Dr. Martin Luther King, Jr., last night. When they killed Dr. King, they made a mistake, because Dr. King was the one man who was trying to ask black people not to burn down the cities. Now that they have killed Dr. King, there is no black man who will ask black people not to burn down the cities. What it means is that we have gone full swing into the revolution. Last night, thirty-five cities had major incidents—where there was burning and shooting and killing over the death of Dr. King. It is clear more of this will continue. It is going to become more and more a guerrilla—urban guerrilla—warfare, because it is clear that we cannot win with the police in open rebellion. So, more people are now beginning to plan seriously a major urban guerrilla warfare, where we can begin to retaliate not only for the death of Dr. King but where we can move seriously to . . . [the next few words could not be made out] serious revolutions with this country to bring it to its knees. It is crystal clear to us that the United States of America must fall in order for humanity to live, and we are going to give our lives to that cause.

He ended the conversation by sending greetings to "our brothers and sisters in Cuba" and to "Prime Minister Fidel."

The Havana telephone conversation seemed to indicate that Carmichael's desire to avoid arrest for inciting to riot was not the only factor prompting him to urge the black community to avoid gunplay. The police, in Carmichael's view, as expressed to LaGuardia, would win in an open confrontation.

A campus leader at Howard University suggested similarly that the real revolutionaries on the campus regarded the outbreak of rioting in the central city as a mere protest action, rather than a serious revolt. The student expressed the belief that most of the radical black students who listened to Carmichael on the college campus did not riot.

"The end of it was evident—National Guard and tear gas, shootings and jail," the student said.

Some Howard students, of course, did participate in the rioting, and a few were arrested on looting charges.

The Howard open-air rally continued for a while after Carmichael left, but subsequent speakers were not able to hold the interest of the students. At the end, the crowd dissolved into small knots of individuals who engaged in animated conversation in the campus quadrangle area.

As Carmichael vanished, about sixty high-school students on the fringes of the crowd, who had not been very attentive to the speeches, departed. They walked off the University campus and headed down Georgia Avenue, N.W., to 7th Street, following in the wake of perhaps 200 other high-school students who had been moving south down the same streets.

Along the way, the mass of youths was spotted by police, who advised headquarters to expect serious trouble shortly in the 7th Street shopping area.

V

Friday Afternoon: Washington Burns

"It's starting up again, and it looks bad," Police Chief John B. Layton told Deputy Mayor Thomas M. Fletcher on the telephone at 12:30 P.M., Friday, April 5. "I don't think we can handle it alone."

The police radio in the Chief's office was crackling with trouble calls, as the crowds of youths roaming 14th Street, N.W., turned into mobs.

Store windows were being smashed, and the swirling crowds were beginning to loot and burn. Firemen were having difficulty getting through the streets to put out the half-dozen fires that had been set.

A noisy band of 200 high-school students marched down 7th Street, N.W. Merchants on the 7th Street shopping corridor, seeing the smoke from the 14th Street fires overhead, braced for trouble.

Public Safety Director Patrick V. Murphy, Layton's superior, had just left the White House, with Under Secretary of the Army David E. McGiffert, for the Pentagon to assure that troops were alerted for possible nighttime duty on the city's streets. At the White House, the two men had agreed to put the District National Guard on training status, so that it could be called upon to assist the police department.

Meanwhile, Mayor Walter E. Washington was entering the National Cathedral with President Johnson to attend a special memorial service for Dr. King. The Mayor was a key member of the group that had assembled at the White House to proceed to the Cathedral with the President. Before departing, he heard the Chief Executive tell the black and the white leaders that a resort to violence would be "nothing less than a catastrophe."

Now on 14th Street, policemen, equipped with riot helmets, began riding the fire trucks to protect the fire fighters from the increasingly violent crowds.

At 12:50 P.M., Fletcher telephoned Murphy at the Pentagon, where the Director of Public Safety was lunching with McGiffert, in the Secretary of the Army's dining mess. The Deputy Mayor reported that students were pouring out of inner-city schools and that Layton now felt he might need help. The city officials had been preparing for nighttime incidents, but had not expected disorders to flare during the day. Murphy and McGiffert had scheduled a 2 P.M. meeting at the Army Operations Center, with the military brass, to plan the deployment of troops.

The black owner of a 7th Street carryout, which sold Tootsie Rolls, popsicles, and soda pop, was doing a tremendous business, serving the crowds of youngsters.

"Then those kids started coming down the street like a herd of animals, down one side and back the other," he said.

At police headquarters, Assistant Chief Jerry Wilson was ordering all available men onto the streets. At the District Building—Washington's city hall—Deputy Mayor Fletcher was picking up what information he could collect and passing it on to Murphy at the Pentagon.

"What we were feeding him, however, was pretty much rumors," Fletcher said later.

Police rushed to Mount Vernon Square, at 7th Street and Massachusetts Avenue, N.W., to set up a roadblock of squad cars and foot patrolmen to keep the avalanche of youths from reaching the downtown area and the richer pickings toward the southern end of 7th Street.

"On their way back, my window was broken," the carryout proprietor said. "I decided to close up." So did other merchants on the street. The carryout owner went out in front of his store to stand guard, with a loaded revolver in his pocket.

Layton talked directly to Murphy at the Pentagon and told

him he was no longer confident of the ability of the police force to handle the disorder, since it had spread to 7th Street.

As these gloomy reports were received, Murphy and McGiffert were joined at the Pentagon mess hall by Secretary of the Army Stanley R. Resor, Army Chief of Staff Harold K. Johnson, and General Ralph E. Haines, Jr., Assistant Chief of Staff of the Army.

"The wheels began to turn," Murphy remembered later. "Nobody actually said, 'We're going to need troops,' but they began sending out the alerts and planning for the possibility."

At about 1 P.M., the carryout owner saw the first fire set on 7th Street—at Charles Macklin's Furniture Store, near O Street, in two buildings constructed in the 1880's. It had been one of the few 7th Street stores looted on Thursday night.

Soon afterward, panicky civilian employees at the District Building and police headquarters began going home. They were working in the two centers most aware of the crisis in the city, and they could see the rising plumes of smoke a few blocks to the north. There had been no policy decision to send people out of the area, but officials began releasing those they thought could be spared.

By this time, the pattern on 7th Street resembled the situation an hour earlier on 14th Street. Adults, who had been standing by idly when the teenagers first appeared, joined in the looting. By now, a dozen fires were burning on 14th Street, and the looting had spread for blocks along the thoroughfare.

As the President and the Mayor emerged from the hour-long service at the Cathedral, a Secret Service agent handed the Mayor a police intelligence report telling of the trouble on the streets.

"It was an alert, not an alarm," the Mayor said later of the message, which was then, at 1:30 P.M., thirty minutes old. He showed the report to the President and Secretary of Defense Clark Clifford, as they rode back to the White House together.

Awaiting them at the White House was a fresh message from Fletcher: The situation was serious. The fires on 14th Street were spreading. Fletcher said he needed the Mayor's help to evaluate the situation. So did the President: He had the final Constitutional responsibility to call the troops, and he detained the Mayor for a few minutes longer, while more information was gathered.

Eight blocks of 14th Street were ablaze by now, and, as the columns of smoke rose skyward, Washington—primarily white Washington—began to panic. The sight of the smoke was alarming enough in itself. Then there were the incredible rumors. The picture of the supposedly secure capital of the United States in flames lent credibility to the most fantastic stories. Local radio and television stations endeavored to report what fragments of information they could hurriedly glean, but they were unable to quiet the rumors.

Tension and excitement were increasing on H Street, N.E., another major inner-city shopping area, where crowds were collecting. A liquor store at 5th and H streets, N.E., burst into flames—and this section of the city was added to the list of those requiring extraordinary police attention.

Chief Layton again talked to Murphy by telephone.

"It looks very bad," the Chief said. "We need all the help we can get." Layton was asked to join the 2 P.M. meeting at the Army Operations Center.

Downtown, Washington's two biggest department stores, the Hecht Company, at 7th and F streets, N.W., and Woodward and Lothrop, at 10th and F, closed for the day, after small groups of youths ran through the aisles, harassed clerks, and snatched merchandise. Carpenters put up boards behind all the windows and doors of Hecht's.

No one anticipated the chain reaction that the closing of the two big department stores would produce. Many hundreds of employees and customers poured onto the streets. The main shopping arteries, F and G streets, soon were choked with cars that could barely move. Other downtown stores began to close, sending still more employees and customers onto the streets, adding to the traffic congestion.

All over town, office workers more or less simultaneously reached for their telephones. The heavy volume of calls, coming at the usually busy time before the start of a weekend, swamped the city's exchanges.

Downtown office workers—both federal employees and those on private payrolls—then did what came naturally. They began piling into their automobiles to head for home. The trek, as it picked up momentum, created one of the most massive traffic jams in the city's history.

Deputy Mayor Fletcher asked the Civil Service Commission to stagger the release of the many tens of thousands of typists, clerks, and 6fficials who wanted to go home, but it was too late. Their flight could not be slowed. Just as the schools had failed earlier in their effort to keep pupils in class, the government now was unable to prevent its work force from fleeing the area. The general disorder, to which the released school children were already contributing, spiraled.

It was every man for himself on the road. Traffic piled up at every intersection as motorists attempted impossible left turns and jammed the traffic lanes. In some cases, cars were stalled on blocked streets for hours.

Traffic signals became meaningless. A man with an overcoat and umbrella on his arm, at 15th and L streets, N.W., was one of many private citizens who tried to untangle the hopelessly snarled traffic.

At the corner of 17th and M streets, two firemen got out of a city ambulance and escorted it on foot through a maze of cars going nowhere.

On 7th Street, bands of youths moved south, block by block, from above R Street, breaking into stores and looting. Adults stood by, at first, but then followed the youngsters through the smashed windows and doors. At Leventhal's Furniture Store, at 7th and Q streets, N.W., teenagers pulled lamps, chairs, and bedding through smashed windows, set mattresses on fire, and threw them back into the store. Before firemen could get through the snarled traffic to this store, the fire had spread to apartments overhead and around the corner, gutting all the buildings.

The carryout owner, still standing guard outside his store, watched the disorder grow. "I saw kids, five and six years old, come out of liquor stores with bottles in their hands and throw them at police cars and other cars driven by whites," he later reported.

"One of those kids came up to me and said, 'Look at those potato chips,' and I said, 'This is my store,' and he looked up and said, 'Oh, yes sir,' politely and walked away.

"Another bunch came by, an older group, and one of them said, 'We gonna burn this motherfucking place.' When I said, 'This is my place,' he looked at me hard and cold, like what I said didn't make any difference.

"Then I put a pistol in his face and I said, 'If you touch anything in that store, I'm gonna shoot you in the face.' When he saw my gun, he started running, and he's probably still running."

Officials who went out to discover what was happening were caught in the jam—as the first troops summoned were to be, also. Chief Layton and Warren Christopher, U.S. Deputy Attorney General, separately battled the traffic crawling across the Virginia bridges. Both men were trying to get to the 2 P.M. meeting with Murphy, McGiffert, and the military, at the Army Operations Center.

Emergency alerts to be ready to move on thirty minutes' notice had already gone out to about 3,000 troops, who had been placed on standby status Thursday night. The troops were located at Fort Myer, in Arlington, Virginia, a few minutes from downtown Washington; at Fort Belvoir, Virginia, thirty minutes away; at Fort Meade, Maryland, an hour away; and at Fort Bragg, North Carolina, six hours away.

These troops were to supplement the 1,750 men of the National Guard, for whom a call-up for night duty had begun at 12:30 P.M. The guardsmen could not be assembled on thirty minutes' notice, because they had to be called to duty from their places of employment by telephone, and this process had been slowed down by several hours because of the massive telephone tie-up, which knocked out the dial tone on many exchanges.

Attorney General Ramsey Clark was still in Memphis. As the acting head of the Justice Department, Warren Christopher attended the Pentagon meeting to make certain that, in keeping with the nation's traditions, federal troops would be moved into an American city for police duty only as a last resort. Not surprisingly, he insisted on taking a personal look at the riot area before giving the President his recommendations. (Established procedure requires local authority—in this case, Mayor Washington and his police aides—to certify the existence of a situation of "serious domestic violence." Review by the Attorney General is the next step, with the President making the final decision on sending the troops onto a city's streets.)

Christopher asked Pat Murphy and General Haines to go along on his reconnaissance. Unable to get a military helicopter immediately, he borrowed Chief Layton's car, which was equipped with a two-way police radio. Layton, himself, went back across the bridge to police headquarters in Washington and moved into his command center, where he was soon joined by representatives of the military.

Mayor Washington, at the White House with Presidential aide Joseph Califano, was still making telephone calls to obtain information for the President. The Mayor relayed the latest police reports from the streets, while Califano checked with the military. Even here, dial-tone failure delayed their calls.

No formal decision had yet been made to call troops, but, as the increasingly desperate nature of the situation became evident, it was plain that troops probably would be used. The Mayor readily accepted a suggestion that Cyrus Vance, who had been the personal representative of the President during the Detroit riot of 1967, be called upon to coordinate the National Guard, the Army, and the police. It was now shortly after 2 P.M. Mayor Washington returned to the District Building to resume direction of the operations there.

While General Haines changed into civilian clothes, Christopher returned to Washington and, at 2:45 P.M., personally delivered to the White House the necessary executive order and proclamation for the President to sign, authorizing the use of federal troops in Washington and federalizing the District National Guard—an action that was required if they were to carry arms on the streets. But there were further steps to be taken.

The White House sent the documents to the District Building to get the signatures of the Mayor, Murphy, and Layton. The Mayor's signature was affixed at the District Building, Layton's at police headquarters, and Murphy's after he returned from the riot-area tour with Christopher and General Haines. Presidential aides insisted on getting all three city officials' signatures. No one in a key position was going to be able to say later that he had not given his consent.

By now, policemen, wearing gas masks, had started using tear gas to break up the crowds. At 7th and P streets, N.W., three scout cars massed in the intersection, and policemen started tossing canisters of gas. The crowd that had been looting and burning the liquor, discount, and less expensive clothing stores, between R and M streets, fled toward Mount Vernon Square and hit the more expensive men's shops near the Square.

A black man in his twenties, wearing sunglasses, a jacket, and slacks, was standing in the middle of 7th Street, between L and M.

"You don't want to get hurt, go home," he shouted at the crowds still moving south on 7th. "It ain't worth dying for. If you love Martin Luther King and all he stood for, please go back. At least let him get in the ground."

He was a plainsclothesman, working as a "counterrioter" to keep the people from pushing down to the police roadblock at Mount Vernon Square. But no one paid any attention to him.

As the crowd kept moving south, the police at Mount Vernon Square started walking north, wearing gas masks and forming a solid line that spanned the width of 7th Street. They moved up about a block, and then began firing tear gas into the oncoming crowd. A tear-gas canister exploded at the feet of four teen-aged girls, loaded down with clothes. They screamed, dropped their loot, and ran. Three blocks of 7th Street, north of the Square, were cleared of people, but only for fifteen minutes. That afternoon, the Washington police, lacking sufficient manpower and experience with gas as a crowd-control device, succeeded only in moving rioters from one place to another.

Christopher, Murphy, and Haines moved into the riot area, and General Haines called the Pentagon to recommend that the troops start moving toward the city. But the three touring officials found themselves trapped in the traffic. It would be almost 4 P.M. before they could extricate themselves from the riot area and before Christopher could reach a public telephone, in working order, to place the call to the President that would order the soldiers onto the city's streets.

The riot-torn 7th Street ghetto area, a shabbier section than 14th Street, had once been the heart of Washington's Jewish section. As the Jews had moved gradually northward and eventually out of the area, the blacks had moved in. But Jewish merchants remained—selling appliances, furniture, liquor, discount and second-hand merchandise, and high-fashion men's clothes.

As fires burned along much of a ten-block strip, from Florida Avenue south to within a block of the police blockade at Mount Vernon Square, a woman clerk in a television repair shop at L Street said to a passing newspaper reporter, "They told me last night they were going to ruin 7th Street, and they did."

The reporter saw a Cadillac, parked in front of the Cavalier Men's Shop, being filled systematically with suits, slacks, coats, and accessories, from metal racks of merchandise that were rolled out of the store. Two men pushed a grand piano down an alley outside a music store, while youngsters sailed 45-r.p.m. records through the air. Three girls loaded lamps, shades, and other small items from a nearby furniture store into a Volkswagen.

"Where were the police while this was going on?" angry merchants later demanded. In some cases, they were standing by helplessly—outnumbered and overwhelmed, some seemingly frozen by the futility of arresting one looter, while hundreds of others milled around them. There were cases of policemen (and, later, of troops) making no effort to disperse looters, because they had other assignments deemed to be more important at the moment. One such assignment was maintaining the blockade at Mount Vernon Square to keep the crowds out of the downtown area. But authorities insisted later, at Congressional hearings, that the police had orders to enforce the law and arrest looters when they could. And even in the worst hours on Friday afternoon, they did. From noon Friday until 8 P.M., they arrested 250 persons.

At about 3 P.M., scores of youngsters and some adults out-flanked the police at Mount Vernon Square and showed up on the southern end of 7th Street. Looters darted around homeward-bound workers, who were waiting impatiently for buses, and broke into the display windows of furniture, sporting goods, and clothing stores. The feared attack on the downtown shopping area had begun, but police moved in quickly, using riot sticks to chase the invaders out of the stores. For the first time Friday, there were enough policemen in one area to do this, but not enough for them to take time out to make arrests.

Young children, six to ten years of age, were among the looters. A boy of about ten was asked what he was doing, as he emerged from a window of the Olympic Sporting Goods Shop with a baseball glove and some athletic shirts.

"Oh, we're just helping out," he answered with a grin.

Employees of some stores stationed themselves near windows and doors to discourage the marauders. Two large German shepherd dogs guarded one front door. A furniture-store owner sat in a rocking chair in the display window, smoking a cigar and cradling a shotgun in his lap. He waved as children ran by his window, which was left unbroken.

Roving bands of older youths and young adults, many in cars, began hit-and-run forays into the western end of the downtown shopping area, which runs along F and G streets to 14th Street, and beyond, to within a few blocks of the White House. Their targets were some of the city's more fashionable men's shops and shoe stores.

Newsmen watched from their offices at the National Press Building, at 14th and F streets, as a half-dozen youths shattered the plate-glass window of Bruce Hunt's, a popular men's clothing store on F Street, and climbed in. Seconds later, the youths, with looted clothes stuffed inside suits and sport jackets, rounded the corner onto 13th Street, past a bus-stop queue.

"Hey, man, you pregnant?" a younger boy called after one of the looters as he ran by.

One of a pair of twenty-year-olds started wrapping a cloth around his fist to break the window of the Massey Shoe Store on 13th Street. A police car pulled around the corner and screeched to a stop as the two men started to run. A policeman jumped out, grabbed one of them, and pushed him into the back seat of the car. The second man was cornered by a policeman from another patrol car, who placed the looter against a building and pulled stolen clothing from inside his coat.

Three men loaded clothing, transistor radios, and some beer mugs into a white Corvair on G Street, between 13th and 14th. They slammed the lid shut at the sound of a police siren, jumped into the car, and sped away. A man in the front seat waved looted shirts out the window at bystanders.

A police car, meanwhile, had pulled up in front of a Hahn's Shoe Store, on lower 14th Street. Officers arrested four youths at gunpoint, as they came through the store's smashed window.

Another police car pulled up in front of Bruce Hunt's, where looting had resumed. The car's siren sent most of a knot of men in and around the store off in all directions. A patrolman leaned out the car window and shouted to a middle-aged man, who was carrying a pair of orange slippers, "Put those back, or I'll take you in for housebreaking."

The neatly dressed man shrugged and returned the slippers to the Bruce Hunt show window.

Despite the efforts of the police, the roving bands cleaned out Rich's and Hahn's shoe stores, as office workers and tourists watched from the sidewalk. (After it was all over, clerks at the two shoe stores found each other's merchandise inside their stores. Looters had apparently moved from one store to the other and had made their own informal exchanges.)

The windows of D. J. Kaufman's branch, at 14th and I streets, a high-style clothing store, with many black customers, were broken into early in the afternoon, while the clerks were still inside. About 3 P.M., the employees abandoned the store on instructions from the proprietor.

After that, looters streamed in and out of the windows and doors, carrying out expensive clothes on hangers and in boxes. A young black woman stood at the corner of a park, near D. J. Kaufman's, and yelled a warning across the street whenever a police car came near. The looters would be out of the store and around the corner by the time a patrol car arrived. As soon as the police were gone, the looters were back in the store. At one point, a panel truck backed up onto the sidewalk in front of the store's main show window, and clothes were loaded directly into the truck.

Shortly after 5 P.M., a car pulled up in front of the now-empty store. One man got out, went into Kaufman's, poured gasoline all over its wall-to-wall carpeting, and set it on fire. Before the firemen arrived, the fire spread to a restaurant next door, and both buildings were gutted. This was one of three downtown stores to be set afire.

The other D. J. Kaufman's store downtown, near 10th and E streets, just a traffic triangle away from Pennsylvania Avenue and the Justice Department, was hit next. The plate-glass front window of this store had been installed that morning, replacing one shattered the night before. After it was broken again, two Cadillacs and a Lincoln Continental, all late-model convertibles with white tops, pulled up in front. Their occupants, Negro men in their twenties, carefully carried Italian alligator shoes and expensive suits out of Kaufman's and put them into the open trunks of the cars.

The riot came nearest to the White House that Friday afternoon when the display windows of Lewis and Thomas Saltz, an exclusive men's clothing shop, were broken and the contents looted. Heavy wooden partitions at the rear of the windows prevented the looters from getting into the store. Saltz's is located on G Street between 14th and 15th—a little more than two blocks from the White House.

The police did succeed finally in chasing the rioters out of the heart of downtown Washington. But that was the authorities' only success Friday afternoon.

Even as 14th and 7th streets, N.W., began to burn in the early afternoon, youths from 7th Street had moved a half-dozen blocks eastward to join the crowds on H Street, N.E.

Before the riot, the twelve blocks, from 3d Street, N.E., to the big intersection of H, 15th Street, Bladensburg Road, and Maryland and Florida avenues, had been a compact replica of the ghetto commercial strips along 7th and 14th streets, N.W., which were now burning. Crowded with liquor stores, groceries, carryouts, and cheap cut-rate stores, as well as smaller and less imposing branches of the variety, clothing, and specialty-shop chains represented on 14th Street, it was a logical target area.

Like the shopping areas of 7th and 14th streets, H Street, N.E., found its customers mainly in a hinterland, at the far end of the strip, where many thousands of blacks lived in congested slum and near-slum housing. Many of the looters on all three streets were residents, primarily youngsters, who poured out of the heavily populated adjacent areas to invade stores they knew well as customers.

The disorders on H Street, N.E., followed the pattern of those on 7th and 14th streets. Unusually large crowds, consisting predominantly of youngsters, began gathering shortly after 1 P.M., when the smoke could be seen rising over other parts of the city. H Street had also been the scene of preriot disturbances and was regarded by police as a trouble spot. Here, again, fires were set in the early stages of the disorder, and fire trucks drew large and frequently hostile crowds.

All over the city, fire-fighting units took special precautions to protect themselves. The open cabs of fire trucks were fitted with wooden roofs and shielded on the sides with chicken wire. Axes and other fire-fighting equipment were placed out of reach of bystanders. There was one consolation for firemen during the riot—the number of false alarms dropped sharply.

Between 1 and 3 P.M., scores of youths began descending on H Street, N.E., from 7th Street, N.W., and the eastern end of downtown, as the looting and burning became widespread. Two dozen badly outnumbered policemen tried to protect stores from the crowds of 1,000 or more persons rushing through the streets. A policeman, with a shotgun, successfully guarded a Safeway supermarket; patrol cars protected the big Sears Roebuck store on Bladensburg Road, near the eastern end of the H Street strip. The police, who had been cautioned not to use their guns against crowds of looters, relied on heavy volleys of tear gas—more than was used on 7th and 14th streets—in an effort to keep rioters away from untouched stores and to chase them off the shopping street. Officers, in twos and threes, stood in the middle of intersections and fired grenades at anyone moving.

But the crowds had control of the street, and it wasn't long before half the stores between 3d and 10th streets, N.E., were looted and burned. Fire-bombers were particularly active. Deputy Fire Chief Robert T. Huntington believed that many, if not most, of the fires were started by Molotov cocktails.

Many H Street fires were ignited at the rear of the buildings, a fireman later told Senator Robert C. Byrd of West Virginia. In one case that night, rioters threw bottles and stones to prevent the firemen from reaching the back of a building where a fire had been set, he said. He described fighting a fire between 9th and 10th streets in two small buildings on Friday night.

"We had these buildings just about under control, when a large building next door, Western Auto, was ignited with the use of a fire bomb—apparently gasoline. We saw the bomb ignite, but we didn't see who brought it into the building. At the time, there were maybe hundreds of people going in and out of the building, taking stuff out."

The sacking of Morton's store, at 7th and H streets, at about 4 P.M., produced one of the day's most spectacular blazes. There, a youngster smashed a show window of the clothing store with the palm of his hand. Then, using the arm of a mannequin from inside the window, he knocked out all the remaining show-window glass, but he could not break the special impact-resistant glass in the front door. A masonite partition denied access to the store from the show windows, which were quickly stripped bare. However, someone was able to shatter the door glass with a heavy cinder block, thus opening the inside of the store to invasion. A portly woman, who accompanied a group of youngsters to the store, shouted and gestured at them to go inside and really loot it. After they departed, with loaded arms, a man, who had been standing on the sidewalk watching the spectacle, removed a gasoline-filled cola bottle from under his coat, lighted it, and tossed it through the shattered doorway. It was a perfect hit. The gasoline exploded, lifting the roof of the store, nearly demolishing the whole building, and starting a fierce fire.

Witnesses said the man had done the same thing at two other stores down the street. They were struck by the fact that he showed no interest in looting, only burning. Undoubtedly, he was one of a number of "professional" arsonists who specialized in setting fires that day.

The fire-bomber presumably failed to see a teen-aged boy still inside Morton's. Twelve days later, when the rubble was cleared from the site, the boy's body, burned beyond recognition, was found in the rubble. He was never identified. The coroner reported that the victim had been a Negro, aged fourteen to seventeen, who had been burned alive.

An examination of the ruined remains of the store later revealed that Morton's had been looted only partially when the arsonist went about his work.

Two blocks down the street from Morton's, a thirty-four-year-old construction worker was killed sometime Friday afternoon, when a wall of the burning I-C Furniture Company, near 5th and H streets, N.E., collapsed on him. Firemen found his body in an alley alongside the store, shortly before midnight. The victim, Harold Bentley, who lived four miles away, near the border with Maryland, had been subject to hallucinations and epileptic seizures. But he had improved so much during a voluntary stay in St. Elizabeth's, the federal mental hospital in southeast Washington, that he had been allowed to leave the hospital for work each weekday and to stay at home over weekends.

"We had great hopes for the future," his wife said later. "He was taking his medicine and had no seizures since getting leave from the hospital. He was home Friday for lunch, and then left for the hospital to get his weekend pass and medicine. That was the last time I saw him."

The unidentified teenager and Bentley were the fourth and fifth persons to die in the riot.

By 5 P.M., the rioting had spread eastward, across the Anacostia River, to an isolated but rapidly growing area of the city known as Anacostia, where racial outbreaks had long been expected. Predominantly white before 1960, this section now has more than 200,000 of the city's 833,000 inhabitants, and more than 150,000 of them are black. Washington's far northeast section, the upper half of Anacostia, is almost all black; most of the whites who lived in Anacostia occupy portions of the lower half, the city's far southeast section. The bulk of the city's public housing projects are in Anacostia; but it is also an area where both blacks and whites occupy neighborhoods—some of them integrated—with tree-lined streets and a definite suburban look. Anacostia also has pockets of old, rundown housing for blacks. Continuing tension and periodic clashes have marked relations between the police and the area's black residents.

While 14th, 7th, and H streets burned out of control Friday afternoon, there had been relatively little concern for this area across the river. Looting and burning had been sporadic, as groups of youths in their teens and twenties moved from place to place by automobile and on foot, hitting scattered stores and shopping centers. Altogether, about fifty stores were looted in Anacostia; about one-fourth of these were set on fire.

When the first reports of trouble in Anacostia were received, police commanders in two precincts sent officers in twos and threes to patrol neighborhood shopping areas on foot. Although policemen in the inner-city riot areas had been warned to avoid using their guns while dealing with rioters, no similar reminders were given to the policemen on riot watch in Anacostia. They began shooting Friday evening, and two suspected looters were shot and killed by police bullets.

Three policemen, patrolling in a shopping center at Minnesota Avenue and Benning Road, N.E., heard a burglar alarm sound in the Young Men's Shop, at about 6 P.M. They found the glass smashed in and several looters coming out with clothes.

One officer, Private David L. Tompkins, grabbed a looter and ordered him to stand facing the outside back wall of the store. Tompkins then stood about 3 feet behind the man, guarding him with a revolver, the hammer cocked. As others came running out of the store, one empty-handed youth turned and ran blindly between Tompkins and his prisoner, striking the end of the barrel of the policeman's gun. It fired, and the youth, Thomas Williams, who would have been sixteen years old in eight more days, fell, fatally wounded by a bullet that entered his body just below his left armpit. He was the sixth person to die in the riot.

Williams had been dismissed at 2:15 P.M. from Carter Woodson Junior High School because of the rioting. Described by his mother as a "quiet, good boy," who attended confirmation class at his Lutheran Church every Sunday, he had walked his sister home and gone to play basketball at a nearby recreation center. He left the center at about 5 P.M. An hour later and four blocks away, he died.

A coroner's jury later ruled that the shooting was accidental. But testimony at the inquest showed that Tompkins and another policeman with him had fired a total of seven shots at or over the heads of fleeing looters, before the shooting of Williams occurred.

After this incident, word was passed to the entire force to exercise particular care in the use of firearms. Pat Murphy later explained that the police department did not approve of the firing of weapons over the heads of rioters as a warning. "Any bullet travels many city blocks and can strike anything," he said. "No policeman should use his gun unless he is prepared—and justified—to shoot to kill."

The shooting in Washington was limited to one section, Anacostia, and one day, Friday. But there were several shooting incidents. Three hours after Williams was shot, three policemen patrolling a two-block strip of stores along South Capitol Street, near the southern city limits, heard glass breaking, and ran toward Al's Liquor Store, a block away.

Private Albert Lorraine, arriving ahead of the other two officers, saw a man backing out of the broken liquor-store window. The man suddenly "whirled around," about "12 to 15 feet" away from the policeman, Lorraine later testified at an inquest, holding a "shiny object . . . menacingly" in his outstretched hand.

Lorraine, his gun already drawn, fired one shot immediately and then two more, as the man ran across the street and down an alley. The suspect was found dead in the alley, with a bullet wound in his back. Homicide detectives found a small, sharp piece of glass, with the suspect's thumbprint on it, next to his body.

The man was Ernest McIntyre, a twenty-year-old janitor who lived with his wife and daughter about a block from where he was shot. He had no police record and had carried no loot out of the liquor store. He was the seventh victim of the rioting, the second and last to die in gunfire.

In both these cases, the question afterward was whether the policemen had followed written police policy in shooting to protect life or to apprehend a fleeing felon "when all other means had been exhausted." Burglary in Washington is a felony. Tompkins and Lorraine were cleared by the U.S. Grand Jury, but the two shooting deaths produced an angry reaction from the black community and helped trigger a demand for citizen participation in the control of the police at the neighborhood level.

By the time the burning and looting and shooting hit Anacostia, the smoke from the fires in the inner city hid whole sections of the sky and made it look as if much of the city, the capital of the United States, was burning—or soon might be.

Washington's fire department has had one of the best insurance ratings in the country and a comparable reputation for its ability to respond to and extinguish fires quickly. It had remained alert to the possibility of daylight rioting Friday, and had kept normally off-duty men in the firehouses, thus increasing, from thirty-two to sixty-four, the number of available engine companies.

Under a plan that had been worked out in advance with suburban fire departments, the Washington firemen were also aided by sixty engine companies from the Maryland and Virginia suburbs. Volunteer fire departments came from farther away, one unit driving down from Lebanon, Pennsylvania. Many of these out-of-town firemen stayed in Washington for twelve hours or more Friday.

But all this was not enough to deal with the more than 500 fires set that day. About 200 were burning all at once during the peak of the rioting, late Friday afternoon. In many instances, gasoline was the fuel, spreading the fire quite rapidly. In some cases, the quick, hot fury of the blazes astonished even the fire fighters.

Some huge fires, like the one at Morton's on H Street, were fought by a single engine company. In most cases, the firemen stayed at a burning building long enough to water it down to smoldering, before moving on to the next fire. But scores of damped-down fires rekindled and had to be fought again.

By 4 P.M., on H and 7th streets, the beleaguered firemen were forced to leave some buildings burning, while they turned hoses on nearby structures to keep the fires from spreading.

Some inner-city residents, including youths, helped the firemen, by holding their hoses and bringing them chairs and coffee as they stayed on the street overnight, watering down buildings.

But many others harassed the firemen.

A black fire fighter, helping to put out a blaze in the O Street Market, at 7th and O streets N.W., was starting to move the hose from that building to a fire on the opposite corner of the intersection, when he heard a white fireman say, "Don't do this."

"He came over to me and he said, 'They cut the hose,' and he had the section of the hose in his hand."

Later, the same fire fighter reported he was trying to determine the reason for low water-pressure, when he found water squirting through a small hole in the hose. A youth was standing nearby with a butcher knife, ready to enlarge the hole. He saw the fireman coming, and walked away.

On H Street, one fireman remembered, looters coming out of a liquor store "hurled Miller High Life bottles of beer at us, pint bottles."

Another fireman, who spent nearly four hours fighting the blaze at Morton's, on H Street, was bothered by the steady stream of looters pushing by him in an alley alongside the burning store.

"The alley was used as a freeway for looters," the fireman said later. "You know, they just kept coming through the alley with all kinds of merchandise, television sets, clothes, radios, everything."

Earlier, at the corner of 7th and Q streets, a black man had tried to stop a group of teenagers who were starting a fire, with burning pieces of cardboard and paper, inside the Quality Clothing Store.

"Don't do that," he shouted. "My mother lives on top of that store, and she can't get out of her bed."

The man was thirty-six-year-old Clarence James, a bus driver and the son of Annie James, fifty-two, who lived in a second-floor apartment over the store. Mrs. James weighed 450 pounds and was bedridden.

Clarence and his younger brother pleaded with the youths in front of the clothing store. But they ignored Mrs. James's sons, and the building burst into flames. Before firemen and her sons were able to get Mrs. James down the fire escape, she had inhaled too much smoke.

"I'm dying, I'm dying," she told Clarence. "I want to see my family and friends. Don't take me to the hospital right away."

According to her daughter, Mrs. James had been a "generous and loving" woman, who had cared for more than forty foster children and had adopted several others. To please his mother, Clarence put her in his car, picked up her eighty-nine-year-old father, who lived nearby, and drove past the crowds and burning buildings to visit relatives. When she lost consciousness later in the day, Clarence took her to a hospital, where she later died. She was the eighth person killed in the riot, and the fifth fire victim.

The fires spread at the rate of twenty and thirty new starts every hour, while thousands of people continued to loot and burn at will, in a mad carnival spirit. One fire fighter later told Senator Byrd, "The whole time I would imagine the only thing that really kept me going was the fact that I fully realized that eventually the military police and troops would come and stop it. But as the day wore on, it didn't look like they would ever get here."

VI

Friday Evening To Saturday:
The Troops Arrive

It was an incredible sight for Captain Leroy Rhode, commander of the 3d Infantry's D Company, as he led 150 men over Memorial Bridge, across the Potomac River, into Washington.

Immediately ahead was the Lincoln Memorial. To the right was the Washington Monument. In the distance was the Capitol, obscured by billows of smoke coming from fires in the center of the city.

The time was 4:40 P.M., April 5, 1968. Captain Rhode, a rifle platoon leader in the first Army unit sent into combat in Vietnam three years before, was now leading the first federal occupation of the streets of Washington since the "bonus marchers" were forcibly evicted in 1932.

Cars on the bridge and Constitution Avenue pulled quickly to the side in deference to the jeeps, driven by Rhode and his Armed Forces Police escort, and the olive-drab trucks, carrying men and equipment.

"People usually ignore a military convoy around Washington," Rhode, the stocky son of an Army officer, observed. "But on that day, they cleared the way for us."

The "Old Guard," as the 3d Infantry is known, is a largely ceremonial, honor-guard outfit. It is stationed at Fort Myer, in Arlington, Virginia, just across the river from Washington. That Friday, its assignment was to protect the Capitol and the White House, as part of "Operation Cabin Guard," the Pentagon's detailed plan for dealing with a riot in Washington.

By 5 P.M., the men in D Company were mounting machine guns on tripods, on the white marble steps of the Capitol, and setting up a command center, under the frescoed dome in the rotunda.

"There I was, twenty-six years old, and with a hell of a responsibility," Rhode said later, "especially since those were fellow Americans we might have to face out on the streets."

A few minutes later, another company of the 3d Infantry surrounded the White House. Banks of huge floodlights were turned on at the edge of the White House grounds, bathing the Executive Mansion and the lawns and trees around it in an eerie, sunbright light.

There was no immediate or prospective threat to the Capitol and White House that Friday afternoon; the troops were desperately needed in the center of the city, where the fires were burning, but the "Cabin Guard" plan covered all contingencies.

At 5:30 P.M., the first 150 soldiers of the 6th Armored Cavalry, from Fort Meade, Maryland, arrived in jeeps and 4-ton trucks on H Street, N.E., which was being looted and burned by rioters. The troops wore the unit's yellow kerchiefs around their necks and black, rubber gas masks over their faces. Holding unloaded M-14 rifles, with sheathed bayonets, on their hips, the soldiers marched toward the looters, who darted back and forth across the street.

Other 6th Cavalry and 3d Infantry troops moved onto 14th and 7th streets, N.W. Smothering, sour-smelling tear gas, fired by the police, mingled with the thick smoke that hovered over all three shopping strips. As soldiers dispersed the crowds, police paddy wagons raced up and down the streets, picking up looters who had been stopped by the soldiers and arrested by police. By midnight, 6,600 troops had restored temporary order, and were patrolling the streets and enforcing a dusk-to-dawn curfew.

Thirty-six hours after Captain Rhode crossed Memorial Bridge, there were 13,600 federal soldiers and D.C. guardsmen on duty in Washington. Not since the Civil War had so many American troops occupied an American city.

Everything went according to the Pentagon's "Operation Cabin Guard," plan, although telephone problems and traffic snarls, caused by the flight of residents from the downtown area, slowed the call-up and movement of the first troops. Thursday night, the troops had been placed on an emergency alert; at 1 P.M., Friday, they were told to be ready to move on short notice; and, at 3:30 P.M., they actually started toward Washington.

The Washington riot-control plan was prepared after the bloody 1967 summer riots, and was regarded by the military as "an extraordinarily thorough plan." The "Cabin Guard" blueprint was just one of the Army Operations Center's bookshelf of plans for controlling civil disorders in American cities.

It called for the use of well-prepared, elite military units, with strong professional-soldier traditions. These units had been trained thoroughly in the latest riot-control techniques, which emphasized restraint in the use of physical force. All of the outfits earmarked for Washington were substantially integrated, and a number of units had black soldiers in key command posts.

The 3d Infantry, from Fort Myer, and the 91st Engineer Battalion, from Fort Belvoir, Virginia, had faced anti-Vietnam-war demonstrators at the Pentagon in October, 1967.

The 82d Airborne Division, from Fort Bragg, North Carolina, had served on the streets of Detroit during the 1967 riot. It was commended for its restraint there, in contrast to the Michigan National Guard, whose troops shot wildly and indiscriminately.

The 503d Military Police Battalion, also from Fort Bragg, had served at the Pentagon. Previously, it had seen duty in Oxford, Mississippi, when James Meredith enrolled at the University of Mississippi in 1962, and in Selma, Alabama, during the 1965 march and demonstrations led there by Dr. King.

The "Cabin Guard" plan assigned specific troops to particular police precincts, and, in February and March, officers of each military unit had toured their assigned precincts with Washington police officials.

Within three hours of Dr. King's death, and one hour after Thursday night's rioting on 14th Street became serious, the first alerts went out to selected Army units, with orders to be ready to move to Washington.

Captain Rhode had just returned to his apartment, at 11 P.M. that night, from the Cherry Blossom Week military show at Fort Myer, when he was ordered by telephone to report back to the post immediately.

The troops were not called into the city on Thursday night, but the alert was continued. On Friday afternoon, after the Pentagon became aware of the daylight outbreak of rioting on 14th, 7th, and H streets, the alerts were stepped up. First 3,000, then 6,000, troops were ordered to be ready to move toward Washington on thirty minutes' notice.

It was at that time that Deputy Attorney General Warren Christopher, who was responsible to the President for recommending the use of troops in the city, General Ralph E. Haines, Jr., the designated "Task Force Washington" commander, and Pat Murphy went out to tour the riot areas.

By cutting in and out of side streets, the three men were able at first to move quickly through the heavy traffic. On 14th Street, they saw block after block of burning buildings and observed that looters vastly outnumbered policemen. Then, at about 3 P.M., they reached 7th Street and saw that the situation there was at least as bad. At that point, they decided to get troops moving toward Washington.

But their only link with the outside world then was a two-way car radio to police headquarters—a broadcast channel that could be overheard on other radios. They felt they had to use public telephones to talk to the President, the Mayor, or the Pentagon, but the lines were jammed. Frantically, the three officials drove from gas station to gas station on 7th Street, trying to find a pay telephone on which they could get a dial tone. The first time that General Haines, wearing civilian clothes, got out of the car to try a phone, he was hit on the shoulder by a flying stone.

When Haines was able to get through briefly to the Pentagon, he told Army Under Secretary McGiffert that he thought the first troops should be started toward the city. McGiffert sent out the orders to move the troops.

At 3:30 P.M., the 6th Armored Cavalry troops left Fort Meade and started south, in trucks and armored personnel carriers, on the Baltimore-Washington Parkway. With their metal armor and treads, the personnel carriers looked like tanks. By 3:45 P.M., the 91st Combat Engineers left Fort Belvoir and were heading north on Route 1 to Washington.

At about this time, in police headquarters, a twenty-eight-man military command staff for "Task Force Washington" had moved in to share Chief Layton's office and adjoining rooms on the fifth floor. Direct telephone lines to the Pentagon and, later, to the White House were installed. General Harris W. Hollis was put in charge temporarily, while General Haines was on the streets. At 3:58 P.M., after crossing heavy traffic to get a look at H Street, N.E., where the rioting was now the worst, and after another desperate search for a working telephone, Deputy Attorney General Christopher got through to the White House. He recommended that troops be put on the city's streets immediately. Mayor Washington, at the District Building, was put on the phone to President Johnson, to tell him directly that the city needed "everything we can get" in the way of troops, thereby confirming his earlier written request.

At 4:02 P.M., while still talking to the Mayor on the telephone, the President signed the proclamation and an executive order empowering the military to restore law and order on the streets of Washington.

"I . . . do command all persons engaged in . . . acts of violence to cease and desist therefrom and to disperse and retire peaceably forthwith," the proclamation read.

The executive order, in addition to sending federal troops into the city, called 1,750 members of the D.C. National Guard "into the active military service of the United States . . . for an indefinite period."

Earlier, while Mayor Washington was at the White House, President Johnson had offered him the assistance of Cyrus Vance, as a federally paid consultant to help quell the riot and coordinate strategy for the Mayor. The former Under Secretary of Defense and Presidential trouble-shooter, during the 1967 riot in Detroit, had been reached at his law office in New York. He flew immediately to Washington and battled the traffic jam to get into the city from National Airport.

As troops neared Washington's city limits, from the north and south, Vance arrived at the command post in police headquarters. He promptly conferred with city, police, and military officials there. It was agreed, as Vance had suggested in a report prepared after the Detroit riot, that the military emphasis would be on the use of overwhelming numbers of men, on tear gas instead of bullets, and on an early, strictly enforced curfew. Moving to carry out the plan, Mayor Washington, at 5:20 P.M., proclaimed a curfew, to begin at 5:30 P.M. and to last until 6:30 A.M. Only police, firemen, doctors, nurses, and sanitation workers were exempted. Everyone else was ordered to stay off the streets and out of public places during the thirteen-hour period. (Action was later taken to permit essential employees of the news media and emergency crews of the public utilities to move about.)

The Mayor's proclamation prohibited the day or night sale of all alcoholic beverages, firearms, ammunition, gasoline and other flammable liquids, except gas pumped directly into a vehicle's tank. Only policemen and soldiers were allowed to carry guns, explosives, flammable materials, or dangerous weapons.

Before the curfew was made public, 3d Infantry and 6th Cavalry troops arrived in Washington and, after careful staging, moved in force onto the three looted and burned shopping streets, 14th, N.W., 7th, N.W., and H, N.E. Encountering very heavy traffic just outside the city, the 6th Cavalry troops split up into companies of 175 men each and took separate side-street routes to their staging area at the U.S. Soldiers' Home, two dozen blocks north of the worst rioting in northcentral Washington. They arrived there shortly before 5 P.M.

As the first company of 175 men reached the soldiers' home, their commander, Colonel Clayton Gompf, sent them immediately to the H Street, N.E., area, in the Thirteenth Precinct, where police felt the rioting was at its worst.

Captain Dan Speilman, a chubby, boyish-faced, unsmiling West Point graduate and Vietnam veteran, commanded the first company of men on H Street, N.E. "I was eager to get going," twenty-four-year-old Speilman remembered later. "We moved as quickly as we could."

It was 5 P.M., and whole blocks of H Street, from 3d Street

west to 14th Street, N.E., were burning. Hundreds of people were still roaming the street and looting unburned stores. The police were strung out, about five men to a block, frantically firing tear gas at the crowds. The firemen had to pass by some burning buildings to hose down and protect others still untouched.

"I was supposed to go and make contact at the police precinct station house first," Speilman said later, "but it looked even from a distance as though I'd never get through the crowds or the fire. So I just headed for the highest columns of smoke."

On the way, at 13th and Florida Avenue, N.E., where no policemen were in sight and stores nearby had broken windows, Speilman's men found a crowd of about 150 persons.

"We dropped off ten men to disperse them," Speilman said. "They were very militant. One man swung at me with a two-by-four. They yelled black-power slogans and other things."

At his order, the first tear-gas canisters thrown by federal troops were used to break up the crowd.

"We reached H Street, N.E., at about 5:20 P.M.," Speilman said. "It was pretty much chaos there."

The police had managed to drive the largest crowds of people into the side streets by using tear gas, which still hung in the air. But there were still hundreds of looters, moving quickly from store to store, on H Street. They took armfuls of booty to homes and alleys nearby, and then came back for more. Half the buildings between 3d and 14th streets were burning.

Assistant Police Chief Jerry Wilson and Deputy Chief Raymond Pyles pulled up in a police cruiser to talk to Speilman. The three men decided first to block off the eastern end of the H Street strip and then to sweep the streets clear of rioters.

Empty troop-trucks were used to block off the big intersection where H and 15th streets, Bladensburg and Benning roads, and Florida and Maryland avenues, N.E., converge. With Wilson and Pyles, Speilman then led his men west on H Street, toward the fires and looting.

At first, they formed the shoulder-to-shoulder, riot-control wedge they had learned in training. But the rioters darted back and forth from sidewalk to sidewalk, ignoring the soldiers marching down the middle of the street.

"The people just kept on with what they were doing," Speilman said later.

So, Captain Speilman then split up his men in groups of ten each, plus a sergeant; the groups spread out and moved with sheathed bayonets thrust forward toward the clusters of people on the street. Assistant Chief Wilson moved down the middle of the street, using a bullhorn to tell the crowds to leave H Street and go home.

"We were really in combat-type formations," recalled Sergeant Edward Dera, a married, twenty-one-year-old soldier from Niagara Falls, New York, who led one of the ten-man groups along H Street.

"We asked people to go home. If they didn't react immediately, we would walk toward them with our rifles and they usually would move. Some people refused to move, and we warned them we would use tear gas if they didn't. After I warned them again, we put on our masks and I'd throw the gas. That always moved them."

As the soldiers moved along H, past 13th, 12th, 11th, and 10th streets, men were dropped off in front of untouched stores and at the mouths of alleys and side streets, where the rioters had fled. Sometimes, one or two soldiers on a corner were responsible for controlling a group of fifty to 100 people massed on a side street.

By the time Speilman reached 9th Street, N.E., he had no more men. To the west, in front of him, there were still scores of people looting stores and hindering firemen. Behind him, his thinly strung-out troops were protecting H Street, although scattered looters were still able to move freely.

"What's the use of sending troops if they don't send enough?" Deputy Chief Pyles asked in frustration.

Captain Speilman sent out a radio call for help. At 6 P.M., another 175 soldiers met Speilman at 9th and H streets, N.E. They were commanded by Captain Tim Donovan, a twenty-seven-year-old ROTC graduate and Vietnam veteran from Bristol, Connecticut, who is the father of three children.

After conferring with Speilman and the police, Donovan took his men in trucks back to the six-way intersection at 15th and H streets, N.E., got them out of their vehicles, and led another sweep down H to 8th Street, dropping off reinforcements on street corners already manned by Speilman's men. "We were able to reach into the alleys down the side streets, and into the stores," Donovan said later.

Now, rioters who resisted the troops or persons found in stores or on the sidewalk "carrying things that seemed out of place" were stopped by the troops and told to wait for the police. The soldiers had the authority to "detain" individuals in this way, but not to make official arrests.

The Ninth Precinct police, reinforced by some CDU members, showed up in paddy wagons and patrol cars to take away persons stopped by the troops. The soldiers filled out forms detailing each prisoner's offense. Few persons resisted detention by the troops. In many cases, they were rounded up and guarded, in groups of a dozen or more, by just one or two soldiers.

"Those caught in stores by tear gas were, of course, very docile," Speilman said. "But most of the others were cooperative, too. I did not sense a lot of bitterness toward us."

Speilman was struck by the fact that "most of the people we were catching did not seem like the kind to be doing this sort of thing. I felt that others started this and were long gone by the time we came."

"We seemed to be picking up kids with a pair of new shoes and adults that had been bystanders and got caught up in the atmosphere of it.

"And there were the drunks. I was disgusted by the large percentage of people that were drunk that night, from twelve years old on up. They must have started drinking that looted liquor right away. We caught drunk people still carrying cases of it."

Before 10 P.M., troops on H Street, N.E., were reinforced, and all but sporadic looting was ended for the night. The reinforcements established a roadblock at the western end of the shopping street and then swept eastward to meet the other troops at 8th Street, N.E., thus sealing off the whole strip.

As firemen battled blazes that had been burning for hours in some stores, the troops helped police round up more than 500 rioters, who were variously charged with looting, disorderly conduct, drunkenness, and violation of the curfew.

The cellblocks at the Ninth Precinct station house and other nearby precinct houses were filled to overflowing with prisoners, at one point. Police who had just acquired sufficient support to make substantial numbers of arrests were then told to hold off for a time on all but the most serious cases. Hundreds of prisoners were moved to the municipal and federal courthouse cellblocks to permit arrests to be resumed in the Ninth Precinct.

Meanwhile, in northwest Washington, two companies of the 6th Cavalry, each with 175 men, occupied 14th Street, with one unit holding the section south of Euclid Street, in the Thirteenth Precinct, and the other unit holding the northern end, in the Tenth Precinct.

Shortly after 6 P.M., 6th Cavalry troops left their trucks at 14th and S streets, N.W., and began moving north, along both sides of 14th Street, while an officer shouted "march, march, march," in cadence. Men were dropped off at each corner to enforce the curfew.

Except for a few bands of looters, rioting had slowed down on 14th Street, although fires were still burning in the northern section. Many bystanders remained, and some resented orders to move. As the troops started up the street, angry youths began throwing bricks, bottles, debris, and verbal taunts at the soldiers. The troops replied by donning gas masks and scattering the youths with tear gas. This procedure was repeated several times along the way, as the troops ran into occasional resistance.

Unexpected but welcome help was provided by three black men in a station wagon, "counterrioters" who shouted at persons on the sidewalk to go home. When they reached a jeep carrying Captain John R. Johnston, twenty-four-year-old company commander, ROTC graduate from Rowley, Massachusetts, and Vietnam war veteran, one of the men from the station wagon got into the jeep.

"If they did not leave the street when I asked them," Johnston said, "this fellow took the microphone and told them to go." Johnston did not learn his name.

By 9 P.M., two full 700-man battalions occupied and sealed off the upper and lower ends of 14th Street, and 350 men were being moved to H Street, N.E., bringing that area, too, up to battalion strength.

About 300 men of the 3d Infantry patrolled the hard-hit area of 7th Street in the Second Precinct, after crossing the Memorial Bridge, at about 8 P.M.

"It looked like a ghost town," Specialist Fifth Class Robert Baker, twenty-four, said later. "No cars on the street on a Friday night; everything closed up; nobody near the Washington Monument when we went by it."

The curfew had succeeded in clearing the downtown area.

As the troop trucks turned north and moved up 7th Street, twenty-one-year-old Private First Class Richard Zimmerman, from Brooklyn, could not believe what he saw. "I guess it was like how I always imagined Berlin must have looked after World War II," he remembered. "Everything was burned, gutted, and crumbling."

His commanding officer, Colonel Joseph Conmy, forty-nine, said it looked exactly like what he had seen during the war. "It definitely looked bombed-out on 7th Street," he said. "I'll never forget it."

The 3d Infantry troops had little difficulty at this hour. They occupied 7th Street N.W., from K to S streets, and helped police round up scattered looters. Troops in trucks and jeeps were driven through neighboring streets "to show the people we were there in force," Conmy said.

Late Friday night, Marines who staffed the training school at Quantico, Virginia, relieved Captain Rhode's men at the Capitol, permitting them to strengthen the rest of the 3d Infantry in the Second Precinct.

Sealing off the three streets made it easier for police to catch and arrest hit-and-run looters still moving through back alleys and side streets. More than 300 persons were arrested for curfew violations between 8 P.M. and midnight, as the policy of rigid enforcement took effect.

The troops had effectively placed clamps on the three main trouble areas. But there were large sections of the city—potential centers of major trouble—where the danger existed that sporadic rioting could flare up.

Anacostia, where police bullets had killed two persons on Friday, was just such an area. To prevent the disorders from spreading, 700 troops of the 91st Engineers, from Fort Belvoir, were assigned to the far southeastern section, and a 150-man company of the National Guard was assigned to protect the far north-eastern section.

The Engineers were stationed at four large shopping centers and other locations to answer emergency calls, starting about 8:30 P.M. Their notion was "to make a show of force" to help disperse looters in shopping centers. The troops moved through the section with a police escort, because, as their commander, Colonel S. C. Smith, explained later, "We really couldn't find our way around down there." The preriot inspection tours, which had proved so valuable in the inner city, had not been made in Anacostia.

"The precinct officials and I took one group of troops to a supermarket being looted by nearly 100 people on Alabama Avenue, S.E.," Smith said. "As soon as they saw us coming in jeeps and trucks, they cleared out of the store and ran away."

It was 9:30 P.M. when a company of National Guard MP's, under Captain Thomas S. Connell, Jr., a black post-office research engineer, was placed on duty in the far northeastern section.

The police and guardsmen picked ten shopping areas that had not been hit by rioters for the troops to guard. Other National Guard MP's patrolled the precinct with police in jeeps.

"The streets were still packed with cars late that night," Captain Connell remembered. "Most of the people apparently just wanted to see what was going on. It was a carnival atmosphere . . . everybody happy and gay. A lot of people greeted us as we went along with cheers and smiles. We encountered little bitterness that night."

The D.C. National Guard was 25 per cent black; one military-police unit was 40 per cent black; there were black officers in charge of integrated troops, as in the regular Army. In federalizing the D.C. Guard, the President was permitting their use for riot control, as though they were regular Army troops. Without that order, the Guard technically was available only as an un-armed auxiliary to the police—primarily for traffic duty.

When troops were called to duty in riots elsewhere in the country, it had been the practice to use National Guard troops before summoning regular Army troops. The Guard answered the call of the state governors, and, frequently, guardsmen were available in sufficient numbers to meet initial emergency demands. Because Washington, D.C., has a relatively small National Guard establishment, it had been generally assumed that federal troops would be used from the outset in any major riot, especially since the new tactic of using overwhelming numbers of troops to quell disorder required it.

In Washington, it was fortunate that this was so. The Guard call-up required summoning guardsmen, by telephone, from their places of employment and homes—a process that took hours, due to the telephone and traffic snarls. D.C. guardsmen were not ready to leave the National Guard armory until long after the federal troops had arrived.

The Guard call-up had been arranged on a "buddy system." Five persons at the armory were to call the first group, which, in turn, was to call five others, and so on, before reporting to the armory. The telephone tie-up resulted in waits of twenty minutes or more for a dial tone, and many hours passed before some guardsmen were reached.

The first guardsmen to trickle into the armory included a fingerprint specialist at the FBI, a systems engineer at the post office, a foam-rubber wholesaler, a newspaper reporter who was working in Philadelphia, Washington Redskin football player Jerry Smith, who was vacationing in Florida, and Baltimore Oriole pitcher Pete Richert (formerly of the Washington Senators), who was at a spring exhibition game in Atlanta. It had been easier to get in touch with the last three men than with many guardsmen right in Washington.

One member of the Guard, Captain Stanley J. Haransky, a trucking industry trade association official, had been at a meeting in Los Angeles. When he saw television films of Washington's Thursday night disorders, on the Today Show, Friday morning, he took the first plane to Washington. Haransky reached his Annandale, Virginia, home at 4:30 P.M.; his wife had his uniform and shaving equipment ready. In fifteen minutes he was on his way to Washington.

When they got to the armory, the guardsmen found no equipment. A sportsman's show occupied both the main floor and the basement of the armory and the Guard's trucks, jeeps, and other equipment had been taken to Camp Sims, in far southeastern Washington.

Guardsmen, who were sent across the Anacostia River to bring back the equipment, ran into the heavy traffic jam. And when they finally made it to Camp Sims, they found that the shopping center next to it, at 15th Street and Alabama Avenue, S.E., was being looted and burned by rioters.

"Those stores are exactly one yard away from the Camp," the Guard commander, General Charles L. Southward, said later. "We were worried that the fire might make it inside. So the men helped fight it, and they put barbed wire up along our wall to keep rioters away from the guns and stuff inside.

"Then, as our men drove the trucks and jeeps out of there, they had to dodge rocks and bricks. It was murder."

In spite of all their problems, the D.C. National Guard was ready to go onto the streets starting at 9 P.M. The first of its two 700-man, military-police battalions ready for action was assigned to protect firemen in their stations across the city and to accompany them on calls to riot areas.

These guardsmen slept in the firehouses, slid down poles with the firemen, and raced alongside them in MP jeeps to fires. They dispersed crowds at fire scenes and detained rioters who harassed firemen. Occasionally, they used tear gas. (Use of the guardsmen in this fashion was another lesson learned from the Detroit riot in 1967. In that city, rioters had so impeded the fire fighters that they were forced to let whole sections burn out of control, adding greatly to the over-all property damage.)

The military plan called for the protection of the power and water supplies against possible sabotage, and guardsmen were assigned to this task. They were also called up to stand guard duty at public buildings, including police headquarters, the District Building, and the D.C. Stadium.

At about midnight, Mayor Washington and Cyrus Vance made a tour of the riot areas. At a 1:20 A.M. televised news conference, the Mayor described the city as "quite calm," with the fires "contained," but with sporadic looting continuing in some stores that had been damaged by fire.

"We talked with police and with the federal troops and

National Guard," Vance said, "and were informed that the coop-eration among them was excellent. The situation appeared to be quieting down and, as of the moment, to be in hand."

After midnight, with the number of troops on the city's streets rising to 6,600, they spread out into tree-lined white and black neighborhoods and began enforcing the city-wide curfew much more strictly. Soldiers, who had been in Washington for several long hours, rested in troop trucks and on the floors of neighbor-hood laundromats and drugstores. Church and civic groups and residents of many occupied neighborhoods began bringing coffee, sandwiches, and pastries to the soldiers.

The streets were now saturated with law-enforcement man-power. About 3 A.M., two young teenagers, out after the curfew, threw pebbles at four soldiers patrolling Georgia Avenue, just north of the devastated commercial strip along 7th Street, N.W. Within minutes, the two youths were surrounded by two dozen soldiers and ten police cars, containing more than thirty officers, and were arrested.

Overnight, another 5,000 soldiers moved toward Washington. Army support units came north in trucks from Fort Lee and Fort Eustice, in southern Virginia. Paratroopers and military policemen were airlifted, as well as equipment, jeeps, and trucks, in huge C-130 transport planes, from Fort Bragg, North Carolina.

By dawn, the occupation of the capital of the United States by its own military forces was well established.

About 6 P.M., Friday, a new Cadillac pulls up to the D. J. Kaufman men's store 36
on E Street, N.W., for a load of expensive clothing.

On H Street, N.E., only store fronts remain standing. 37

By order of President Johnson, federal troops roll into the city. Third Infantry soldiers from Fort Myer in Arlington, Virginia, enter Washington near Memorial Bridge and head for positions at the Capitol and White House *(left)*.

38

39

40   41

South of the White House, the 3d Infantry sets up its communications equipment.

The 6th Armored Cavalry troops from Fort Meade, Maryland, become the first to see riot action on H Street, N.E. *(two photos at left)*. They helped clear the area of people and enforced the curfew.

Cavalrymen form a human wedge to sweep along H Street, N.E. *(above)*.

Cavalrymen set up a command post at 14th Street, N.E. *(below)*.

44

Thursday night, fire destroys the Pleasant Hill Market *(above)*. By Friday afternoon the adjacent liquor store and Judd's Pharmacy on the corner of 14th and Fairmont streets, N.W., were burned *(below)*. The fire spread through the four-story apartment building, leaving it a shaky shell *(right)*.

45

46 →

Before dawn on Saturday, troops and police man strategic checkpoints.

At dawn, Saturday, a soldier stands guard in the rubble at 8th and **H** streets, N.E., near where the body of a youth was later found.

Daylight begins to bare the wreckage that the rioting of Thursday and Friday has left. Armed soldiers, tense and tired, watch and wait in the relative calm that the curfew has provided. One soldier's outpost is 7th Street and Florida Avenue,

N.W. *(above)*. Another guard oversees jagged structures at 5th and H streets, N.E. *(below, left)*. At 7th and H streets, N.E., a mangled mannequin lies in a heap of trash as citizens chat with troops or simply stare *(below)*.

53→

52

One of several unfounded reports of sniping sets off this tense incident at 6th and M streets, N.W., and prompts a major response from both police and soldiers. Police in search of a sniper invade a building and yank the residents out as soldiers keep a large crowd from forming. Even a little girl is whisked up by the police. No sniper is found, but a Mercedes is overturned. Two white men in the car manage to flee.

54

55→

A Safeway supermarket at 14th and Chapin is sacked on Thursday night. A crowd forms as looters remove merchandise in buckets through the door and in cartons through a shattered window. The store is stripped bare.

By Saturday, the Safeway has become a mass of twisted girders and charred rubble. Fire destroyed the building when disorder resumed Friday.

As fires rage Saturday afternoon, a Special Operations Division policeman with 58 shotgun poised scans roofs at 9th and L streets, N.W.

VII

The Occupation of Washington

The first full day of the occupation of Washington—Saturday, April 6—was to have been the big day of the annual Cherry Blossom Festival, with a parade, a sports tournament, and the crowning of a queen, chosen by the spin of a wheel from among the state societies of the city. These organizations—social offshoots of the various Congressional delegations—are predominantly white. The Negro majority in the city has never been involved in this tourist hoopla, sponsored by the Board of Trade's Convention and Visitors' Bureau.

When the Festival was canceled, tourists focused their cameras on the riot areas, rather than on the Tidal Basin and its glory of blossoms.

The worst-hit sections of 14th, 7th, and H streets were cordoned off by troops. But tourists could look up the 14th Street hill and see smoke, still coming out of dozens of smoldering shells of buildings, and fire hoses, snaking across the street. They could look up 7th Street and see, in place of stores that had stood two days earlier, block after block of rubble, bricks, and debris spilling over onto the sidewalk and into the street. At the corner of 7th Street and Florida Avenue, N.W., a tired soldier stood with his rifle in front of a block of blackened, brick-front walls, with cavities where doors and windows had been. There were no rooms behind.

Even in residential neighborhoods, strollers happened onto burned-out holes in clumps of neighborhood stores on Capitol Hill, along nearby 8th Street, S.E., and in shopping centers at Minnesota Avenue and Benning Road, N.E., on Rhode Island

Avenue, N.E., along Good Hope Road, S.E., at Wheeler Road, S.E., and the District line. And downtown, across from the Justice Department, on Pennsylvania Avenue, tourists photographed the smashed windows of the ransacked D. J. Kaufman's men's clothing store. Acrid smoke and tear gas hovered in the cool air of the clear spring morning.

On 7th and 14th streets, N.W., 6th Infantry troops, wearing gas masks, made sweeps along the shopping strips, helping the police arrest scattered looters and tossing tear gas at gathering crowds and into looted stores.

A teenager shouted at the soldiers, "When are you going to shoot someone? You haven't killed anyone yet."

The appearance of troops, in force, on the shopping strips most affected by the rioting sharply diminished the disorders there. Looting and burning on a major scale occurred throughout Saturday, but much of it was away from the big troop-concentrations. The targets were mostly shopping centers in fringe areas and isolated, unprotected stores.

The rioting on Saturday morning never reached the proportions of Friday afternoon. Fires were the biggest problem, as arsonists, generally using Molotov cocktails, set 120 more blazes. Suburban firemen were again called upon to help.

On many of the sidewalks and street corners of neighborhoods where furious looting had taken place the night before, soldiers, policemen, and black residents seemed in a relaxed mood that Saturday morning. One group of soldiers showed some black children how the walkie-talkies worked. A ten-year-old, in the midst of a group of soldiers, stood at attention, with his own toy rifle slung over his shoulder.

But in Anacostia, where 2,000 paratroopers from Fort Bragg, North Carolina, were relieving the 91st Combat Engineers from Fort Belvoir and the D.C. National Guard for duty elsewhere in the city, about 200 youths gathered around a supermarket on Benning Road, N.E. For more than an hour, soldiers and youths stared at each other in a tense confrontation. The soldiers successfully faced down the youngsters.

Throughout the occupation, the objective of the military commanders was to avoid violence, even to avoid physical contact with citizens. Serious confrontations between soldiers and rioters were nearly always handled with the military version of tear gas—a chemical irritant known as "CS." It rarely inflicts any permanent injuries and is psychologically more effective in dispersing crowds and momentarily disabling attackers than are bullets or clubs.

"CS has a strong burning sensation that attacks your eyes, nose, and even your skin," a 6th Cavalry officer said. "It makes you feel like you're being burned and smothered at the same time. All you want to do is get out of it so that you can breathe."

The irritating effects of tear gas linger for hours in open places and for days and even weeks inside buildings. Soldiers and police tossed tear-gas grenades into unoccupied stores and effectively kept looters out. During the April riots, Washington police alone fired off 8,000 canisters of tear gas, an enormous quantity. How much more the military used, in canister form and in machines designed to saturate an area quickly, is not known. The use of tear gas was a fundamental aspect of the policy of restraint that governed the conduct of the police and the troops.

Troops and police were under rigid, although different, instructions about the use of weapons. The police always carried loaded sidearms and were prepared to use them, but only under certain specified circumstances and not against a crowd of looters. The troops were not permitted to load their weapons without authorization. Each soldier carried a plastic card that spelled out his special orders for riot-control duty.*

---

* The text of the card reads:

SPECIAL ORDERS

For members of the Army engaged in Civil Disturbance Operations

1. I will always PRESENT a NEAT military APPEARANCE. I will CONDUCT MYSELF IN a SOLDIERLY MANNER at all times and I will do all I can to BRING CREDIT UPON MYSELF, my UNIT, and the MILITARY SERVICE.
2. I will BE COURTEOUS in all dealings WITH CIVILIANS to the maximum EXTENT POSSIBLE UNDER EXISTING CIRCUMSTANCES.
3. I will NOT LOAD OR FIRE my weapon EXCEPT WHEN AUTHORIZED by an OFFICER IN PERSON, when authorized IN ADVANCE BY AN OFFICER under certain specific conditions, or WHEN REQUIRED TO SAVE MY LIFE.
4. I will NOT INTENTIONALLY INJURE OR MISTREAT CIVIL-

There was no quick-reaction loading and firing at snipers by the troops, as there had been during the 1967 rioting, particularly in Detroit and Newark. In fact, there were only a handful of occasions when rifles were loaded—and they were reported to have been fired only three times.

Many of the young soldiers on duty in Washington worried about what they would do if they had to shoot. Specialist Fourth Class Jack Hyler, of the 503d Military Police Battalion, fretted about this, as he led four jeeps down a narrow, residential street, off 14th Street, N.W., on the way to a fire set by arsonists.

"I noticed a large group of kids following us down the street," he said later. "They were yelling things and threatening us. Physically, we were trapped by the rowhouses, solid on each side of the street, and the fire burning out of control at the other end.

"I started worrying about what we should do if those kids tried to attack us—use gas, load our guns, or what.

"But then people came out of the houses on the street and told the kids to go away and leave us alone—that we just had a job to do. The kids dispersed and there was no trouble."

Hyler remembered the incident as "typical of the cooperation we usually got. Only the teenagers harassed us. And that really didn't seem to be racial, just against authority."

A Vietnam war veteran who had worked in refugee and pacification programs, Hyler "felt badly about what was happening to the people in 'Nam.' " But the soft-spoken, twenty-three-year-

---

IANS, including those I am controlling, or those in my custody NOR will I WITHHOLD MEDICAL ATTENTION from anyone who requires it.

5. I will NOT DISCUSS OR PASS on RUMORS ABOUT this OPERATION.

6. I will IF POSSIBLE LET CIVILIAN POLICE MAKE ARRESTS, but I CAN IF NECESSARY TAKE into TEMPORARY CUSTODY rioters, looters, or others committing serious crimes. I will TAKE such PERSONS TO the POLICE OR designated MILITARY AUTHORITIES as SOON AS POSSIBLE. It is my duty to DELIVER EVIDENCE and to COMPLETE EVIDENCE TAGS and detainee FORMS IN ACCORDANCE WITH MY INSTRUCTIONS.

7. I will ALLOW properly IDENTIFIED REPORTERS and RADIO and TELEVISION PERSONNEL FREEDOM OF MOVEMENT, unless they INTERFERE WITH the MISSION of my unit.

8. I will AVOID DAMAGE TO PROPERTY AS FAR AS POSSIBLE.

old white soldier from Chattanooga, Tennessee, seemed to feel worse about his occupation duty.

"It was mighty hard to have to take up arms against Americans in Washington. I kept thinking, 'These are my people.' It would have taken a lot of thought before I'd strike another American. Violence would have been hard."

Saturday continued to be a day of looting incidents, fires, and one death. In the morning, Thelma Dixon, who lived several blocks from the worst rioting, on Allison Street, N.W., received a telephone call from the police. They asked if her son, Ronald James Ford, twenty-nine, was missing from home. They had found his body just outside the playground fence of Cardozo High School, on 13th Street, N.W. His throat had been cut open, and a trail of blood led to the broken plate-glass window of a looted store, nearby. He was the riot's ninth fatality.

Later that morning, at 16th and F streets, N.E., the huge, 70-foot-tall American Ice Company warehouse—once used to store ice blocks, in the days of home iceboxes—caught fire. An adjacent supermarket had been looted and fire-bombed on Friday night. Firemen, too busy with other calls to completely extinguish the blaze, had left two hoses for residents to use in wetting down nearby buildings, while the remains smoldered. Heat from the fire may have caused the thick, dry cork interior walls of the icehouse to burst into flame.

A large crowd gathered around the firemen fighting the huge blaze. At first, the onlookers were quiet. Then, at noon, a television camera appeared.

"We want a soul brother for fire chief," a spectator shouted at a black fireman. The fireman grinned.

As the camera and microphone sought out those in the crowd who were vocal, the talk grew bolder. Soon there were angry shouts. Four squad cars arrived, and policemen moved into the crowd, poking with riot sticks and gruffly ordering everyone to disperse. The crowd resisted and pushed back the police, who detonated tear gas.

A group of guardsmen arrived and interposed themselves between the crowd and the fire fighters and police, warning that there was danger of the building collapsing or of an explosion from several thousand pounds of ammonia in an adjacent building. The crowd backed up and became calmer.

One of several unfounded sniper reports was turned in, at the corner of 6th and M streets, N.W., about noon Saturday. It triggered a tense incident. A new Mercedes car had been overturned in the intersection by a group of youths, and the two white men inside, one of them a wealthy building contractor, had been chased away. Third Infantry troops, ordered to the scene, prevented a large crowd from forming, while police went into the building where the sniper was reported to be. (Actually, it was the building into which the youths had fled, after overturning the car.) Inside the four-story apartment building, the police argued with several of the black residents, arrested them for disorderly conduct, and pushed and pulled them down the stairs and out of the house, in some cases using the business end of revolvers and shotgun barrels as prods.

"What were they doing?" a woman on the sidewalk called out.

"Go on back home," a policeman yelled back.

Washington Post reporter Stuart Auerbach moved through some bystanders to ask what had happened, and a white plainclothesman, with a drawn gun, ordered, "Get out of here. You are going to be shot."

It was an ugly moment.

Then, from the fringes of the mass of troops and people on the street, came Public Safety Director Pat Murphy and Assistant Police Chief Jerry Wilson. Murphy was angry.

"Request, *request* the people to go back to their homes," he told policemen on the sidewalk. "No curfew is on. Be courteous to these people."

Murphy moved all of the policemen off the street and left the soldiers to disperse the crowd quietly.

At about 2 P.M., while looters still flouted troops and police, popular, black soul-singer James Brown appeared on television, introduced by a city official.

"I know how everybody feels," Brown told the television audience. "I feel the same way. But you can't do anything by blowing up, burning up, stealing, and looting. Please go off the streets. From one brother to another, go home."

Not long after that, the Mayor announced that the curfew would begin at 4 P.M., an hour and a half earlier than on Friday, "because of the heavy traffic and the large number of citizens on the street." The order was aimed as much at the hordes of sightseers getting in the way of firemen and police in the riot areas as at the scattered groups of youths still setting fires. At 4 o'clock, police cars cruised the city's streets, announcing the curfew over their loudspeakers.

By 5 P.M., the main thoroughfares downtown were nearly deserted. Only thinly spaced soldiers and policemen could be seen on the sidewalks in front of the government buildings on Pennsylvania Avenue, the department stores on F Street, and the hotels and new office buildings on K Street.

Instead of gathering in the parks to enjoy the pleasant evening weather or heading for the neon lights of the night-life strips along M Street in Georgetown, 14th Street downtown, and upper 14th Street in the ghetto, Washingtonians were forced to stay home. The parks were empty. The neon lights never went on. The go-go girls did not dance. Thousands of tourists left the city early, and hotels and restaurants, which usually count the Cherry Blossom Festival as their first lucrative weekend of the spring tourist season, were deserted.

In some neighborhoods, black and white, people appeared on front porches and lawns, and basketballs bounced on a few off-street playgrounds, sandwiched between row houses in the inner city. Elsewhere, people peered anxiously at the street from behind the glass doors of apartment buildings in which the curfew had imprisoned them.

On many blocks, Army jeeps would drop off two to four soldiers, who would then stand guard in the middle of the street.

One of the larger fires, still burning at nightfall, Saturday, was consuming a shopping strip of five stores on Southern Avenue, S.E., right on the border between the city and Prince George's County, Maryland. As firemen fought the blaze that spread through all the stores, cars of Prince George's County policemen were parked just across the boundary line. The suburban policemen had gas masks, tear gas, Canine Corps dogs, shotguns, and rifles. Two state policemen, with high-powered rifles, were stationed atop a liquor store on the Maryland side of the line. Others poked gun barrels out from behind store walls.

They were watching about 300 people, mostly youngsters, looting a grocery store, delicatessen, and liquor store, just inside Washington, half a block from the Maryland line. The Prince George's County police had specific authority from County Commissioner Gladys N. Spellman to shoot, if necessary, to stop any looting that spilled over into the county.

D.C. National Guard Major Robert Donlan remembered "being scared stiff" when he saw the police across the state line, "armed to the teeth, just waiting." As Guard MP's under his command tried to disperse the crowd, Donlan went into the intersection with a bullhorn.

"I told the people in Washington to stay within the city limits and go home. I told them if they crossed into Maryland they would probably be shot. Nobody crossed the line."

The predominantly white suburbs remained jittery during the occupation. They were fearful of sympathetic outbreaks in the pockets where blacks lived and were worried that rioters from Washington might decide to break across their boundary lines.

Alexandria, Virginia, a historic old Southern city just across the Potomac River from Washington, was the suburban area most seriously affected. Windows were broken on Friday and Saturday nights in about a dozen stores, and half of them were looted. Police made two-dozen arrests to break up large crowds of youths in their downtown shopping section, not far from a ghetto area.

On Saturday night, in Fairmount Heights, Maryland, police reported that they were fired upon from a car carrying three Washington Negroes. No gun was found when the car's occupants were arrested. A Prince George's County, Maryland, elementary school was set on fire, and three stores were looted during the rioting. A coke-bottle Molotov cocktail was thrown through the plate-glass window of the new Rockville City Hall, in Montgomery County, Maryland, late Saturday night, and started a small fire, which did little damage. A white teenager was arrested and charged with the fire-bombing.

Several fires, which police attributed to arsonists, broke out in Arlington and Fairfax counties, in Virginia, but there was no looting or gathering of large crowds in either county.

On Saturday night, Washington police and federal troops set up checkpoints on nearly every major street leading in and out of the District on the Maryland and Virginia borders. They checked outgoing cars for contraband and all incoming vehicles to see if their occupants had legitimate reasons for being in Washington after the curfew. Even incoming trucks carrying "emergency food" signs were searched carefully, after troops found one truck containing marijuana.

Inside the city, after the curfew went into effect, a press conference called by the Black Student Union of Howard University, to be held at SNCC headquarters, was canceled when a tear-gas canister was detonated in the office. The group charged that the police did it, but the police insisted that a stolen grenade had gone off inside the office. Half an hour later, someone threw a tear-gas grenade into the Twelfth Precinct station house. The police put on gas masks and continued to do their work inside.

The police and soldiers were enforcing the curfew very strictly, arresting hundreds of people, even though the streets now seemed quite empty. Between 5:30 and 9:30 P.M., 600 people were arrested for curfew violations, and only ten for looting.

"The curfew and its tight enforcement is having an effect," Cyrus Vance said at an 11 P.M. press conference. "The city is secure."

Another 1,000 people were arrested for curfew violations before dawn Sunday. By then, the total number of persons arrested since the rioting began Thursday night reached more than 4,000. More than half of those arrests were for curfew violations, and one-fourth were for looting.

Captain Thomas S. Connell, Jr., black commander of one company of the 171st Guard MP Battalion, said later that he thought both his men and people in the community reacted better than he thought they would during the occupation.

"The main problem we had," he said, "was verbal abuse. The people on the street heckled our Negro troops, especially with stuff about why were they, soul brothers, guarding the white man's property. But the men paid no attention."

Although relations between the troops and citizens were generally free of open hostility, there was an underlying touchiness.

One afternoon, Captain Leroy Rhode, of the 3d Infantry, found about 100 people shooting craps on the sidewalk of a small side street near 7th Street.

"We were supposed to break up all large crowds," Rhode remembered, "so I sent in about forty men. They had gas masks on as a precaution. It was a mistake. Everything got tense right away. I thought we would have our own riot right then and there. One guy yelled, 'Kill the sons of bitches, they're going to gas us.'

"Right away, I pulled everybody out. Then I sent in just three men, and without gas masks or tear gas. They just stood around and watched. Nobody got mad this time, but the people didn't like to be watched by soldiers while they shot craps, either. So after a while, the game broke up and everyone drifted away."

Some troopers favored a tougher approach.

"If they give you any bullshit, smash them in the face with the butt of your rifle," a 6th Cavalry sergeant told soldiers at Mount Vernon Square, at the foot of the smoldering ruins of the 7th Street, N.W., shopping strip.

A late-model Pontiac went right by a 7th Street checkpoint, farther south, and headed toward the square. Twenty soldiers, led by the tough-talking sergeant and carrying rifles with bared bayonets, rushed into the street and stopped the car. They ordered the young black couple inside to get out and stand up against the side of the car. With the points of bayonets touching their backs, the young man and woman were searched.

"Why don't you go do this in Vietnam, Jack?" the black youth asked the sergeant, who, like the rest of the soldiers surrounding the car, was white.

"Well, we do it here, too, right?" the soldier answered. The search was finished. The couple was released and ordered to get home immediately.

On Saturday night, and until the end of the occupation, off-duty troops bivouacked in senior and junior high schools throughout the city, Gallaudet College for the deaf, one or two police precinct parking lots, the U.S. Soldiers' Home, and East Potomac Park. They slept in bedrolls on school gymnasium floors and in tents on park grass. Most of the military units had complete messes, which served hot food at their bivouac areas. But soldiers eating during duty on the street had to be satisfied with cold, ground beefsteak from olive-drab cans. Jeeps, trucks, and armored personnel-carriers were lined up on asphalt playgrounds and on the outfields of high-school baseball diamonds, where command posts were also set up. These command posts were complete with sophisticated radio equipment, sprouting long antennae and guarded by soldiers with automatic rifles.

One company of the elite 503d Military Police Battalion, from Fort Bragg, North Carolina, went right to the Twelfth Precinct, Saturday night, to help patrol the street with eleven jeeps.

"It was quiet there," the company commander, Captain C. Lee Lockett, a twenty-seven-year-old black officer from Abilene, Texas, said later. "Our main job was to get a feel for saturation patrols in the city, to decide how we could best help the police watch for looting and attempted burnings, now that the worst was over."

On Sunday, the 503d MP's were sent to all precincts in the center and north of the city, including those encompassing the riot areas of 14th and 7th streets, N.W. They worked out round-the-clock, antilooting patrols with the police. Policemen rode with the MP's in jeeps, and MP's provided extra personnel for police cars. Each vehicle had both police and military radios and could be directed by either police or military commanders.

April 7 was Palm Sunday and Washington's first day of almost complete calm since the assassination of Dr. King. It was a day of new incongruities: families in their finest clothes, walking to church past burned-out buildings, sooty debris, and armed troops; soldiers wearing folded palms in their helmets; sermons touching on the triumphal entry of Christ into Jerusalem, the slaying of a modern black martyr, and the furious destruction of a riot.

On 7th Street, N.W., near O Street, in a block filled with

gutted buildings, Sol Green, thirty-one, one of the street-corner "regulars" of the area, wandered through the rubble that had been the Carolina Market. At about 9 A.M., he tripped over a man's body. Green lit a match and recognized his friend, Cecil Hale, who was known to Green and the other regulars only as "Red Rooster."

Red Rooster was one of the ghetto's cartpushers. Every day, up and down 7th Street, he pushed a homemade conglomeration of three or four supermarket carts, in which he put the pop bottles he collected and turned in for pennies.

When Green found him, dead of smoke inhalation, Red Rooster was wearing the navy-blue overcoat, black pants, and work boots that he wore every day. He was the tenth victim of the riot, the sixth to die as a result of the burning.

A block north of the Carolina Market, firemen fought a blaze that rekindled in a partly burned dry-goods store. They put it out quickly and left. A week passed before the seventh fire victim, the eleventh person killed in the rioting, was found there. He was William Paul Jeffers, forty, who had just been discharged from the Air Force, after nineteen years' service. On Palm Sunday morning, he had left his home, eight blocks from 7th Street, "to look for work clothes," his sisters later said. That night, a teenager, who would not give his name, appeared at the Jeffers' home and told the sisters that he thought Jeffers had been killed in a fire on 7th Street. He said they both had gone through a rear basement-door of the dry-goods store, only to find that smoke was still rising from burning debris inside. The youth found a trap door and made his escape, but Jeffers did not.

Seven supermarkets in or near the riot areas were opened on Sunday, from 1 P.M. until just before the 6 P.M. curfew. Customers flocked to them, finding the shelves half-empty, milk and bread very scarce, eggs broken, and some items—catsup in one store— curiously out of stock entirely.

Soldiers and policemen lined the front of each store and patrolled the parking lots behind them. Inside, soldiers armed with rifles, without bayonets, stood guard by the cash registers.

The only incident that interrupted Sunday night's quiet occurred at a remote shopping center at Benning Road and

50th Street, S.E., in Anacostia. Two 82d Airborne paratroopers, standing guard in front of a supermarket there, heard three shots, which they thought were fired at them from woods adjacent to the shopping-center parking lot.

Dozens of policemen and more soldiers quickly converged on the shopping center and surrounded it and the woods. Tear gas was fired into the woods to flush out the suspected sniper, but nothing happened. The soldiers then fired flares to illuminate the wooded area, but the flares touched off a brush fire.

The fire was put out before it did any real damage, and a black man, armed with a .22 caliber derringer pistol, was arrested by policemen near the edge of the woods, on a residential street. The police said it appeared that the gun had been fired recently, but, lacking any other connection between it and the soldiers' sniping report, they charged the man with carrying a concealed weapon.

A half-dozen persons with guns were found and arrested during the twelve-day occupation, but only two were known to have shot at policemen or soldiers: one was a man in a car, who fired on a Prince George's County, Maryland, police car at the city limits; the other, an armed looter, who shot at soldiers as he ran out of a liquor store. Both men were captured without the authorities' returning the gunfire.

The recommended response to a sniper is to assign a sharpshooter to pick him off. There were many sniping reports during the period of rioting, but the vast majority of the reports proved unfounded. Most of the "sniping" reported by soldiers or policemen turned out to be tear-gas grenades being detonated, beer cans and bottles exploding in fires, and firecrackers exploding in metal trash cans. When the police and soldiers feared that a sniper report might be true, they sealed off the area, put sharpshooters, armed with high-powered, scoped rifles, in key positions and on roofs, and made careful searches where the sniper was reportedly located.

The curfew received an unexpected test early on Monday, April 8. Police had a report that SNCC would defy the curfew by sending a caravan of automobiles to Richmond, Virginia, where SNCC leader H. Rap Brown was awaiting a hearing on extradition to Cambridge, Maryland, on charges of inciting to riot. There was a rumor that an attempt would be made to free Brown.

At 5:25 A.M., Lester McKinnie, Washington director of SNCC, and two other young men opened the 14th Street headquarters' door and stepped onto the sidewalk. Immediately, four senior police officers, including Deputy Chief Charles R. Burns, approached the SNCC doorstep.

"Don't you know there's a curfew on, boy?" Burns demanded.

"Don't talk so loud to me," McKinnie answered. "You can talk to me like a man. I'm standing right here."

Burns lowered his voice and repeated, "There's a curfew on. You can't come out of these buildings until 6 A.M."

Police converged from all directions. McKinnie agreed to go back inside. Precisely at 6 A.M., McKinnie and several others left SNCC headquarters and headed south for Richmond. By the time they arrived, the hearing, one of a seemingly interminable series on the extradition question, was over.

The city made its first attempt to return to normal that morning. Schools were opened for an abbreviated class day that ended at 1:30 P.M. Most undamaged stores opened for business, with a 4 P.M. closing time to allow for the 6 P.M. curfew. Soldiers were out in force on all commercial streets and in front of and inside many stores.

Fred Wulf, a seventy-eight-year-old retired house painter, died at the Washington Hospital Center that Monday. While police were still chasing the last of Thursday night's rioters from 14th Street, N.W., Wulf, a white man, had been found unconscious on the sidewalk, at New Jersey and H streets, N.W., several blocks from 14th Street. A witness told police that the old man had been attacked and beaten by a group of black youths. Doctors said that pneumonia had more to do with his death than the head injuries he had suffered. But the authorities listed Wulf's death as the twelfth and last of the riot.

Early Monday, at the city's prison complex in Lorton, Virginia, prison officials heard rumors that disorders were planned for

Tuesday, the day of Dr. King's funeral in Atlanta. At 10:45 A.M., a suspicious fire started in the prison's furniture repair shop. It was put out easily, but three more fires were started between 6:30 and 7:30 P.M., in the clothing-issue building, a dormitory, and the reformatory administration building. A fire bomb was thrown through a window of the administration building. Some prisoners refused to go back to their dormitories for bed checks.

Prison guards restored order with little trouble while the fires were being put out. At midnight, a group of 91st Combat Engineers arrived at the prison complex, marched around to make their presence known, and stood guard until dawn. There was no more trouble.

On Tuesday, April 9, Mayor Washington and his wife went to Atlanta, with other dignitaries, to attend the funeral of Dr. King. The Mayor postponed making a definite decision on his departure until the last moment, to assure himself that the occasion of the funeral would not be used to resume the rioting in Washington. There was some uncertainty because the schools and stores were closed, but the city remained calm. More than 11,000 soldiers, still patrolled the streets.

By Wednesday, it was clear, at last, that the city's crisis was over. It was professional baseball's opening day at D.C. Stadium, and 32,000 persons watched the Washington Senators lose to the Minnesota Twins, two to nothing. There were no incidents.

Thereafter, the troops began curtailing their patrols, preparing to leave and turning back to the police department primary responsibility for maintaining order in the city.

The ordinary crime plaguing every big city was absent in Washington during the final days of the occupation. On Tuesday, for the first time in the memory of one fifteen-year veteran policeman, there was not a single prisoner in the lockup at the station house for the Ninth Precinct, the highest crime area in the city. There was not a single reported robbery throughout the entire city.

Day by day, the hours of the curfew were reduced. The hours on Tuesday, April 9, were 7 P.M. to 5:30 A.M.; on Wednesday, 10 P.M. to 5 A.M.; on Thursday, midnight to 4 A.M. By Friday, the curfew was eliminated altogether. Meanwhile, the Mayor had authorized the resumption of liquor sales.

On Saturday, April 13, the troops began leaving the city. Few were on the streets Easter Sunday.

On Monday, April 15, Mayor Washington issued a proclamation terminating the state of emergency.

By the following day, April 16, twelve days after they were summoned, the last of the troops left.

During the occupation of the capital city, the Mayor, Presidential trouble-shooter Cyrus Vance, Task Force Washington's Commander General Ralph E. Haines, Jr., Public Safety Director Pat Murphy, and their aides spent most of their waking hours in the police headquarters' command center, down the hall from the Task Force Washington "war room"—where a large wall map of the city showed trouble spots and troop concentrations.

Deputy Mayor Thomas Fletcher said later that the decisions made during the occupation of the city "were all done around the table," in the office of Police Chief John B. Layton. "Cy Vance was always there with the book he prepared after Detroit."

The "book" contained the lessons learned from the mistakes made during the 1967 riot in Detroit, where Vance served as the President's special representative. Vance was in on every major decision, always suggesting or questioning, rather than ordering, and getting along very well with Mayor Washington and ranking police officials.

"I felt he was the eyes and ears of the White House," said one police official, who sat in on many impromptu meetings with Vance. "But you'd never know it, the way he acted. He didn't throw his weight around."

At first, police and military officials wanted the curfew, which was in effect for six consecutive nights, to cover only riot-affected sections of the city. Mayor Washington disagreed, saying it would only be fair if it were city-wide and enforced evenly throughout. Vance seconded the Mayor, and that is the way it was done, although police and soldiers were more lenient in the white, far northwest neighborhoods of the city than in black areas.

Vance's Detroit book has become the bible of the U.S. riot-control effort, with much of it reflected in the recommendations of the National Advisory Commission on Civil Disorders. At the back of the book, Vance had a dozen pages of "lessons" learned in Detroit, nearly all of which were applied in Washington.

Among the points were:

> More tear gas should be used.
>
> Use of guns by soldiers and police should be sharply restricted.
>
> National Guard troops should be better trained and disciplined and have more Negroes among them.
>
> All soldiers should have written orders, preferably on wallet-sized cards, emphasizing the need for courtesy and restrained use of force.
>
> Careful logs should be kept of riot activity to spot meaningful trends.
>
> Sniper reports should be thoroughly investigated and not answered immediately by return gunfire.
>
> Street lights in riot areas should be left on and not shot out by troops.
>
> Officials of all branches of authority should participate in decision-making and arrive at clear, concise orders.
>
> The communications systems of the police and the troops should be integrated so that each can talk to the other.
>
> Curfews should be strictly and fairly enforced.

Taking stock after the rioting and occupation had ended, the city listed twelve deaths that were riot-connected in some way—seven from fires. About 1,190 persons were injured, few seriously. Many were treated for tear gas or smoke inhalation. The injured included fifty-four policemen, twenty-one firemen, and twelve soldiers; none was seriously hurt.

More than 7,600 men, women, and children were arrested. Of the 6,500 adults picked up, 4,000 were charged with curfew violations, 1,000 with looting, and 750 with disorderly conduct.

The total money cost of the riot, including direct property damage, the cost of bringing in troops, city government expenses, and indirect business losses, exceeded $27 million.

VIII

Fair Trial: The Rioters in the Courts

"If any of you know any of the defendants, please step up and identify yourselves. You may be able to help us."

It was midnight, Friday, April 5. Judge Tim Murphy had just gone on the bench, as part of an extraordinary effort by the Court of General Sessions to handle an anticipated torrent of riot arrests. Police and federal troops had begun sweeping the streets and arresting large numbers of rioters. Even as the first groups of prisoners reached the court, dozens of relatives and friends lined the brightly lit corridors, hoping to obtain their release.

In one of his first cases, Murphy released a man charged with disorderly conduct, after the defendant agreed to stay off the streets at night and to call his lawyer on Monday morning.

"You immediately go straight, directly home," the judge told him. "Please stay out of trouble."

In another mahogany-paneled courtroom, Samuel Jones, charged with petty larceny, appeared before Judge Alfred Burka. He was released, after he promised to remain with his wife and stay out of trouble.

"Mr. Jones," Burka said. "If you fail to appear in this courtroom on May 16 of this year, you're subject to a year in jail or a $1,000 fine or both."

The authorities were clearly concerned that rioters, if released, would return immediately to the streets.

"If you're picked up again between now and the day of trial," Judge Burka warned Jones, "your bond will be $50,000. Stay out

A man runs to the rear of Manhattan Auto's parts department as another vaults over the counter. Looters had already removed adding machines and other office equipment. Later, the building burst into flames.

Soon after rioters enter Manhattan Auto's parts department, buildings across the street, including Manhattan's accessories shop, are engulfed by fire and thick clouds of smoke, attracting a group of curious spectators. Nearly forty automobiles are destroyed by the intense heat of the fire.

By Palm Sunday, the fires along 7th Street have taken their toll. Behind the street light are the remains of Manhattan's west-side accessories store near R Street *(above)*. The scarred cars are in Manhattan's main showroom on the east side of the street *(below)*.

An aerial view of the 7th and R streets, N.W., area shows the rubble on the west side of the street—all that is left of Manhattan Auto's accessories shop and the two adjacent buildings. The company's burned-out showroom is on the east side at the corner.

64   Saturday night's curfew, more rigidly enforced than Friday night's, brings the heart of the capital to a virtual standstill. K Street, N.W., is nearly deserted.

66

Curfew violators are stopped and searched on Maryland Avenue, N.E. When no suspicious articles are found, they are dismissed with a stern warning.

65   Connecticut Avenue's usual army of strollers is replaced by the real Army.

On 14th Street, N.W., apartment-house dwellers are curfew "prisoners."

Two soldiers do patrol duty at 15th and F streets, N.W.

This was the scene on lower 7th Street after looters stripped and dismembered the clothing store mannequins and tossed them aside.

71

A priest stops to talk with two soldiers on guard duty in front of a looted liquor store *(left)*. A laundromat becomes a cramped barracks for weary soldiers during the first hectic night of the occupation *(above)*.

On Easter Sunday, the rubble of the rioting sharply contrasts with the finery of a woman and child.

WOHLMUTH
NOW AT
714 7TH ST. N.W.

73

75

Providing for relief and recovery is an awesome task. Chain stores open on Sunday under military guard *(above)*. General Ralph E. Haines, Jr., and Mayor Walter E. Washington lead a busload of civic leaders and newsmen on a tour of damaged areas *(above, right)*. A woman, forced out of her apartment by the burning, sits on the street corner and waits for help.

74

At the Capitol, Marine Corporal Michael Hicks poses for sight-seers.

of the area. This is no fooling-around matter. Stay out of trouble."

Judge Milton Korman was beginning to hear cases involving curfew violations and disorderly conduct. Although the curfew had been in effect only a few hours, these cases were flowing into court faster and more smoothly than the more serious and more complicated looting cases.

Many persons arrested that day for disorderly conduct never appeared in court. They were released, at police precincts, after posting bonds of from $10 to $25, which they had the option of forfeiting. But the curfew was a new experience for the city's legal system, and there was no standard way to deal with such cases. On Friday night, some judges released defendants on their promise to return for trial; others set bonds of from $300 to $500. In one dramatic instance, $10,000 was required.

The exchange between Marvin Martin and Judge Korman was not untypical:

"How do you plead?" the judge asked.

"Not guilty, Your Honor."

"Make the trial May 16th," the judge said. "What were you doing?"

"Visiting my sister," Martin replied.

"I never saw so many people visiting sisters in my life," Judge Korman snapped. "Suddenly they've got a love for their sisters."

Judge Murphy heard the not-guilty plea of a man who had reported for work at a social club before the curfew was announced. The club had not closed until an hour after the curfew had gone into effect, and he had been picked up a few blocks away. Judge Murphy, a former prosecutor, verified the man's story by telephone and dismissed the charge.

Murphy then set a two-hour grace period, in curfew cases, for anyone who could give a valid reason for having been on the streets. Pressure-packed, round-the-clock riot justice had begun in the Court of General Sessions.

Earlier on Friday, Chief Judge Harold A. Greene had realized that a flood of riot cases was about to inundate the eighteen-judge court. He had placed the tribunal in continuous session, with some judges—mainly younger ones—going on the bench at 9 P.M., and others starting at 9 A.M., Saturday.

It was obvious that a riot would place immense strains on a court that lacked the space and personnel needed even for its routine workload. Some preliminary planning for a possible mass-arrest problem had been done, but little had been decided when the riot struck.

Judge Greene, forty-five years old, had been appointed to the bench, in 1965, from the Justice Department, where he had been chief appellate lawyer for the Civil Rights Division. His appointment had been part of a continuing Justice Department effort to reform the court, which had fallen into the rut of dispensing mass justice in an automatic, impersonal, and slipshod way—a failing of municipal courts in many American cities. Murphy, Burka, and Korman were among the new judges placed on an expanded General Sessions' bench.

As the first cases started to flow in (150 adults had been arrested Thursday night), assistant U.S. attorneys, who prosecute serious crimes in Washington, began to tackle the required paperwork. Normally, a D.C. police officer signs his name twenty-seven times before an arrested person is brought before a judge. The policeman fills out three forms before the prosecutor decides what charges to place. Then, the policeman has to swear out a formal complaint. Similar systems operate in most major cities and invariably break down during a crisis. The Justice Department had devised a simplified arrest form for use in the event of a riot in Washington; but, at the time of the April riots, it had not yet been printed.

On Friday morning, many police officers who had made arrests went off duty, exhausted, without completing their paperwork—thus creating, at the very start, a backlog that was to grow to mountainous proportions.

The judges had to make sure that prisoners were dealt with fairly and knew their rights. This is always important, but it becomes crucial in riot cases, since any feeling that the courts are arbitrary can add to the disorders. The judges had to balance this need against pressures to deal severely with the rioters, particularly with regard to bail and sentences.

A pall of smoke was hanging over the courthouse buildings Friday afternoon. There was a touch of tear gas in the air and the wail of police-car sirens.

The judges decided against holding formal trials in even the simplest cases, thus sparing themselves the need to make hasty decisions that they might later regret. The National Advisory Commission on Civil Disorders had recommended that trials and sentencing be postponed until after the riot period, "when community tensions are eased." During a riot, arresting officers cannot be spared from street duty to appear in court, witnesses are hard to find, unprejudiced juries may be difficult to assemble, and prosecutors are likely to be less flexible.

In Baltimore, where municipal judges made a different decision, curfew violators were tried, convicted, and sentenced to terms of up to thirty days in jail within a few hours after their arrest. The overwhelming majority of Washington's curfew violators were held in custody overnight, released, and subsequently fined $25.

After the judges decided against holding full-dress trials, the setting of bail became the key question. In 1966, Congress had adopted the Bail Reform Act, which applied to the federal courts, including all courts in the city of Washington. Judges were expected to release as many persons as possible, on their promise to appear for a future hearing, without requiring bail in the form of cash, property, or a costly bond, purchased from a bail bondsman. The idea was to relieve the poor of the expense of bail, with the judge appraising the likelihood that the defendant would appear as ordered. (This appraisal was based partly on the defendant's roots in the community.) The penalty for nonappearance is up to a year in prison and a $500 fine.

U.S. Attorney David Bress told Judge Greene, at 3:30 P.M., Friday, that he hoped the court would use sparingly its discretion to release prisoners. Judge Greene suggested that Bress make the argument in open court.

At the time, an assistant U.S. attorney was urging Judge Justin L. Edgerton to set bail for a woman charged with looting. Judge Edgerton disagreed and released the woman on her promise to return. Bress then took the next case. He told the judge that there were unsubstantiated reports that some of those arrested for looting Thursday night and released that day had returned to the riot areas. He argued that, before releasing anyone, the judges should (1) make sure the defendant had roots in the community, (2) find a third party or organization to supervise the defendant after his release, and (3) get a promise from the defendant not to return to the looting scene. Judge Edgerton applied Bress's recommendations and set $500 bail.

Shortly afterward, the judges met to discuss the bail situation. There seemed to be a consensus in favor of Bress's recommendations, although it was clear that each judge retained individual discretion. In most later cases, bail was set at $1,000, although some judges, who had reputations for toughness, required higher bonds. A few judges continued to adhere strictly to the Bail Reform Act procedures.

Word of the judicial consensus precipitated a revolt among about thirty defense lawyers, who objected to the imposition of an arbitrary bail standard. Some of them left the courthouse and did not return that weekend. One of them said there was nothing a lawyer could do for a client, under the circumstances.

Judge Greene, who stayed in the courthouse night and day during the riot period, told a delegation of lawyers that defendants were going to have to do more than say, "I will be good," before they could be released, during a riot, without bond. The judges were getting calls from frightened residents, black and white, who implored them not to release rioters until the city cooled down. (The fear that released rioters would return to the streets immediately, to riot and loot again, appears to have been exaggerated. Twenty-seven cases of repeaters were listed, but the U.S. Attorney's Office only considered nine to be cases of double looting.)

The volume of arrests soon created a shortage of lawyers to protect the rights of defendants and prevent the judicial process from degenerating into a kangaroo court. The judges knew that riot-arrest pressures in other cities had produced mass procedures, without benefit of counsel.

Judge Greene asked John E. Powell, president of the District Bar Association, to issue a call for defense attorneys. But Powell feared the bar group would be held liable if a volunteer were injured, and Judge Greene did not want to acknowledge publicly that the court was in serious trouble. So he and Powell decided to send out an unattributed radio and television appeal.

Since the appeal was unattributed, it did not disclose the fact that the Washington Bar Association, an organization composed primarily of Negro lawyers, had not been consulted, whereas the much larger District Bar Association, a racially integrated but predominantly white group, had been contacted. Alexander Benton, president of the Negro group, later criticized Judge Greene for not calling the smaller, black lawyers' association.

Some of the black lawyers who practice regularly at the court were aggrieved that none of the three Negro judges on the court was present at the meeting to work out bail policy. One of the three was ill, and the other two had not been assigned to work that Friday. Nor were they called in to participate. There was a feeling among some Negro lawyers that several white judges were openly displaying hostility toward Negro defendants and their attorneys, by setting "astronomically high bonds."

The flow of riot cases to one judge was shut off after it became evident that he was gaveling them through arbitrarily. When this judge was asked to reconsider what a lawyer considered be an unreasonable bond, the judge, a white man, said to the attorney, "I've told you to shut up. I've ruled in this case."

A Negro attorney later commented, "That's an affront to your manhood—not only to your professional standing. Some of those white lawyers would stand there, but I refused to take part."

Both Negro and white lawyers were among the courthouse "regulars" who protested the bail bond policy, and some left because they did not want to work as volunteer lawyers in their usual courtrooms.

But the unattributed appeal did the trick. A large number of attorneys responded, joining those "regulars" who remained. The overwhelming majority of volunteer lawyers were white, drawn from a large pool of downtown attorneys with prosperous civil practices. Although there are not nearly as many black attorneys in civil practice, Negro lawyers also volunteered. The turnout more than supplied the needs of the court.

There was resentment by some black attorneys at the influx of white lawyers. Many of these white newcomers to the court had never handled criminal cases and were unfamiliar with the court's routines. One black lawyer commented, "They didn't even know where the cellblock was."

Although the chief prosecutor at the court, Joel D. Blackwell, was a Negro, almost all his staff members were white, as were fifteen of the eighteen-judge panel. Thus, it turned out that most proceedings during the hectic riot period involved black defendants, prosecuted by white men and defended by white men who were appointed by white judges.

Once the decision had been made not to try cases or hold preliminary hearings over the weekend, the lawyer's role changed sharply. Normally, judges defer setting bond until the D.C. Bail Agency has interviewed the defendant, checked his statement, contacted relatives or employers or friends, and looked up his police record. The judges asked the lawyers to concentrate on assisting in this bail check. They began rousing employers out of bed at 4 A.M. to verify the defendants' statements. Families were questioned, and some were requested to come to court.

Saturday morning, the corridors of the Court of General Sessions were jammed, as scores of relatives and friends wandered around, seeking to find out what had happened to those arrested. Walking briskly by were young members of leading law firms and young government lawyers, who had responded to Friday night's public appeal.

There were some unusual encounters. A woman, in soiled clothes and a head bandage, approached a young man carrying an almost-new briefcase and asked him to help find her husband. The counsel for the city's biggest bank elbowed his way through the crowd to ask a newsman what was going on. A former prosecutor argued with one of his successors over the treatment of one of those arrested.

Scarcely more than 10 per cent of those arrested had been brought into court. Most were waiting—in precinct houses, in the cellblocks of the Court of General Sessions and the District Court, in the cellblock of police headquarters, and in the D.C. jail.

Saturday afternoon, Dean David McCarthy, of the Georgetown University Law Center, arranged to have Legal Aid Agency lawyers and graduate-school legal interns set up a briefing course for the volunteer attorneys who were unfamiliar with the court's procedures.

The backlog of paperwork began to diminish, and things began to move. Policemen appeared in the courthouse to transcribe their scribbled notes into formal statements and sign the complaints. As the file of complaints grew larger, so did the number of prisoners.

The task of matching up complaints with prisoners was almost impossible. Normally, a policeman arrives in the court at the same time his prisoner is taken to the court's cellblock. Because of the heavy volume of cases, officers were separated from prisoners, and prisoners were separated from the papers describing their crimes. At one point on Saturday morning, the deputy U.S. marshal in charge of the court's cellblock reported that he had 150 signed complaints and 150 prisoners, but none of the complaints matched any of the prisoners. Lloyd Cutler, senior partner of a major law firm, attempted to help sort out the confusion in the cellblock. He found that the single marshal on duty faced the problem of matching names and prisoners, while answering busy telephones and handling many individual requests for information.

As prisoners were matched up with charges, they were brought into court, told of the charges against them, and assigned attorneys. One lawyer said he was a member of the bar of the highest court of Virginia and of the U.S. Supreme Court, but not of the District of Columbia. "You're a member of the bar here now," the judge said, with a grin, and asked him to pay the fifty-cent admission fee.

As Saturday wore on, the anger of the crowd in the corridors began to rise. A woman sat on the floor sobbing. She said her husband had been arrested Thursday night, and she could not find out what had happened to him.

"Is this any way to treat us?" she shouted. "It's just like Nazi Germany!"

She told a minister, who urged her to go home, that she would stay "until I find out what they've done to him." Someone took her to a quiet corner while the minister attempted to locate her husband.

Scurrying about the courthouse, Judge Greene cajoled and threatened officials to hurry in their work of processing prisoners. Marshal Luke Moore insisted that his men were doing their best to match prisoners and complaints. The U.S. Attorney's office insisted that it was preparing the complaints just as rapidly as it could find the policemen who made the arrests. The police department said it was releasing policemen to prepare the papers as rapidly as it could. Judge Greene constantly reminded them that a sense of unrest was arising from the long delays. The disappearance of friends and relatives could upset the calm that seemed to be settling over the city.

Confusion increased as to the identity and whereabouts of arrested rioters. Relatives and friends of missing persons pressed the police for information. Wives visited precinct stations, to be told that there was no record of their husbands' arrests. They would be sent back to the court where, once again, there was no information.

About midday, Saturday, a group of volunteer government lawyers arranged to set up a courthouse information service to answer inquiries about persons arrested. Law students and members of religious orders assisted. The volunteers visited each of the fourteen precincts, the jail, and the District Court cellblock to obtain the names of prisoners. On Sunday, Monday, and Tuesday, the service handled more than 2,000 inquiries.

Still ahead was the flood of curfew violators, expected on Saturday night. Police Chief Layton directed that curfew violators be treated by police as a separate class of offenders. They were to be booked at the precinct and taken to the alcoholic rehabilitation center at Occuquon, Virginia, to be photographed and held overnight. The next day, they were to be driven back to the precinct, released, and given a citation—not unlike a traffic ticket —instructing them to appear in court. Because of a shortage of vehicles to transport the prisoners, the release process often took most of the day. Between 6 P.M. Saturday and noon the following Wednesday, 1,768 persons spent a night at the old workhouse facility.

Officials struggled with the backlog of looting cases, which could not be handled in the routine way established for curfew cases. It was likely that some persons arrested on Friday would not get into court until Monday, and those arrested after Friday would have to wait in custody even longer.

Of the 225 persons waiting in the court's cellblock Saturday afternoon, only twenty-five had been formally charged. In addition, there were several hundred persons, who had been charged, waiting elsewhere in town to appear in court.

Private Edward Mulligan, a member of the police department's efficiency evalutation office, helped cut the red tape. He asked the U.S. Attorney's Office to define the minimum amount of information needed for a complaint. He was told that complaints could be filed if the name and age of the defendant and the place of the alleged crime were known. Mulligan persuaded the Justice Department that police officers need not swear to complaints personally; he could do so for them. Mulligan then gathered the needed information and personally took it to the U.S. Attorney's Office. There, the charges were typed, and he signed them.

Defense lawyers subsequently challenged Mulligan's shortcut, but Judge Greene ruled identification by the arresting officer, at a later preliminary hearing, would cure any deficiency in the formal complaint.

Mulligan and Police Inspector Aubrey C. Woodard began using the District Court cellblock as the principal staging point. Prisoners were brought there from the precincts; Mulligan secured the pertinent information and sent the prisoners to the General Sessions courthouse.

In midafternoon on Sunday, Judge Greene was told that five women had been waiting for more than eighteen hours in the court cellblock, without being charged. There were no facilities there for resting, and the sanitary facilities were inadequate. He ordered the women brought before him and told the U.S. Attorney's Office that it had thirty minutes to file formal charges. In twenty-nine minutes, the judge called the women again. Charges were presented against four of them, and the judge released the fifth.

Two lawyers then produced the names of forty persons who claimed they had been in the cellblock for forty-eight hours or more. Between twenty and thirty of these were released in the next hour, when no trace of them could be found in police records. In the mass confusion of the two days, the reason for arresting them had been forgotten; either the arresting officer had not made a report or it had been lost.

The hallways and courtrooms of the courthouse were jammed all day Sunday. The staff of the Bail Agency and the volunteers had done a remarkable job of locating relatives and bringing them to court to vouch for the defendants. In many instances, they brought substantial amounts of money for bond. Oddly, most of the professional bondsmen who work in the Court of General Sessions were not around. Those who were there were reluctant to take a chance on bailing out persons they did not know. Thus, ironically, a man with a prior police record, who was known by bondsmen, had a better chance of getting out on bond than a man with a clean record.

By 4 P.M., Sunday, a total of 4,200 persons had been arrested, half of them for violating the curfew. About 700 arrested on charges of disorderly conduct had been released at police stations, after posting collateral. Of the 1,300 who had been charged with felonies or serious misdemeanors, about 900 had been processed. But the processing was not going smoothly. One court-appointed lawyer described a scene in which he tried to confer with his client:

"It was in the jury room behind Courtroom 18. There was a very long table and lots of chairs. Marshals were guarding the room, but it was a crowded, sweaty place. There were about twenty-five defendants waiting there, along with lawyers and representatives of the bond agency. All the lawyers were white. All the defendants were Negro. Most of them had not been arrested before and didn't understand what was going on. They had a basic mistrust of telling us their stories, and we couldn't do much for them until they did. But I don't blame them."

The police department had established an assembly line at the District Court cellblock to fingerprint and photograph those arrested. Photographs, stapled to the papers of the particular defendant, helped to solve one of the problems plaguing the marshals. Some defendants had refused to give their names or had used phony names. When the marshal called out the phony name, no one in the cellblock would answer.

"You sure you're not Billy Smith?" Police Private Mulligan asked one man.

"No," the man said. Mulligan told him he wouldn't be able to get back the valuables taken from him at the precinct unless he gave the name he used there.

"Man, I had $300 in that wallet," he said. "Let me ask my buddy what name I gave."

All weekend, lawyers grumbled at the tightened bail procedures. Monday morning, the judges met again and agreed to resume full use of the Bail Reform Act. At that time, the processing of prisoners had almost caught up with the flow of arrests, which had dropped off sharply on Sunday.

The American Civil Liberties Union filed a suit, Monday morning, seeking the immediate release of all those in custody who were unable to make bail or who had been held more than twenty-four hours without seeing a judge. The suit was dismissed that day by District Court Judge Curran. The ACLU complained of the delays in bringing the individuals into court and objected to the way the Bail Reform Act had been modified. It also objected that curfew violators were, in effect, sentenced by police to a night in custody whenever they were held overnight before they got their citations.

Judge Greene then denounced the ACLU at a public courthouse ceremony. His court had processed more than 1,800 defendants in a little more than seventy-two hours and would complete its handling of all those under arrest by 9:30 P.M. that night, he said. Top officials of the District Bar Association and many of the volunteer attorneys supported Judge Greene's view. But the predominantly Negro Howard Law School Alumni Association issued a strong resolution attacking the court, saying that the judges had illegally suspended the Bail Reform Act and had kept defendants in jail needlessly.

There were still about fifty jailed prisoners who would not give their names. A Negro activist, Rufus "Catfish" Mayfield, former head of Pride, Inc., a black self-help group, went into the cellblock and came out with the correct names and addresses. He said he had an agreement with Judge Charles W. Halleck to release most of them to his custody without bond.

Between April 5 and 10, the U.S. Attorney's Office had charged

1,468 persons with felonies or serious misdemeanors. Of these, the judges had released 664 on their pledge to return, and another 311 had posted bail in one form or another. The remaining 493 were jailed when they could not make bail, but, in the next two weeks, 407 of these were released, either when the judges reduced the bail previously set or when the defendants found funds. The figures indicated that the judges had continued to use the Bail Reform Act, but had released only 45 per cent of those charged under it, instead of the usual 55 per cent.

There had been, of course, a number of mishandled cases. One man, charged with disorderly conduct—an offense on which defendants normally can post $10 to $25—was held in $5,000 bond. One man, charged with violating the curfew, was held in $10,000 bond, and another, in $5,000. In other cases, persons got lost in the system. Robert Skelton, a twenty-seven-year-old postal clerk who lived at 1816 Irving Street, N.E., was arrested and charged with looting at 8 P.M., on April 5, and was taken before a judge the next day. Bond was posted for him that day, but court officials could find no trace of Skelton or the papers in his case. Finally, on April 10, he was found in the D.C. jail and released.

Almost forgotten in the struggle of the judicial system to keep up with the volume of arrests were the 1,114 juveniles picked up by police. In Washington, youths under eighteen whose offenses require judicial attention are referred to the badly overworked Juvenile Court, whose operations have been the subject of much controversy. This court did not meet over the riot weekend.

In general, those juveniles charged with more serious riot offenses faced two or more charges, ranging from curfew violations to burglary, assaulting police officers, or throwing rocks and bottles. Six out of seven of those referred had prior records, and one out of two was either on probation when arrested or had another case pending. A total of 194 cases were sent to Juvenile Court, but only sixty-one were considered riot-connected. Chief Juvenile Judge Morris Miller later told a Congressional committee that the three-judge court did not have the "judge-power" to arraign the youths in those cases until June or later. Those youths who denied the charges would not be tried for at least six months. (In adult riot cases, the Court of General Sessions had misdemeanor trials under way in June. Federal District Court felony trials began in July.)

A total of 117 juveniles were charged with burglary or attempted burglary (the looting charges), while 535 were listed as curfew violators. Others were charged with disorderly conduct or, because of the minor nature of their offenses, were released by the precincts, without further proceedings. In only seventy-four cases were juveniles held overnight in the city's Receiving Home—in most cases because their parents could not be located immediately.

Police juvenile officers held hearings on more than 750 riot cases that were not sent to court. The officers talked to the youths about the offense and to their parents about such matters as discipline, home life, and school work. Some of the cases involved children of ten to thirteen years of age, although the average age was sixteen.

"The children would tell us they saw other people picking up things in the street and out of store windows, and they just did it, too," Lieutenant Charles H. Calderwood, a juvenile officer for sixteen years, said. Many of them, he said, were not "bad," but were caught up in the contagion of the rioting.

No one in Washington was entirely satisfied with the administration of justice during the riot period. Those in positions of authority made their share of mistakes. But many legal experts concluded that, as judges, prosecutors, and court officials learned by doing what they had never done before, they performed better than had their counterparts in Detroit, Los Angeles, and Newark, in the past, and in Baltimore, during the week of nationwide rioting. (At one time, Detroit had more than 4,000 persons in custody, with 1,000 held for days in an underground garage; other prisoners were held in police buses for periods of more than twenty-four hours. Bonds were rarely set at less than $10,000, and often went as high as $50,000 and, in a few cases, up to $200,000. Two weeks after the riot, about 1,200 persons remained in custody.)

The crisis in the adult courts over releasing riot offenders on bail was an issue of the moment. But it soon faded. By

April 25, the number of defendants still in custody was down to sixty-seven.

U.S. Attorney Bress was subject to some community pressure to drop charges against defendants who had been caught up in the "contagion of the rioting." Bress decided to take a tough line, except where innocence could be clearly established. Officials of Howard University called him on behalf of an honor student who protested his innocence of looting charges and whose record was such that, in other circumstances, he would have been given the benefit of the doubt. Bress sent the case to trial, and the youth was acquitted and allowed to participate in a military scholarship program, which started the following day.

With respect to that case and looting cases against six Howard University coeds, Bress explained, "I did not feel in good conscience that the charges against them could be dropped."

Nor did he "feel it would be fair" to drop a case against a soldier, in Washington on emergency leave from Vietnam, who was arrested inside a record store with a handful of records. In that case, he received "quite a few" calls from Army officials and from friends of the soldier's family.

There were, of course, cases where clear mistakes were made. On Friday night, Bress was called by the owner of a liquor store, who said he had left an employee in the store to protect it. When the police arrived, they arrested everyone, including the employee. His release was arranged.

Similarly, no charges were placed against a woman found empty-handed inside a looted Safeway food store. She said she was looking for her fifteen-year-old nephew. A check in the neighborhood confirmed that she had a reputation of keeping a strict watch on the youth.

One attorney said he was prepared to admit in court that his client stole items from a store. He said he would argue that the requisite criminal intent was lacking during the general looting "festivities," since local residents viewed all property as "public" during that period.

In some cases, lawyers told Assistant U.S. Attorney Harold Sullivan that their clients, frightened that they would be mistaken for looters, ran into looted stores when they saw police approaching. One was so frightened, Sullivan commented, that he ran upstairs to the room containing the safe.

Later, as the cases were processed, many charges were dropped or were reduced from felonies to misdemeanors. By July 2, a total of 356 persons had been indicted, mostly on charges of second-degree burglary and engaging in a riot. In most instances, the preliminary hearings, which began on the Tuesday after the riot, were short. The policemen would describe the circumstances of the arrest and then identify the defendants. In about forty cases, defense lawyers staged lineups in the courtroom, demanding that the officer pick the defendant out of a group of persons. In one such lineup, the policeman identified as the defendant a court clerk, instead of the man charged.

Prosecutors, who were to handle the hundreds of cases, were troubled about the inadequacies of evidence obtained in the heat of rioting. They were also worried that lawyers for many rioters would raise the "contagion of riot" defense for their clients.

By the time the most serious looting cases were being tried by the Federal District Court, the Court of General Sessions was already proceeding well into its roster of lesser cases (attempted burglary and petty larceny). The sentencing pattern generally varied, from probation to a year in jail.

Judge Burka, who was assigned a first batch of looting cases, followed the practice of giving probation to defendants with no previous record, particularly if they indicated remorse. From the bench, he explained that he was distressed by the way the riot was handled, saying, "Apparently no effort was made to instruct the public that looting would be punished by arrest and prosecution." (One high-ranking public official privately expressed astonishment at this comment, wondering why it was necessary to tell citizens that stealing was against the law.)

Burka asked nine men, who pleaded guilty to riot-connected offenses, "If you had heard that looters would be shot, would you have been on the street?"

Not surprisingly, the answer each time was a simple "No, sir." The threat of arrest and swift prosecution also would have deterred them, they agreed.

Nevertheless, the judge placed on probation virtually all

defendants with no prior criminal records. Plainly, he, too, had accepted the "contagion of riot" theory.

"It appears that, somehow, many people in the city just didn't consider that the police would act," he said. "The public came to believe that what was done in a group was all right, although the same act committed by an individual would be punished."

In discussing the case of Nathaniel Dobbs, a fifty-one-year-old dishwasher, Judge Burka commented:

"If I don't send Mr. Dobbs to jail, it is tantamount to saying everyone with a clean record is entitled to one looting. But if I do, where is a man who has a wife, four children, another on the way, who has been working steadily to support his family?"

He sentenced Dobbs to 360 days in jail, but suspended the sentence and put him on probation for two years, during which time the sentence could be executed if Dobbs got into trouble again. Burka followed by the same pattern—one year's probation and a $100 fine—in other cases in which the defendant had no prior record. But he sent James M. Carroll, thirty-one, to jail for 360 days for carrying a pistol without a license. Carroll, like the others, had a record of steady employment, but, unlike the others, he had a police record dating back twelve years.

Judge Halleck imposed the maximum one-year sentence on three men who had been arrested the Sunday of the riot outside a grocery store, where one of them was loading wine and beer into the trunk of a car.

"I remember reading that this was a city of remorse," he said. "Well, here stand three young men who have given no indication of remorse . . . and who can't have any possible excuse because they did it on Sunday. . . . Their acts under these circumstances were willful and without justification or excuse. . . . This court, at least, will make clear that deliberate violators will be dealt with sternly."

All but a handful of the defendants who appeared before the various courts were black. The D.C. Bail Agency records of 869 serious cases included only twelve in which whites were charged with riot-connected offenses. None of the juveniles sent to the Juvenile Court by police were white. Although exact figures were not available, it was also evident that few curfew violators were white.

Of the twelve white adults who were arrested, the cases of five were referred to the grand jury, for possible indictment. One of these cases involved a special policeman who was charged with assault with a dangerous weapon, after a Negro youth was shot and wounded in the leg at a playground. In another case, a college sophomore arrested for curfew violation was also charged with carrying marijuana. The other three were jointly accused of firing four shots and slashing the car tires of a man with whom they had a dispute. The grand jury did not indict them, and the case was referred to the U.S. Attorney's Office in General Sessions, for prosecution as a misdemeanor.

There were also two cases of whites being charged with re-- ceiving stolen goods. In one, a service-station attendant was charged with illegal possession of two television sets, a stereo set, and two air conditioners, but the charge was dropped when the arresting policeman did not appear in court. The grand jury is weighing bringing new charges in this case. In another, a Maryland restaurant owner was charged with receiving stolen goods, after police found large quantities of liquor and clothing in his car. But the government could not establish who owned the property, and it dropped the charges.

"You won't believe this," the man told police, "but I got all of this for $150 from some fellow I don't know."

An eighteen-year-old white youth convinced the prosecutor to drop a charge of carrying a dangerous weapon. He claimed he had picked up the .22 caliber pistol as he fled a house in the riot area, after a group of Negro youths tried to break in.

In one case involving a white defendant, Judge Burka sus- pended a $25 fine, even though the defendant pleaded guilty to walking the streets (on the Saturday afternoon of the riot) with a .38 caliber pistol, a 9-mm. revolver, and a hunting knife strapped to his belt. He claimed to be a soldier who had just returned from Vietnam and wanted "to help the Army." A few days later, Burka sentenced an eighteen-year-old Negro youth to a year in jail for possessing a .22 caliber pistol without a license. The difference, Burka said, was that the eighteen-year-old had "criminal intent—he said he wasn't going to let anybody give him any trouble." (After two months, the judge relented and suspended the remainder of the youth's sentence.)

Curfew violations represented the largest volume of riot-related arrests—a total of 4,049. During and after the riot period, many questions were raised about selective enforcement of the curfew.

Although the police and the military would have preferred to restrict the curfew to the riot-torn areas, it was imposed on the whole city, to avoid the charge that it was being enforced in a discriminatory way. However, the authorities maintained stricter patrols around the affected areas, which were mainly inhabited by blacks. And, in applying the curfew, policemen and troopers tended to look mostly upon Negroes as potential rioters. Thus, carloads of homeward-bound, Negro paper handlers from *The Washington Post,* dressed in their work clothes, were more than once brusquely ordered out of their automobiles, made to lean against the hood of their cars, and frisked. Homeward-bound white newsmen, dressed in business suits, were rarely required to leave their automobiles. Instead, they were asked politely, "Going home, sir?" and were waved on their way.

The legality of the curfew itself was challenged in court, prompting the District government to ask Congress to spell out its power to impose curfews in the future. Although Judge William C. Pryor, of the Court of General Sessions, upheld the city's power in curfew cases, his decision is being appealed.

As soon as the riot was over, the D.C. government, the Justice Department, and the courts jointly commissioned a committee, headed by attorney Lloyd Cutler,* to see how well the judicial system functioned in the crisis. The Cutler group offered seventy-four specific recommendations for changes in detailed procedures, many of which were put into effect immediately. The streamlined procedures of the emergency period were generally approved.

---

* Lloyd Cutler was named executive director of the National Commission on the Causes and Prevention of Violence by President Johnson after the assassination of Senator Robert F. Kennedy.

The committee also called attention to the need to improve the administration of justice under "normal, noncrisis conditions."

"Before the system can be expected to work well in a crisis, it must be made to work better on a normal day," the Cutler report said.

The group emphasized that it was not offering any formulas to prevent riots. Its goal was to present a "plan for the administration of justice under emergency conditions in a manner that helps to diminish, rather than aggravate, disorder, treats all persons fairly, and earns the respect of the entire community for the rule of law and the institutions that enforce it."

The Stern Family Fund financed a study, by attorney and author Ronald L. Goldfarb, that looked beyond the evident defects in the judicial apparatus to the way society treats persons arrested in such emergencies. Judges, the Goldfarb report suggested, should afford defendants an opportunity to make restitution, instead of imposing fines or imprisonment, except in "compelling cases." And the report stressed that "solving the problems in the administration of justice during a riot is less crucial to the life of this community than solving the problems giving rise to the riots."

IX

The Looters

"Whitey don't care about what's been happening to me. Why should I be upset about taking something from him? Whatever I got is really mine. Ain't but one way you gonna get anything from the white man, and that's take it," Al explained.

Al is sixteen and a ninth-grade student. He took part in the looting along Washington's 7th Street on Friday afternoon, April 5, concentrating, he told a reporter later, on the stores between T and New York Avenue. Most of his loot consisted of clothing.

"I got several suits, a few pairs of slacks, and some shoes. I got more than I wanted, and I gave some away to my friends. It was easy looting. The cops didn't give a damn about who was taking what, and I just dug in like everybody else."

His looting, he said, had nothing to do with Dr. King's murder. He would do it again if he had the chance. Right now, he is thinking about quitting school.

"I ain't getting nowhere. I drop out, come back, and drop out again, and the only reason I come back is my old lady begs me to. School ain't got shit for me."

"I was hoping they'd burn the whole town down."

Those were Earl's words—the words of a rioter, specifically a looter. In some ways, Earl (his name, like Al's and others to follow, is fictitious) was not an average rioter. A twenty-three-year-old graduate student at Howard University, he is majoring in philosophy. His father is a doctor, and his mother is a public school teacher. But in two important ways he is typical—he is young and black.

"After the memorial services for Dr. King, we went over to the place on 14th Street where they were rioting," Earl said. "There was burning and looting all over the place. We were just standing there, talking to people on the street, when a crowd broke into Hahn's Shoe Store. Two girls from school came up, and they asked us why weren't we getting in on the action. After thinking about it for a minute, we couldn't do anything but start taking a few things. I got nine pairs of shoes, all my size, and all good shoes, too. The girls got a larger number of shoes.

"There was a black cop standing outside and he smiled at us," Earl said. "He asked one of the girls, 'What're you doing in there, sister,' and gave her a light tap on the behind with his night stick. At first we were afraid, but, after we saw how the cops were reacting, we lost all our fear."

After leaving the shoe store, the four drove toward Earl's apartment.

"Then we saw this liquor store being hit. Everybody was taking care of business. All of us went in. We took our time and got single bottles of good whisky. I got stuff like Jack Daniels, J&B, Cutty Sark, Old Granddad, Beefeater's. We had at least three or four cases of good liquor, about twenty-eight bottles of wine, and maybe twenty bottles of cheap bourbon. We ended up with liquor wall-to-wall in the apartment.

"When we started driving again, we had to pass through some barricades. This was the first time during the thing we felt scared. We felt like we were really going to get caught. The car was obviously full, and we thought maybe somebody might stop us. But we got through all the blockades.

"As soon as we got back to the apartment, we unloaded what we had and went out again for some more stuff."

They returned to 14th Street, where they joined in the raiding of Morton's, a recently opened outlet of a local clothing chain, at the intersection of Monroe Street.

"We stuffed the back seat with things. The place was burning, and I thought maybe the girls might get hurt, but we got out all right, so everything was okay. The building wasn't in danger of falling down, but it was starting to burn pretty well, and you never could tell what might happen.

"We left Morton's and started driving down 14th toward Columbia Road. We went on past a Safeway store on Columbia. The windows were out, there were no cops, so we decided to help ourselves.

"We wanted meat, but somebody had beat us to it. But we got several frozen turkeys, some canned goods, and other things like vegetables and a little fruit. We also got some soda. There were some cigarettes left, too. They had hardly been touched, so we copped some of them."

Earl said he had no moral convictions about what happened.

"I was hoping they'd burn the whole town down. I'm not particularly fond of Washington. I'm not sorry about anything. All I worried about was whether black people would get hurt. All the white stores in town could burn down. I wouldn't care.

"Dr. King's death was a tragedy. Everybody I saw out there said whitey shouldn't have done it, and things would never be the same. I felt like striking back, maybe making up for what I hadn't done. I always stood back and refused to be an activist. Before, my only way of helping in the civil rights movement was to work in the poverty program. If another riot occurred, I would not let hate overcome me. But I'd have just enough greed to cause me to take what I needed, instead of what I wanted.

"We gave away much of the loot. Anybody who asked us for anything, we gave it to them."

Earl gave some of the liquor to his parents, who disapproved of his action but accepted the loot. Of course, he and his friends kept much of the booty. On Saturday of the riot week, they had a community meal in his apartment.

"We had a ball," he said, ". . . just a ball."

Pat is twenty-one years old. An unemployed high-school graduate, she has been married for four years, but has no children. She and her husband live in northeast Washington. Her parents are working people; her father, a laborer, her mother, a domestic. On Friday afternoon, Pat and some friends drove to a supermarket in the Safeway chain.

"I don't remember exactly where, because of the excitement in the car. I got three bags of groceries. I was nervous and scared, but I had to take what I could. I couldn't get as much as I wanted."

After being driven home, she unloaded the groceries and went back outside for more looting.

"While I was looking around in a variety store for items to steal, I turned around when I heard this noise. It was a policeman, and he had a gun in my face. Friends told me later that I fainted. At that moment, the policeman and his partner were called away. I wasn't arrested. I guess I was just lucky.

"My husband," she added, "acted just like I'd been somewhere partying. He didn't say anything bad about what I'd done. I wouldn't do it again. I think so much of my life that I wouldn't risk it like that again. That gun in my face was enough to shake me up."

Nancy is seventeen. She lives in the northeast section with her parents. She does not attend school. On Friday afternoon, she looted a drugstore on Division Avenue and took "four or five large bags," loaded with perfume, cologne, hosiery, and miscellaneous household medical items.

"I hid the stuff in the alley so that I could go back and get more."

The girl explained that an alley near the store was used as a general storage place for looters while they cleaned out the drugstore. Why did Nancy loot?

"It had nothing to do with Dr. King's murder. The manager was nasty and mean, and the bastard overcharged."

Linda is nineteen and a native of Washington. Like Nancy, she lives with her parents in a northeast neighborhood. She is single, a high-school graduate, and earns $120 weekly as a keypunch operator for a government agency.

"Me and some friends went over to southeast Friday and took some stuff from this drugstore. We got film, clocks, pole lamps, wall plates, mops, and clothes. There weren't any police around, so we weren't afraid."

Later, she and her friends—a woman and two men—looted a men's clothing store, taking suits, sweaters, and sport coats. Then, at about 8 P.M., they went to the northwest section, to 7th Street, and helped loot the Cavalier Men's Shop.

Why did Linda loot?

"I did it because I knew I could get away with it and because everybody else was doing it. Most of the stuff I didn't need, but I wanted to do it."

Joe is seventeen, a native Washingtonian, and an eleventh-grader at a vocational high school. He took part in the looting along H Street, starting on Friday afternoon. He said his take consisted of clothing and jewelry, all of which he kept.

"I did it because everybody else did it," he said. "I think most of the people on 14th Street did it because of Dr. King. His office is down there on 14th Street. But the people on H Street were out there to get what they could.

"I'm not sorry about what happened. Why should I be? My house is okay. I think a lot of people are sorry because they lost their homes and they don't have anywhere to shop. But I'm all right."

The above interviews with a handful of Washington residents involved in the rioting Friday, April 5, seem to support the conclusions of Dr. Leonard J. Duhl, special assistant to Secretary Robert Weaver (Department of Housing and Urban Development) and a distinguished psychiatrist, formerly with the National Institute of Mental Health, and Dr. Jacob R. Fishman, associate professor of psychiatry at Howard University. Both these men believe that, without Dr. King's assassination, the riot would not have occurred when it did, but that his death was not necessarily a motivating factor for most rioters.

"The assassination was deeply meaningful to some; but to

others, just a significant straw on a pretty weak camel's back," Dr. Duhl told a reporter.

Dr. Fishman, who was tear-gassed when he visited the riot area the Saturday following Dr. King's murder, said he detected "a spirit of euphoria" among the most brazen looters. He said it seemed to be "a vicarious release from emotional tension and a condition of group excitement, the infection of hysteria, in which the anonymity of being in a crowd encourages participation."

But he said that many of the law-breakers he observed "later appeared depressed," when they realized the extent of damage to their neighborhoods.

Dr. Fishman also pointed out that "many rioters are going through adolescence, which is for most people a difficult period —an explosive, unpredictable time, when a person is caught between dependence and independence, childhood and adulthood, between getting and not getting." For ghetto youths, the period is doubly difficult, he said.

The looters went about their plundering in a variety of ways. The ordinary looter might break a window, move in, snatch what he could, and then run off, having opened the gates for others. To many, looting became a sport, a game of tag, or a bizarre version of cops and robbers, with the idea being to see how much could be grabbed before the police came.

Joe, a high school senior, admitted he had made quite a haul. He did not dare bring all the goods home, because he knew his mother would disapprove. He kept the merchandise in a friend's garage and planned to bring it home gradually, so that his acquisitions would not attract attention.

Asked why he looted, he replied that it was an easy way to get something for nothing. Besides, it was an adventure. He had seen looting on television and wanted to get into the action.

"It was not a racial thing," he said. "All those windows were broken and all those stores were open, so why not take what you could get?"

Joe was typical of the looter caught up in the crowd. This type of looter swarmed in with others, after someone else had smashed the windows. Frequently, he grabbed anything he could reach, although, when there was time, he shopped. The Peoples drug chain reported that Easter baskets were extremely popular with looters in all seven of their stores that were raided. Unquestionably, many looters used the baskets to carry away other more desirable merchandise.

Then there were the "rip-off artists" and other systematic looters, who went to a specific store and looked for items to use or sell. Morton's 14th Street, N.W., store was robbed of its entire stock of expensive leather coats on Friday afternoon by rip-off artists who knew exactly what they wanted. These coats were stored in a locked closet, out of sight, on the third floor. They were carried off by thieves who bolted upstairs, went directly to the locker, broke it open, and made off with the contents.

One Howard University student, Steve, who ran a black market in his apartment, was just such a rip-off artist. This twenty-six-year-old entrepreneur bragged that he had single-handedly cleaned out "Mr. Man," by stripping a men's clothing store on 14th Street, Thursday night. (Later, it was suggested that this had been a mistake; the looter did not know that the store was owned by a black man.)

The floor of Steve's apartment was covered with clothes—bright pastel slacks, knit pull-overs, belts, socks. There was also electronic equipment—two turntables, two lamps, perhaps a half dozen speakers, and two tape recorders. All of the articles on the floor were for sale, except the electronic equipment. "Not at any price," Steve said.

Another student came in to make a purchase, casually looking over the merchandise. He tried on slacks and chose four pairs—bright green, yellow, lavender, and blue—at $8 a pair. Steve provided a suitcase for the contraband, cautioned the purchaser about the curfew, and took his money.

Steve did all his looting on the first two nights of the riot.

"I was glad it happened," he said, "because I was able to make quite a bit of money out of it. I was not worried about the danger because, on that first night, the police were too disorganized to be effective."

Another looter who was thinking of money to be made was Harry, a teenager with a police record, who looted a liquor store and then set it on fire. Any loot he sold "would be clear profit," he said. He admitted setting the fire, but claimed it was not out of hatred for the owner. "I just thought it was the thing to do," he said.

Homeward-bound residents got glimpses of Friday afternoon's looting. Dozens of young blacks could be seen streaming across Franklin Park at 14th and I streets, N.W., their arms filled with merchandise from the D. J. Kaufman store. One carried a stack of pastel-colored trousers; another was loaded with boxes of shoes. On upper 15th Street, a block away from the action, it looked like a parade breaking up. Two policemen directed traffic, while looters moved west on Park Road, some rolling new galvanized trash cans, heavy with "liberated merchandise," along the sidewalk. One man carried five blankets of assorted colors in their original plastic wrappings. A woman carried a stack of little girls' dresses slung over her shoulder, knapsack style. Small children in the crowd clasped games and toys. Two feeble, elderly women were loaded down with loot; one was pushing a grocery cart, stacked high. Behind her, four men struggled under the weight of a 6-foot-tall potted palm. It was apparent that there were more women than men in the crowd.

Late that afternoon, a man walked into a furniture warehouse that had already been looted extensively.

"Sorry, fellow," the warehouse manager said. "There is nothing left. It's all gone. We're clean."

The man pushed the manager aside, saying, "I take my own inventory."

He finally found two rugs and carried them out.

Reporters and photographers on the streets during the disorders described the typical looter as inexperienced and, in some cases, unsure about what to do next. This generalization was not true of all. For the vast majority, it was the first riot, and many found the experience exciting, even thrilling. Later, they could supply reasons for their actions, but few expressed having felt revenge or hatred while they gathered the goods.

A white photographer reported an encounter with a liquor-store looter, whom he started to photograph in the act.

"Don't you go taking my picture," the looter told him, "or I'll bash your head in."

The photographer removed his hands from the camera, which was suspended from his neck, and held his empty hands out.

"I'm not taking your picture. See."

"You're a good guy," the looter said, and handed him a fifth of whisky through the shattered window.

Liquor played a large role in the looting. For people like Jim, a thirty-nine-year-old alcoholic, acquiring liquor was the primary interest. Pulling a bottle from his pockets, Jim said, "I was out there. I got whisky—that's all . . . and I got stone drunk.

"I didn't think it would happen here. I didn't think that King was that much a part of colored people. But he was a powerful man, a good man. If I ever loved a man, I loved King. But I can't go out and dig him up, so that's all I need to talk about him."

Jim came to Washington from a small Georgia town eighteen years ago, leaving behind a wife and a daughter. He was a construction worker, he said, and he hoped he could live long enough to get an old-age pension.

Many middle-class persons, both white and black, prefer to believe that it is only the Jim's, a very small proportion of the population, who actually loot and riot—the "riff-raff" of society, uneducated, unemployed, unconnected. But the best estimates suggest that perhaps 20,000 persons actually rioted during those wild, early April days in Washington. This figure would involve approximately one out of eight persons in the ten-to-fifty-nine age group, who live in the immediately affected areas.* And studies made by the National Advisory Commission on Civil Disorders of those who participated in the 1967 riots in other American cities suggest that the "riff-raff" theory is far from valid. To the extent that the Commission could find a "typical" rioter, he was an unmarried Negro male, between the ages of fifteen and

---

* See Appendix I.

twenty-four, "in many ways very different from the stereotypes."
The Commission found:

> He was not a migrant. He was born in the state and was a life-long
> resident of the city in which the riot took place. Economically his
> position was about the same as his Negro neighbors who did not
> actively participate in the riot.
>
> Although he had not, usually, graduated from high school, he was
> somewhat better educated than the average inner-city Negro, having
> at least attended high school for a time.
>
> Nevertheless, he was more likely to be working in a menial or low
> status job as an unskilled laborer. If he was employed, he was not
> working full time and his employment was frequently interrupted by
> periods of unemployment.

A careful study of more than 850 Washington rioters arrested
for serious crimes in April, 1968, tends to support the general
picture painted by the Commission. Records of the D.C. Bail
Agency, which interviewed most of the 1,468 persons arrested on
felony charges, were made available to *The Washington Post*
for analysis. (The Bail Agency did not cover juveniles. Yet, more
than 15 per cent of those arrested were juveniles, with an average
age of sixteen years.)

Almost 90 per cent of those arrested were Negro males.* Only
9 per cent were women (an interesting commentary on police
arrest patterns, since it was evident to witnesses that women con-
stituted far more than 9 per cent of the participants). White
males made up the remaining 1 per cent.**

It was definitely a young man's riot. *The Washington Post*
study shows that the average age was just short of twenty-five
years, while nearly four out of ten were between the ages of
twenty-six and forty. (The average age of the entire group would
be lowered by slightly more than a year if arrested youths, under
eighteen, had been included.) There was a sharp tapering off in
the ages of the looters. For example, the group aged twenty-one
to twenty-five was approximately 50 per cent larger than the

---

* See Appendix II for more detailed analysis and explanation of these and
succeeding figures, as well as additional information on persons arrested.

** The Washington Bail Agency listed twelve white males with riot-con-
nected offenses. The total was too small to develop reliable data, but their
average age was about two years older than the black rioters.

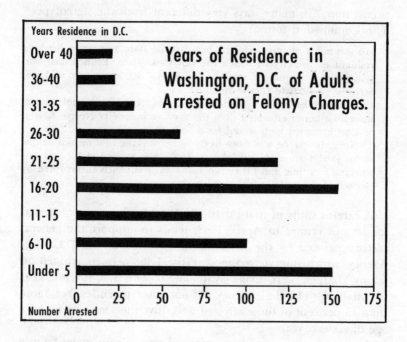

Years Residence in D.C.

Years of Residence in Washington, D.C. of Adults Arrested on Felony Charges.

Over 40
36-40
31-35
26-30
21-25
16-20
11-15
6-10
Under 5

0   25   50   75   100   125   150   175
Number Arrested

group aged twenty-six to thirty and twice the size of the group aged thirty-one to thirty-five.

It was a hometown riot. About four out of five rioters had lived in Washington for more than five years; four out of ten, more than twenty years; and one out of three was born in Washington. Paradoxically, the length of time the rioters lived in Washington is, in part, a reflection of the number of youths who have lived here all their lives. Those not born in Washington were clearly a product of the historical northward migration of Negroes. Half of the group were born in the Eastern Seaboard states south of Washington, with the largest number coming from North and South Carolina, but they generally had moved to Washington early in their lives. Only twenty-seven came from four border states, including Maryland, and only fifty-four came from twelve northern states.

It was not a riot of the city's most impoverished and deprived. The typical rioter could not be considered well-off, but the rioters' hourly or weekly earnings indicated a median earning potential of about $4,000 a year. Among married rioters, two out of three earned above this level, and two out of three unmarried rioters earned below this level. (Average individual income for Washington blacks is now about $3,500, with family incomes averaging above $6,200. The figure of $1,700 is considered the poverty level for individuals; $3,300, for families.) Incomes among those arrested increased with age, from an average of $2,800 for those under twenty-one to $5,000 for those in the forty-six-to-fifty age bracket. Above age fifty, income dropped off sharply, with those fifty-six and older indicating an income of $2,500 a year. Women rioters were paid substantially less than the men; three out of four women earned less than $4,000 a year, while less than one out of two men were in that pay bracket.

It was a workingman's riot. At least three out of four had so-called blue-collar jobs. Only one in eight was unemployed. Smaller numbers were white-collar workers, housewives, students, or military personnel. A handful worked for the federal or D.C. governments. Most of the blue-collar workers had average annual incomes in excess of $4,000.

It was a riot of dropouts. A large proportion had lost interest in school after reaching adolescence. Only one-third of the arrested rioters had finished high school. One-third started high school, but did not graduate. One-third dropped out along the way, before the end of junior high school, with one rioter reporting absolutely no education, five dropping out after the first grade, eight after the second grade, and eight after the third grade. The educational breakdown was roughly typical of Washington's Negro population, except for those at the upper end of the scale. Only a tiny fraction of the part of the black population that went to college was arrested in the rioting.

It was a riot largely of first offenders.* About 54 per cent of the men and 86 per cent of the women had no previous arrest records. Just one of the twelve whites arrested had a prior criminal record. Of those twelve, five were charged with having

---

* One note of caution: Data on those who were not arrested was unavailable. Were those arrested likely to have been the most venturesome, or simply the ones least skilled in eluding the police?

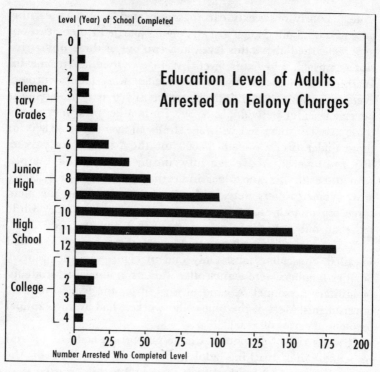

Level (Year) of School Completed

Education Level of Adults Arrested on Felony Charges

Elementary Grades: 0 1 2 3 4 5 6

Junior High: 7 8 9

High School: 10 11 12

College: 1 2 3 4

Number Arrested Who Completed Level

weapons in their possession. The same charge was placed against thirty-six of 759 blacks.

It was riot that included government employees. Since Washington's principal industry is government, it is not surprising that there were government employees among the looters. Just how many were involved cannot be determined, but twenty-seven federal employees and fifteen municipal government workers were arrested for riot-connected offenses.

Naturally, the participation of government employees drew fire from many congressmen. After hearings in April, Congress passed a law directing that, thereafter, anyone convicted of a felony connected with a riot or civil disturbance would be barred from employment by the federal government and the city government for five years. U.S. Civil Service regulations in existence at the time of the April riots also called for the removal of any government employees convicted of a riot-connected felony.

Of the twenty-seven federal cases, eleven were dropped without court action. The first three that were tried resulted in convictions and suspended sentences. Another two left the government service voluntarily, and one was dismissed for misconduct.

A woman government employee, with a master's degree, was one of those arrested in the rioting. But she was lucky. After spending more than six hours in custody in a police station house, she was dismissed without charge by a police sergeant who was moved by her plight. On Friday afternoon, she had gone to 14th Street with two male companions, "to see what was going on." Police picked up all three, after one of the men jumped out of the car and returned with four bottles of liquor from a looted store.

When it was all over, she wrote about her feelings, under the pseudonym P. J. Wilson, in an article for *The Washington Post*:

As I was running up the stairs to my apartment, I realized how close it had been and how much I had really put on the line for some excitement.

For those ten seconds after we got the liquor, I felt that the System had finally given me something for nothing.

White people do not realize the mixed emotions that an educated Negro feels every day. They tell you to go to school and get educated and then they give you some penny-ante job and expect you to feel like the world has been so gracious. But even that white secretary feels that she is better than you because she is white. But I enjoy being a black woman in D.C. I belong to a community where I can walk down the street and speak to people and know that I belong someplace. I was on 14th Street during the looting and burning but no one hurt me or threatened me. I stood in front of a store on 7th Street that had been cleaned out. The men there were talking to me and laughing. When the cops came down the street with the tear gas guns, the men turned around to make sure I was all right. I have never felt like that in a white world.

I went to a black university and I loved every minute of it because there I was fighting for my identity as a woman and a person. Not as a Negro. It felt good, real good. If I ever have any children, I hope they will live in a community where they belong. You can't fight the race issue constantly and find your identity at the same time.

The police were wonderful. The black cops made me proud that I was black. One cop who is about to retire in two years talked to me before he went off duty. He had been on the streets since 8 A.M., and it was now after 11 P.M. He asked me didn't I think it was senseless for them to burn. He said, "I only finished high school and when I first came to Washington all we could do was become messengers and porters." He said, "You have some degrees, what do you say? I have an 8-year-old son and I want him to go to college even if I have to work three jobs to see that he gets there." He added, "We are only burning down our own neighborhoods."

It's nice when I talk to all of my intellectual friends and say that it is all right for us to burn and loot. But the little people do get hurt. My feelings were that most of us who were locked up were only sorry that we had gotten caught. But the black people in this city were really happy for three days. They have been kicked so long and this is the one high spot in their life. Most of the buildings that got burned should have.

There were looters who suffered remorse. Shortly after the riots, there was some enthusiasm for an amnesty scheme to permit the conscience-stricken to return stolen merchandise without penalty. Doing so, it was argued, might help heal the community's wounds. Clergymen held informal discussions on suggestions that churches serve as depots to receive returned loot, but the idea was dropped as impractical and unwise. Some members of the Negro clergy opposed the idea on the grounds that looters and the general public should not be deluded into thinking that the individual's or the city's problems could be solved so easily.

The police department did not object to the plan, but declined to give absolute assurances that the looters who returned merchandise would not be arrested. "We felt it was something we would rather have happen, but not know about," a police official explained.

Some individual looters did deliver goods of negligible value to a Catholic priest, who donated them to the Salvation Army.

There were also instances of looted merchandise being turned in for cash at other branches of the same chain. Friday morning, a big northeast store discovered that an unusually large number of customers were not presenting sales slips when returning merchandise for cash. The sales staff concluded that many of the articles came from another branch that had been looted on Thursday night.

And afterward, for days following the end of the riot, there were the scavengers, who combed the rubble of demolished buildings over and over again.

X

"All You Need is a Match, Man"

A few days after the occupation of Washington ended, *The Washington Post* assigned a reporter to find and interview some arsonists to complete the picture of the April riot that was being assembled for this book. He began at once making contact with persons who might lead him to someone who would talk. At first, he was told that anyone who set fires would not agree to talk for publication. He persisted, suggesting that the interview be conducted with the arsonists wearing masks or hoods so that their identities would not be known. For nearly four months, there was no response.

Then, on August 8, around noon, the telephone rang.

"About the meeting. Do you still want it?"

When the reporter said "yes," he was told to expect another call around 10:00 P.M.

At 10:15 P.M., the same voice on the telephone told him to appear in front of a specified room in a shabby old hotel, in the heart of Washington's inner city. The reporter, who is black, said he would like to have another reporter accompany him.

"No, we don't want anybody else. Just you."

Armed with a tape recorder, the reporter appeared alone at the hotel room and knocked on the door. After he identified himself, he was made to wait two minutes. Then the door opened just a crack. A pair of eyes peered at him from two small holes in a black hood and he was allowed to enter.

The only light came from a lamp on the floor of an open closet. It cast a dull, eerie glow on three hooded figures in the small room. One was the black-hooded man who had opened the door. The other two wore improvised hoods, made from white hotel linen, with jagged holes torn out for eyes and mouths. One had also covered himself with a bedsheet, from his neck to his shoes.

Ground rules for the interview were quickly established. The reporter explained that the information was desired for use in this book and that he might be required to tell the authorities what he knew about the meeting. The trio balked at the idea of using a tape recorder, but agreed when the reporter promised to destroy the tape after the interview was transcribed. Presumably, they feared that their voices on the tape would provide clues to their identity. However, as the interview progressed, they began to warm up to the tape recorder and even orated into it. (The tape was destroyed as soon as the transcript was made.)

The interview proceeded for an hour and forty minutes. The room became stifling hot, and two of the men kept pulling their wet, sweaty hoods away from their faces. One man had a .45 caliber automatic in his belt. Once, hearing a noise in the hallway outside the room, he nervously drew it. The reporter did not, as far as he could tell, know any of the three hooded men.

The purpose of the interview was to learn about arson in the April riot, but, as the session went on, it became evident that the three men were purporting to describe an unknown aspect of the riot—the fact that a small group of revolutionary activists had worked to keep it going.

The three made no claim that they or their group were responsible for starting the disorder in Washington. To this extent, their story parallels the FBI's assessment that there was no plot or conspiracy to touch off a riot in Washington in April, 1968.

They did claim, however, to have performed a catalytic role in the riot, by example and suggestion.

"A lot of areas we went into, man, there was nothing going on till we got there," one of them said.

The scope of their activity was limited, they said, by the relatively small size of their group and because Dr. King's assassination caught them by surprise. They took strong exception to the word "riot," preferring "rebellion" or "revolution" instead. They did not see what happened in Washington as a reaction to Dr. King's murder as much as an assault on a racist system, which, they believe, must be destroyed if black Americans are to survive.

The reporter felt that their basic story, told four months after the events of early April, was not inconsistent with what was known. This, too, was the judgment of senior reporters and editors who listened to the tape and examined the unedited transcript. It was decided that the interview should be published to help in understanding the reactions and attitudes held by some participants in the riot. The transcript was then edited for space and clarity, with less relevant portions omitted.

The reporter assigned numbers to the three men, who had spoken to him as follows:

No. 1: I guess what you want to hear about is what happened after Dr. King got killed. Right?

REPORTER: Right. But specifically about burning.

No. 1: We've had ourselves somewhat organized in this city alone, I'd say, since about February. We felt for quite some time that it has been necessary to protect ourselves, to arm ourselves, in case the beast does decide to come down on us. When Dr. King got killed, of course, it came as somewhat of a surprise to us—a hell of a surprise. It caught some of us off guard. But we still were able to do our thing. We had some of our equipment at close hand, where we could get to it easily, even with the curfew being in effect.

REPORTER: When you say equipment, what do you mean?

No. 1: Cocktails, even dynamite. There were a couple of places in this town that were dynamited. A&P at Benning Road, Cavalier's on 7th Street, were dynamited, and a couple of other places. But to get to burnings and things. We were preparing to make our own move with the slightest motivation, with the slightest incident that we could use to move with. We had the reasons, but, in order to move, you must have the people behind you, also.

REPORTER: You used Dr. King's murder as an excuse?

No. 1: No. That's not the wording I used, brother man. I said we needed an incident that would make it justifiable even in the eyesight of the mass of the people that do not agree with the term "black power." With the mass of people that do not agree with protecting oneself with a piece [gun] such as I have on my side, you see. We had some people who still think that the white man is a good man and he will set us free. Jesus with blue eyes and blond hair. I see the white man as a beast, not only from anybody's terminology but from my own past experiences. I was raised in the South, man; I've dug on it there, you see.

REPORTER: Thursday night, Dr. King was killed. What did you do?

No. 1: Thursday night. I was uptown when I heard the news. I was somewhere between U and Florida Avenue when we heard that Dr. King had been shot, and we were waiting news whether he would survive. Shortly afterwards, we heard that he had died from the gunshot. People were demonstrating, from the beginning of 14th and Florida, down 14th Street, to get the businessmen in that district to recognize Dr. King. This is to show our respect for the man, although our philosophies conflicted, you dig it. But the mass of people fell in behind them. And from that, I think the first window that was broken was at one of the theaters on U Street. And, man, when that broke, that was, like—the shot that was heard around the world when the honkies were fighting against their own people.

REPORTER: What was the first thing? What did you do? You say you got to some equipment?

No. 1: I broke a window.

REPORTER: You broke a window. With what?

No. 1: My foot, man. I put my foot through it. I wear combat boots most of the time.

REPORTER: What was the first place you burned? Or threw a bomb?

No. 1: The first place that I personally burned? My first thing I did was not the part of burning, as such. I believe in a total type thing. So I just stuck the cap on, lit it, and threw it, you know.

REPORTER: You put the cap on what?

No. 1: On a stick of 'mite.

REPORTER: Where?

No. 1: A&P.

REPORTER: What street?

No. 1: It's Benning Road, I forget the exact hundred block. These things don't register too well with me.

REPORTER: How did you obtain the dynamite?

No. 3: Well, like in Maryland and Virginia, they have sites where they keep dynamite.

REPORTER: Construction sites?

No. 3: Yeah. In the District, they take the dynamite back to the place that's doing that job, you know. But like, out in Maryland and Virginia, they keep it in shacks on the site in many instances.

REPORTER: It was stolen from there?

No. 3: It was liberated.

REPORTER: Where did you learn to make Molotov cocktails?

No. 1: I learned in the service. Uncle Sam taught me in Army basic training.

REPORTER: How do you make them?

No. 2: Simply by deposting gasoline into a glass container or plastic container and putting some type of combustible material at the top—and ignite it.

REPORTER: Are you selective about what type of Molotov cocktails you use against a certain surface?

No. 3: When we had time. I know one group of brothers I was with—we didn't have time to do nothing but just pick up and go.

REPORTER: Why didn't you have time? The policemen were nearby?

No. 3: Yeah. Well, the police were in the whole area; they were saturating the area. All we had time to do, like one instance, just drive up, hop out, hit it, and jump back in the car.

REPORTER: Is there a place where Molotov cocktails are made? And are stored?

No. 3: Now there isn't so much—there was a semiplace that was used before to store some gasoline, kerosene, and varsol, you know. We had a place—a couple of places—to store those

things, and we would get it little by little. To build up. Because, like, the guns and everything—we didn't have the
money we have now to buy guns off the street, so we had to
store gasoline and things along with the few sticks of dynamite
that we got and bullets and everything. We even were storing
bullets we didn't have guns for before. But we have guns for
them now.

REPORTER: Why did you use fire after Dr. King was killed?

No. 3: I think what you're trying to say—why did you use fire
instead of bullets?

No. 2: Because fire is more destructive, and it's much faster to
destroy a building or the contents of most of the building with
fire than any other means other than dynamite, and we had a
limited amount of that. We had to hit special places with that.

REPORTER: Why were they special places?

No. 2: Well, because, first of all, like they were the biggest Jews
and the biggest exploiters in the community, and we wanted
to make sure they never did get back.

REPORTER: Why do you want to destroy in the first place?

No. 3: First of all, fire is the only thing that people could identify with. People are not ready for an armed thing right now.
And we were not ready either—for an armed thing. We had
been preparing for both fire and guns, but we didn't have
enough and we didn't feel the people had enough guns. We
knew the pulse of the whole city, because we worked in it,
we've lived in it, you know, we were block workers and everything. And, like, twenty-five of us knew that it wasn't time
for that.

REPORTER: Is that all there are of you, twenty-five?

No. 3: Back in February, when we first started to get together,
we said there was a small knit group that was together, instead
of a large group that wasn't together. Although we had a lot
of mistakes, it was very good. And at the state we are now, we
are very much together. That's why we have enlarged so much.

REPORTER: You have more than twenty-five now?

No. 3: Oh, yes, many more than twenty-five.

REPORTER: Can you give me an estimate?

No. 1: Those who know don't say; those who say don't know.

But, to reiterate, fire relates to the mass of people much more, because it is something they can use easily. All you need is a match, man, a piece of paper, you dig it. Whereas if we got into a whole long thing of using carbines and M-1's and pieces, you see, they would say, "damn, we ain't got this—what you doing shit like that," you see?

REPORTER: Did the fact that the police didn't shoot generally have any influence on your not using guns?

No. 3: No. If they had shot more, we would have just kinda come on out, you know, for the protection of our people. But since they didn't use them, we had decided not to use them. We had said we weren't going to do this thing all the way. But we decided in the beginning, too many black people would get killed for our mistake—for our not being ready.

REPORTER: There were seven people who died in fires. Does the fact that they died bother you? And they were blacks.

No. 3: No. I hate to see them go, but I came to the conclusion and to understand black people are going to have to die.

REPORTER: Are you prepared to die yourself?

No. 3: I think I am. I can't say I am. I believe I am.

No. 2: As a matter of fact, one of my best friends and one of our members in Cleveland got killed—we look on it as a sacrifice and we hate to lose him but he had to go.*

REPORTER: No. 2, what places did you burn?

No. 2: Well, I'll tell you, the first place that I burned was up at Barry-Pate.

REPORTER: Barry-Pate Chevrolet?

No. 2: Right.

REPORTER: How did you burn it, what did you do?

No. 2: I used a Molotov cocktail to start one of the cars. And from there, some of the younger brothers just came on over with gasoline. They saw the fire and then they came on over, turning over cars and so forth, you know what I mean.

REPORTER: What else did you do? Where else did you burn?

---

* In late July, 1968, in Cleveland, a four-hour gun battle between black nationalists and police ended with the death of ten persons, including at least two of the gunmen.

No. 2: We began to hit all along 14th Street. The Temple Grill and on up in that section.

REPORTER: What went through your mind as you were burning the place? Did you get any satisfaction from doing it? Were you avenging Dr. King's death, or what?

No. 2: My thing wasn't because of Dr. King's death, to me, personally, you know. Yeah, I got a satisfaction. As long as I can destroy the beast in any form I can—you know, economically, physically or any other form. But I have to wait my time.

REPORTER: The beast? Meaning who?

No. 2: The honkie, the whiteys.

REPORTER: No. 1, what went through your mind when you burned A&P?

No. 1: You want to know what really went through my mind? I couldn't get through fast enough with one place to move on. Really! You have a realization in your mind that not everybody is there that you would like—every black person wasn't there—so you have to do more than you would normally do, if you follow me. I couldn't strike a match fast enough.

REPORTER: Why did you want to burn?

No. 1: Well, I realize, myself, that the beast was our enemy.

REPORTER: Where do you get this word "beast"? Is that just the latest thing for honkie?

No. 1: Well, it's not the latest thing. It is not a faddish word. It's a description, man, it's a reality. He is a beast. If you dig on his history you see he has done beastly things all his time. I mean, he walks different, smells different. He's a beast, baby. It's quite that simple. I wasn't completely satisfied because the revolution wasn't into a full-scale thing, because our people didn't think it was time for a full thing. In other words, a lot of people are still, what I say, in the Negro state of mind. The Negro state of mind being that of loving the white man or thinking that the white man is not all bad. I got some satisfaction, because I was doing something to hurt him. I know he's an exploiter of our people. Even they recognize the fact. They'll put on the news that in some stores in the ghetto areas, on the day that the people receive their welfare checks, the prices are hiked two and three cents on each item, so they can make a better profit on poor people who are living on welfare as it is.

REPORTER: You want to destroy those stores?

No. 1: I personally want to destroy the system. The system is what suppresses our people and oppresses our people. We have gone through this shit for 413 years. Dr. King, the king of love, got killed because he preached love for all, you dig it. And then, what happened to him? A honkie put a bullet through his head! The man is our enemy. His way of living is our enemy. We are fighting for survival. Not for recognition. If I wanted recognition, I'd take this shit off my head and let you see who I am, but I'm not going to do that.

No. 3: Dr. King wasn't only killed for the reason brother stated. He was also killed because he was one of the ones that attacked the militarism. Every man that attacks and has followers, the man who attacks colonization, is knocked off. They didn't start hating King until he started coming out against the war in Vietnam. Even white Southerners let him come down there for civil rights, but when he got international—when Malcolm [Malcolm X] got international, when Kennedy got international, all of them, you know—this country just can't stand that shit.

No. 1: Dig it. It was in the paper recently, man, that the economy of this country is so much based on the Vietnam war that, because of all their investments there, that if there was a halt to the war right now, that this country would be facing a depression.

No. 3: And so, if we can present Vietnam here, in the major cities over here, if all those were developed into Vietnams, like Oakland is becoming, you know, like Miami is going to be going like that for a while, and like Chicago is going to come, like Boston is getting with it. That brother we got up there—he's been working hard.

REPORTER: This is to organize violence?

No. 3: If you want to call it that, that's what it is.

REPORTER: What do you call it?

No. 3: We call it revolution—for freedom and liberation of black people.

REPORTER: Do you object to the term "riot"?

No. 1: Yes.

REPORTER: Why?

No. 1: Riot is spontaneous. Revolution is planned. It's as simple as that.

No. 2: I'm opposed to the terminology of riot because it's developed by the honkie. It's a term to say that it's something bad. It's just a term used to make us look wild, you know, like we're just a bunch of savages. We have our own terminology, because this is why we're rebelling.

No. 1: If you dig on the thing, I think Webster will tell you that a riot itself is a spontaneous, sporadic, I think, action. What we're doing is not spontaneous, sporadic—shit.

REPORTER: What do you do when somebody makes the allegation that it was a plot—was all planned?

No. 3: I don't think it's relevant. We took advantage of an incident. If it was planned, you see, there would be nothing left of the city. There would be very few white people around here, also.

REPORTER: Why wasn't more burning done?

No. 3: Ah, why wasn't more burning done? I thought it was quite a lot myself.

No. 2: Like, I think that one of the reasons there was not more burning is that we realize the fact that our people were not prepared for the beast. And we know what a savage he is. We know that pretty soon he would begin to shoot them down, you know, like, we were the only protection that they had. Therefore, after we saw them move in, we, like, asked people to go home and get off the street.

REPORTER: So at one point, in other words, you were burning, breaking windows, but at another point you were telling people to go inside?

No. 2: Well, we were asking some people to go inside.

No. 3: Sure. Children and old ladies.

No. 1: Yeah. At some point they were going through that looting thing, man, and the cop he come right up with that shit. Ain't no use in them getting hurt, man, when it's not necessary. Not just for that looting thing.

No. 3: And then, other times, we told them to go on because we were going to burn down, like, a complex or a building, which they would get caught up in.

REPORTER: Were you ever afraid of being arrested by the police?

ALL: No.

REPORTER: Why not?

No. 3: It was easy to get away. See, like, man, like if I was arrested, see, I could give them some story—like, if I was arrested on the spot, I would make it seem like it was just out there. And I just be another looter. Dig what I'm saying?

No. 2: It's no big thing. And if I was arrested, we have attorneys. We have money and attorneys to get us out. Like during the April thing, man, just a couple brothers out of the twenty-five got arrested. And they were just called, like, breaking curfew. In all three cases.

No. 3: And there's no reason to act bad when you get caught like that. You just act cool, just act cool. Say, "damn, man, I was going home," or some shit like that.

REPORTER: Why not be more hostile?

No. 3: Oh, then you get a real rap. You get your ass beat, you know, if you ain't going to get it beat already. You see, when the odds are against you, there is no reason to act the fool and die. We realize there's going to come a time the man ain't going to stop you, and arrest you for looting or curfew, but we going to be up-tight, and we expect that, by then, the majority of the black population in all the cities are going to be up-tight too.

No. 1: You want to hear something that make my bust [arrest for curfew violation] sound a little more funny?

REPORTER: Yeah.

No. 1: They asked me all kinds of questions. They called me a Communist, man. You see, what happened was I went past the National Guard checkpoint. Dude asked me, "Where you going?" I said, "Well, sir, I'm going home, I just got off of work." I got past about five of them, man, then here come the rollers, you dig it, with, I think it was six or seven whiteys and one poor soul brother who had to be the one act most hostile towards us, you see. They saw the walkie-talkies and they busted us. What could they do? The walkie-talkies was not stolen, you see; they wasn't even copped in this city. So they bust us, man.

No. 1: Another thing, too, it's a disadvantage of these honkie cops that move out to the suburbs, 'cause nobody knows the city better than the city-dwellers. There are alleys the cops don't know about. And rooftops can take you plenty of places.

No. 3: Yeah. Since you're talking about that, we are finding that the city is really a jungle in more respects than people in the past, when they refer to it as a jungle, what they mean. This is really like a real jungle, man, a jungle where you have forts. Each block is like a fort in some areas. And, you can survive within those blocks, you know, square blocks, for a long time without the man ever finding you. You can, really.

REPORTER: No. 3, tell me what you did during Friday afternoon.

No. 3: Friday afternoon? Was that the first night?

REPORTER: That's the day after.

No. 3: Oh, yeah. The day after. I went over to Northeast. There were a couple of brothers there. And then a couple of brothers from Southeast came over, too. One main project that I had, mission that I had over there, was the American Ice Company. That thing was, I don't know how many stories high, and we were in the process—me and a couple of other brothers that came over—before this. We were going to try to get that, anyway, at, you know, a convenient time. The King thing came and everything and so we say, okay, we going to go on and get it now. It turned out to be a demonstration of power, man. See, I'll tell you how it turned out. We used dynamite and gasoline to that place, man. When it was all over, the walls had caved in and everything. I want you to go over there and look at it. I don't know if they have cleared the land or not, but they pushed in the walls. The fire was so great, the firemen couldn't do nothing. After we burned it, we watched.* After it

---

* No. 3's story of how the unused American Ice Company warehouse was burned could not be checked. There are no detailed fire-department records on this fire, but it is the prevailing belief of the authorities and persons in the neighborhood that the smoldering remains of an adjacent supermarket ignited the cork insulation of the building's walls, as already described in

started burning good and we went out and the firemen came after a while and everybody was out there watching it—clapping and having a lot of fun, man. From old ladies to little kids. Everybody. The complete spectrum of black people. They were just happy. And the heat from the building spread at least a block. I mean just natural heat. Raw heat.

REPORTER: How did you feel when you watched it burn?

No. 3: Oh, man, I was just so free.

REPORTER: Why?

No. 3: Fire—it brings everything out of me and it's like a cleansing agent.

No. 1: The Bible says fire is a purifier.

No. 3: But let me say one thing. When the fire got going real good, it was feared that the flames were going to shoot over to the street in back of it. And we helped a lot of people move out of the apartments in back of it.

REPORTER: What did you do after that? Where else did you go?

No. 3: Well, I went out to Southeast. Some brothers were out there that we had been working with. And they wanted to try some sniping that night. But not where it would be detrimental to masses of black people.

REPORTER: Do you have any automatic weapons?

No. 3: Yes.

REPORTER: What kind?

No. 1: M-14's.

No. 3: I don't know how much we should say. I don't know how it could be used. Okay?

REPORTER: No. 3, tell me about some of the fires you set.

No. 3: 14th and Park Road.

REPORTER: What specific places?

No. 3: Across from the Tivoli, where the liquor store is. Not across 14th, but across Park Road. And, you know, the Peoples

---

Chapter VII. The 70-foot-high, windowless brick building had only two doorway entrances, both of which were boarded up before the fire. No. 3's account of what happened after the fire started would suggest, however, that he actually saw the structure burn. It should be noted that No. 3's account is off by one day, since the ice house fire was on Saturday. He took note of this inconsistency later in the interview and corrected himself.—*B.W.G.*

Drug Store—and the Hahn's store there and that Wings-N-Things—that grease pot.

REPORTER: Why did you set Wings-N-Things?

No. 3: Oh, man. That honkie been taking black people's money for all—for a long time. Ride down there in Cadillacs and pick up the money. Black man was slaving there, man.

REPORTER: Where else did you burn, No. 3?

No. 3: That day, those were the two main areas I covered. The other days—what I more or less did was help coordinate some brothers that were doing some things like jumping honkies, getting their I.D. [identity card]. We were going to some places and getting money orders, like liquor stores and things, out of the money order machines, things like that—that would help us build. We wanted some things that would be lasting, and we got I.D.'s from white people that came in the area that we beat up.

REPORTER: No. 2, tell me about what you did. Starting Friday morning, when you got up.

No. 2: First of all, I never went to bed. On Friday morning, I got myself in the area of 7th Street. There were quite a few burnings going on.

REPORTER: Set by whom?

No. 2: Set by the people.

REPORTER: You mean just ordinary people?

No. 2: The black masses, yes. There were like a few stores on 7th Street, particularly between the blocks of Florida Avenue and T Street, there were a few of the Jews that we really wanted to get.

REPORTER: Why do you mention Jews in particular?

No. 2: Because they're the biggest exploiters in the black community. I'm just saying that these were.

No. 3: A batch of hypocrites. They say they want to give us civil rights because they went through the same thing, and then take all the money.

No. 2: Anyway, like the fire started from one of the Jew clothing stores, and it, like, it was a lot of gasoline put into that area and it just destroyed, like, the whole block.

REPORTER: What did you do specifically?

No. 2: I went behind the stores on 7th Street and—.

REPORTER: In the alleys?

No. 2: Yes. I wanted to get it in the most effective place I could. So, you know, it started from the alley.

REPORTER: What hundred block was this?

No. 2: I guess that's about 1900 block.

REPORTER: On what side of the street?

No. 2: We were on the west side. After the fire got started, there was another explosion. Which I assume was a gas line. However, there was so many other members with some dynamite who, I understand, has set a couple sticks of dynamite in that area, too.*

REPORTER: How do you use dynamite?

No. 2: Well, we have different means of using dynamite. We have the cap and we, you know, like, have it set from gasoline.

REPORTER: What do you mean, set from gasoline?

No. 2: Well, you know, we'll put it in a deposit of gasoline or soak it around with gasoline and set it from a distance, or we might use a Molotov cocktail to ignite it. And it goes off.

No. 1: One way, you can just set a fire and toss it into it. In other words, the fire be set by ordinary means, paper and matches, get back and toss the 'mite.

REPORTER: Just an ordinary stick and it'll go off? It will explode?

No. 1: Yeah. Hell, yes. It'll go off by contact, man, by impact, I mean. You can detonate it by firing into it, if you don't have caps.

REPORTER: Where did you learn to use dynamite?

ALL THREE: Brothers.

REPORTER: Where this was taught—was a school conducted?

No. 3: Never a formal school. Instructions are going on every day, you might say. Brothers that want to help us out, that want to help themselves out, that want to share their knowledge with other brothers that they found they could communicate with and let this information, you know, share this information. Some brothers have been in the war.

---

* The west side of the 1900 block of 7th Street, N.W., between Florida Avenue and T Street, was completely burned out by fires Friday afternoon and Saturday morning.

REPORTER: Are there many brothers that are involved in your group that are veterans?

No. 3: Yes.

REPORTER: Are there many that are Vietnam veterans?

No. 3: Well, let's say it this way. The new recruits more or less have been—are just coming out of the war.

REPORTER: How many fires, No. 2, do you think you are responsible for?

No. 2: Oh, man, I get carried away so much, I can't really say how many I set. I would say at least fifteen.

REPORTER: What about you, No. 1?

No. 1: Fires, per se? I don't know, around ten or twelve—about three different 'mites. In other words, I'd say about ten fires. See, my district is Northeast and Southeast.

REPORTER: You say district. In other words, that means there was some organization?

No. 1: Some? There is organization, brother baby. There is organization. Don't you realize that, as I said, there's a revolution going on; there must be organization! That's the reason that it was not a riot but a rebellion! There is organization. You have your assigned districts that you work with.

REPORTER: How much did *The Battle of Algiers,* that movie, influence your organization?

(Numbers 1 and 2 said they saw it once after the April disorder. Number 3 said he had seen it once in December and three times since.)

REPORTER: No. 3, why did you go so often?

No. 3: Because I wanted to distinguish in my mind what's particular to this country and black people and what's particular between the Algerian people and the black people there. Because, you see, I know what it means, but now I want to know how to implement this.*

---

* *The Battle of Algiers,* a vivid cinematic re-creation of the beginnings of the Algerian struggle for independence, is the story of how a strong sense of nationalism redeems a young man from years of petty crime and leads him to become a revolutionary guerrilla fighter. It was a hit among black militants, many of whom saw it several times and took notes on the structure of revolutionary cadres and their use of violence. Black militants insist there are parallels between Algeria's struggle against the French and the black man's quest for freedom in America.

REPORTER: How many fires do you think you were responsible for, No. 3?

No. 3: I couldn't tell you, because see—.

REPORTER: How about an estimate?

No. 3: Because see, let me tell you, my job is more or less as a coordinator of groups now. Like I was a floater. I did do certain things like I told you in Northwest. I just have the times wrong. But, anyway, after that I was a floater, to more or less give the brothers direction to what they should do next. And that's why the whole thing was shifted from more or less burning and looting. Brothers didn't do that much looting. They just burned. From that they went to taking checks and things like that. Breaking honkies over the head, when they came through the sites, to get their identification, so that you could use it when everything was over downtown. Now, what we did on that second phase like that was really prosperous, because like the merchandise we got we sold and put back into guns and bullets.

(The reporter asked him to elaborate on the purchase of guns and it was explained that they were bought "off the street.")

REPORTER: But you can get only hand pieces like that.

No. 3: No. That's a lie. No. We had hand pieces then. We don't concentrate on hand pieces that much, anymore. We concentrate on bigger guns.

No. 2: Long guns.

No. 3: And you can get them right on the block. Cats that are in the war, right in this country, at their camps. The brothers take them off the base, piece by piece, man. They doing a good job.

REPORTER: Tell me, what do you think about liquor stores, for instance. Did you burn any liquor stores?

No. 3: Can't stand them. Yeah, I did.

REPORTER: Why?

No. 2: It's in the picture, man. If you seen *The Battle of Algiers*, you seen why.

No. 1: Well, see, whisky has a bad effect on our people's minds. Like when I saw a brother, I'm going to tell you the truth, when I saw a brother breaking into whisky stores to take the whisky, I tried to discourage him. I just set the thing on fire and leave the whisky and let it burn, too, 'cause it's combustible. It burns. But, to loot for whisky, man, it's like a useless thing, because you can't use the whisky against the beast. You see. I hit one whisky store, and the thing burned up and didn't suit me, so I went back and burned it again.

REPORTER: Where was that whisky store?

No. 1: 14th and W.

REPORTER: What time did you set that on fire?

No. 1: I think it was on Saturday. Afternoon. No, it burned on Friday, they got busted again on Saturday.

REPORTER: Who got busted?

No. 1: Some whiteys. You know, whitey's got the nerve to drive through and stuff and see what's going on in the poor stricken ghetto. Well, he was driving through.

No. 3: One thing that I'm mad about because, in terms of the symbol and being relevant to black people, the news didn't report how many white people got fucked over. The news didn't do a good job. They did report a good job on how many niggers got fucked over, but they didn't report on how many white people crawled back to Maryland and Virginia. How many white people got busted and got all the shit stolen from them. We wanted that reported, man, so it could really mean something to black people.

REPORTER: Well, did a lot of white people who were beat up, did they go to the hospitals or to the police or did they just go home?

No. 1: Now, for instance, I kicked that honkie in the head. To get his wallet. I know he had to go to the hospital. He had a hole in his head.

REPORTER: How much of the burning. You said about ten, you said about, what, fifteen? You said you don't know. But just say, all lumped together, maybe fifty places—fifty places that you were responsible for, personally?

No. 3: Let me tell you, I think, man, the majority of the places that were burned were burned by the mass of black people. I don't think the twenty-five of us set all of those fires.

No. 2: Hell, no.

No. 3: But I tell you this. If we didn't set a lot of those fires, a lot of black people wouldn't have went on to burn some other places.

No. 2: That gave them an incentive.

No. 3: We were like an igniting spark in a lot of instances across the city. Like in Southeast, nothing was going on, like that first day out there, man, that first night and the next day, it was nothing going on out there. At all. Hey, listen, that ice house was Saturday, wasn't it? A lot of areas we went into man, there was nothing going on till we got there. But once we started our thing, man, people just took up. A lot of places we went to, we told them what's going on in a different part of town or a different street or something like that and they say, yeah? And we say, yeah, brothers you better get your shit together, 'cause we going to do something right now.

REPORTER: Tell me more about liquor stores, No. 2. What's wrong with liquor stores?

No. 2: Well, I feel that as a revolutionary person, that being that alcohol has an effect on the mind of humans, I don't indulge in alcohol at all.

REPORTER: Did you ever drink before?

No. 2: Yes. I have.

REPORTER: When did you stop? And why?

No. 2: One year, I really began to find the effects of swine and wine. When I say swine, I'm talking about oink; when I say wine, I'm talking about wine, you know, I'm talking about alcoholic beverages.

REPORTER: When you say oink, you are talking about what?

No. 2: Pig, pork. I learned the harmful effects of it.

REPORTER: No. 1, what happened to you to take the jump to go on the other side of the line, to become a revolutionary?

No. 1: You recall past experiences, as far as encounters with the beast, you realize what's going on, and, if your mind is open, it's not as easily subjected to propaganda issued by the whitey. Because you weigh everything. And when I weighed it, man, it came out blackness was the only way. And that revolution is the only way to save our people from genocide.

REPORTER: Where are you going to take us? How much of a revolution can black people mount in this country?

No. 1: I think I can answer your question with a quote. "In a revolution, you either win or die." That's Che Guevara.

REPORTER: Well, Che Guevara, he got messed up.

No. 3: He's just one man that died.

REPORTER: Well, let's talk about the revolution. And how far can you push it in this country?

No. 3: Okay. Well, let's look at it this way. The honkie, the white man, is pushing it far enough for us. Because if you look, like from '60, when the Movement started, and now, look how much more black people are arming themselves and going toward that direction. In context of the world—what's going on in the world—because I think what you were saying is a lot of hangups that Negroes got hung up in and what white papers try to portray, we are a minority in this country, but in the world, we are a majority and in the world, that's what's going on. South America. Latin America. Vietnam, Asia, and Africa.

REPORTER: Why do you want to destroy the white man?

No. 3: Why do I want to destroy the white man? Not only for what he has done to us in this country. He has oppressed us, he told us he made us free 100 years ago, we still slaves.

No. 2: He brutalizes us.

REPORTER: How does he do it today, in Washington, in 1968?

No. 3: He does it. Wings-N-Things—he does it there. He does it by employing us in all them government jobs and not paying us. He does it in Washington here today by not giving us home rule. He does it here in this country by not letting us have nothing to do with who we want to govern at all.

REPORTER: What happened in Washington before April that made you go out and burn places? What did the white man do to you and other black people in Washington, D.C.?

No. 3: It wasn't only in Washington, he did it in a few other places. Let me tell you about some other things. Loan companies. They're rotten motherfuckers, boy.

REPORTER: They don't have any of those in Washington.

No. 3: They have them on the edge, on the borderline.

REPORTER: You didn't burn any of them.

No. 3: They going to burn. They going to go, don't worry. See, like brother mentioned in the beginning, it kind of caught us by surprise. We not making excuses, now dig it. Of course, we are at a stage where we are building and getting ready for something that we would plan and we would react to, not something that the honkie would make us react to. And that's the way it's going to be from now on.

REPORTER: What about the boys with the pastel pants and the $40 shoes?

No. 3: They just been denied that all their lives. And if they can wear it now, well, that's beautiful. It's what's in their minds. Like a lot of brothers have to stick their head out whether they know it or not. They consciously or subconsciously do that to survive. So that they can hustle, so they can put on a white game. Like sisters have to put on wigs, man, so they can pass in the white world, so they can sell their bodies or get their gig [job] or whatever. 'Cause the man don't dig that natural thing. We find a brother that's a Negro, well, we going to try to influence that brother and tell him to get a natural. And tell him the reason why, so he can identify. Like there are brothers right down on U Street, now, man, that got some fine suits and some slick hair, but brother what they got now. They're ready. They get out there at night so they can eat and put something in their house and keep their roof over their head, but they're with us now.

No. 2: For example, I know a few of the brothers out there. One of them specifically is so black, you know, he is a part of our group. He also had his woman out on the block. And when he came to this stage of blackness, like, he took his woman off the block and he got a white woman and he put her out there, using her, you know, and gave his woman respect. Now, I understand that there are a lot of the hustlers in the process of taking their women off the block and finding white women.

REPORTER: There are a lot of women down there on 14th and T tonight.

No. 3: There is a lot of them out there, but listen, brother, you'd be surprised how many we've been able to reach. There used to be none out there, man, that you could even communicate with, man, but now you can communicate with a whole bunch of them.

XI

The Merchants

A month after the riot ended, Washington businessmen were still in a state of shock over what had happened to them. Many were bitter, angry, and frightened. Some felt they had been unfairly singled out.

"We were sacrificial lambs," one businesswoman told Senator Robert C. Byrd, of West Virginia, emphasizing her indignation at the authorities' failure to nip the riot in the bud.

The main economic impact of those days in April was felt by businessmen. By far the bulk of the physical damage—conservatively estimated at $24 million—was to business places. Some homes were destroyed—more than 667 dwelling units—but generally only as an accidental side result of the burning of a commercial establishment with living quarters over or adjacent to it. More than 900 businesses were damaged in some way.

Every conceivable type of business was hit—record stores, drug or variety shops, appliance shops, jewelry stores, repair shops, small manufacturing outlets, dry-cleaning establishments, shoe shops. But the hardest hit were food, clothing, and liquor stores—and liquor dealers took the worst beating of all.

The most severely damaged businesses were in the inner-city areas of Washington. There was some reaching out into the downtown area, but generally with much less destruction and very little burning. Even downtown, however, losses to individual stores were heavy.

One hard-hit downtown merchant described his feelings at the time:

"I loaded up as much of our records as I could and put them in the trunk of the car and told everybody to get out. Then they looted the store. They didn't burn it. And you can imagine. I am sitting home with my wife terrified, watching television, and on the screen is our store—seeing people coming out of the windows and doors carrying arms full of merchandise, the sidewalks lined up with merchandise, cars circling. It made us cry, but we couldn't do anything about it."

All businesses located in the riot areas were hurt by the disorder. Even if a store wasn't damaged, it suffered due to loss of trade, a broken water main, or a burned-out electric line caused by a fire next door or down the street.

Some black businessmen in the ghettos of Washington were hit by looters, although the display of "soul brother" signs on the show windows of Negro-owned businesses generally seemed to protect them. But—and this was a matter of ghetto sophistication—the mere sign was not enough. It did not protect white businesses or those Negro stores in which there was believed to be substantial white ownership. One white-owned furniture-leasing concern posted a sign saying "37 Soul Brothers and Sisters Earn Their Living Here." The sign was torn down within fifteen minutes, and all movable merchandise was carted away by looters.

It was generally the white businessmen who suffered—in a large number of cases, the Jewish businessmen. There are no hard figures on the percentage of white businesses in the inner city owned by Jews, but the total is substantial.

Some merchants armed their employees or hired guards to protect their stores. There were no cases of guards shooting looters, and, generally, the looters bypassed guarded stores.

Many Negro proprietors stayed in their establishments and thus provided visible proof that a black man owned and operated the place. But that was not always enough to keep a store from being engulfed in flames if it happened to be next to a building that was burning. A Negro barber on 7th Street, who kept his shop open all day Friday, stood by and watched the place next door being looted.

"After they got everything out of there," he said, "they were going to set it on fire. I had to go out and stop them. They told me 'We're not going to set your place on fire.' So, I told them, 'If you set that place on fire you'll set me on fire, too.' "

A ghetto merchant, whose store was unscathed, told Senator Byrd, "I am a black businessman. I think the majority of the people in my area are black Americans and they do respect me to a certain extent."

But he felt the civil disorder was not racial. "They were just trying to hurt the people that seemed to have most of the money, which they thought were their enemies to a certain extent."

"People were venting their anger and frustrations," according to George Storey, whose Build Black, Incorporated, was set up after the riot as a community attempt to rebuild portions of the devastated 14th Street strip.

At the height of the looting, there was little concern about ownership of property. A number of dry-cleaning stores were looted of clothing that had been left for cleaning. Six of Washington's thirteen pawn shops were badly damaged, and property left as security was removed. Some of the cleaning establishments were black-owned; none of the pawn shops was, but presumably most of the clothing and valuables in both belonged to neighborhood Negroes.

After the riot, militants like Storey could give many reasons why a particular merchant was hit. This one had surly clerks. That one made a black man feel like a thief when he went into the store to shop. One had no Negroes waiting on customers. Another required Negro clerks to submit to the indignity of asking a white clerk to ring up the sale on the cash register. This one cheated his customers. That one sold shoddy merchandise.

The list of grievances was long, but even Storey readily agrees that they did not apply universally. There may have been some vengeful selectivity Thursday night on 14th Street and again Friday during the excursions into downtown stores, but selectivity was clearly lacking elsewhere when whole blocks and even rows of blocks were looted and burned. Some areas, of course, were more attractive targets for looters than others. Thus, the upper half of the 14th Street strip, with larger and better-stocked stores than the lower half of the area, was heavily looted. Its west side, where the better stores were located, was stripped clean, while some sections of the east side of the street, containing smaller shops, were bypassed.

In the high excitement of the moment, Storey admits that "some innocents were run over." Among them were many white merchants who were leaders in working for civil rights and who often contributed money or merchandise to neighborhood schools and activities. For them, there was a special irony in being the brunt of the riot, although one of them later said that few individuals who rioted knew or had any knowledge of his interest in the black community.

Mortimer Lebowitz, three of whose four stores were looted or burned, was a pioneer in hiring Negroes and promoting them to management in his chain of clothing stores. A former president of the Washington Urban League, Lebowitz had participated with Dr. King in the last leg of the historic march into Montgomery from Selma, Alabama. Another earnest advocate of equal employment was Oscar I. Dodek, president of D. J. Kaufman's menswear stores. One of his shops was looted and burned; the other, looted.

Thursday night's marchers down 14th Street, who directed merchants to close in honor of Dr. King, pointed to the need to find some way to honor the slain leader. White merchants scurried around for pictures of Dr. King to place in their windows. Some took out memorial advertisements in the newspapers. However, a few merchants reported that some white customers complained about the display in Dr. King's honor, as well as the lowering of flags to half-staff.

Police were able to limit the looting of downtown stores to hit-and-run excursions. A combination of chance and design probably controlled the selectivity there. For example, in the heart of downtown (the 1300 block of F Street, N.W.), Bruce Hunt's, a men's store known for its stylish fashions, including imported sweaters and expensive pastel and bright-colored slacks, and Rich's, a shoe store that specializes in fancy imports, were hit by looters who ignored other stores in that block. Among them were one of the city's best luggage shops, an optical-goods store that displayed high-priced telescopes and binoculars, and a well-known jewelry store. Why Bruce Hunt's and Rich's? The two stores were extremely popular among certain groups of Negroes, particularly the juvenile "block boys" who can be found standing on street corners or sitting around all-night laundromats. The stores that were passed by did not enjoy much Negro patronage and therefore were unfamiliar to the rioters.

After the riot, some merchants took a hard look at their practices to see if they had unwittingly added to the disaster. One businessman found out that an overzealous Negro guard had antagonized many of the youngsters patronizing his relatively new clothing store.

"The way he looked at the kids made them feel that he thought they were dishonest," the merchant said. "So the store became a target."

Security arrangements to curb shoplifting evidently were resented. Turnstiles, lines where parcels were inspected, and other protective devices were regarded as indignities not imposed in predominantly white neighborhoods. One record store, Waxie Maxie's, which was burned to the ground, permitted black employees to ring up sales, but a white man at the door made a final tally at a front cash register and checked all packages before the customer was allowed to go through a turnstile and depart.

"It was a very insulting atmosphere," according to Louise Stone, a black jazz writer.

Some of the repeated burnings, it has been suggested, may have been prompted by efforts to destroy credit records. If so, the rioters generally acted in vain. The so-called high-credit merchants customarily move their credit records to other locations at the end of each day, and many of the worst offenders were spared, in any case, because their stores were outside (although close to) the main riot areas.

Clearly selected as riot targets were the inner city's liquor stores. Nearly half of the city's 383 liquor dealers suffered some damage and theft during the riot. No other single class of stores felt such an impact—37 burned, 82 looted of most of their stock, and 52 partially looted. At the time, only 10 Negroes owned liquor stores in Washington, and only 3 of those were among the 171 damaged. The cost of the damage and theft was estimated at $7.5 million by Hilliard Schulberg, executive director of the Washington Retail Liquor Dealers Association. Store shelves were loaded when the riot occurred. In addition to their usual, heavy first-of-the-month inventories, the dealers had added to their supplies in anticipation of Easter and Passover.

Some rioters reached beyond the main shopping streets to loot and burn liquor stores. But most did not have to reach far. There was a very heavy concentration of such stores in the poorer black neighborhoods. The heart of Washington's most crowded ghetto areas (the Second and Thirteenth precincts), where 115,100 persons, 95,600 of them black, are crammed into 3.02 square miles, was served by 84 liquor stores—one for every 1,370 persons.

The actions of many rioters seemed to reflect resentment at the presence of so many liquor stores in the city's poorest, blackest, and most congested neighborhoods.

"These liquor stores have a demoralizing effect on black neighborhoods and on black people," a tall, articulate black man, who called himself Ndamase, said. He was standing on 14th Street after the riots, wearing a faded green field jacket with a Mao Tse-tung button on one pocket flap. "What do you think it does to our children to see black men staggering on the streets? It's all out of whitey's trick bag to contaminate our youth."

Joy Simonson, chairman of the city's Alcoholic Beverage Control Board, is "not sure the inference is warranted" that liquor stores suffered during the riots because black people dislike them. "People just wanted the product," she believes.

Many ghetto liquor stores specialize in the sale of pocket-size half-pints—small packages that yield the dealer about 25 per cent more than he would get for the same amount of whisky sold by the fifth. The half-pint is the staple for the city's drunks—and for its bootleggers, who reap a harvest after the 2 A.M. bar closing hour.

"The half-pint business is a socio-economic phenomenon that turns out to be racial here because you are selling to poor people, and, in Washington, poor people are black," Mrs. Simonson says.

The "basic reason" for the small number of Negro-owned liquor stores, according to Mrs. Simonson, has been "economic, a shortage of capital." In order to get into the liquor business in Washington, you must have money for rent, for fixtures, for stock, and to buy a license from another licenseholder. Because no new licenses may be issued, existing licenses have acquired a cash value that fluctuates. The going rate may be $25,000 or more, depending on the store's location, although immediately after the riot the price of a license in the inner city dropped sharply.

Such matters as the racial composition of the industry, allegations of discrimination in the transferring of licenses, and the over-all relationship of the industry to the inner city are matters that the Alcoholic Beverage Control Board has ignored, but one liquor dealer, who has been in business in Washington for seventeen years, is convinced there is no special antagonism toward liquor stores in the Negro community that can be separated from general antiwhite feelings. He agrees with Mrs. Simonson that the rioters broke into the liquor stores to get the liquor and for no other reason. "It fits everybody," he said. "You can sell it and it can't be traced. It's easy to carry. It's got a high value for a small volume. People like it."

"If we have a bad image," says Morris Stirman, owner of Calvert Liquors, "it is because we haven't been able to communicate with the consumer. This is the real reason. One factor in this might be that Jews have always been afraid of being discriminated against and haven't spoken up."

Neither of these two liquor dealers was hit by looting or arson. One who was, a forty-five-year-old man who has worked fifteen years in Negro areas, told Senator Byrd that, "When this situation came up on April 5, I really sincerely believed I had nothing to worry about because I had done so much for them. I was their doctor, their lawyer, their counselor, their advisor, anything that you—that they didn't know what to do. I filled out their tax papers when they came to me.

"So when I walked out of my store at 2:30 on April 5, I felt I had nothing to worry about.

"That same evening at home, I got a telephone call from one

of my employees telling me that the store was being looted and torn apart. I really couldn't believe it. So, being very much upset, I got into my car with a gun and went down to my place of business and saw what was happening. When I arrived about 6 or 6:30 in the evening, the doors had been busted down, the shelves were practically 100 per cent empty, and there were three policemen in the store with shotguns.

"I said, 'What are you going to do about these people?' About that time there were twenty or thirty people in the store. And he said, 'We can't do a thing. The only thing we can do is shoot tear gas in here and leave.'

"They made no attempt to make an arrest, no attempt to do anything about the people stealing my livelihood. I had a gun in my hand, and I became very bold and told them either get out or get shot. But, of course, I could not stay there all night long. And these people that I saw there were my customers, people that come in the store every day."

Another liquor-store owner, David Bayer, forty, a German immigrant who says he escaped numerous times from prison camps and later joined the Israeli army, asserts that he lost $38,000 to looters during the riot. He claims to be a good friend to his customers and says that several have apologized for looting his store. He also says he understands the mood that struck looters.

"I did the same kind of thing a hundred times," he told a reporter, explaining that during the war he led raids on warehouses "because we needed food." He believes "it's just a matter of one kid saying 'Let's go' to several others."

Liquor stores in the inner-city areas have long served as community facilities. Although they do not open for business until 10 A.M. daily, they stay open later than most stores and provide check-cashing facilities in the neighborhood.

Some stores have a practice of charging as much as 50 cents to cash a check unless a purchase is made. This requirement may have been a source of resentment. Negroes with low incomes rarely get enough money ahead to open a bank account, and many encounter great difficulty cashing their checks—even government pay checks.

For a while after the riot, a number of liquor dealers continued to be threatened and plagued with incendiary fires. One merchant told Senator Byrd that the day after the riot he was informed:

"Oh, there is no sense of boarding up your store because we are going to rip it off and burn the store. And, if you stay there, we will burn you with it. Get out, white man, we don't want you in our neighborhood."

Another group of stores as familiar, as much depended upon, and, it turned out, as vulnerable as the liquor stores were the inner-city food stores—both the small neighborhood shops and the big food chains.

The little, so-called mom and pop shops probably suffered more than the big chain drugstores and supermarkets.

One man on upper 14th Street, N.W., a refugee, was forced to close his food store, not because of his losses to rioters but because of the wave of antiwhite feeling that swept over the neighborhood following the disorder. This man, who owned the "P & G Market," was told by one of his customers "we'll chase you out." And his wife said, "A little kid, three years old, comes in and says her mother told her not to go buy candy at the white Jew store." "The Germans couldn't kill me," the owner said, but he's quitting now because "I didn't have any other choice."

Another man, who was sixty-one and had been in business for fourteen years at the same location, told Senator Byrd he was completely wiped out after rioters stole or damaged $95,000 worth of goods and fixtures.

Some chain food stores were hit much harder than others during the riots, but the evidence does not support a popular notion that specific stores were systematically singled out.

Safeway Stores, Incorporated, had thirteen outlets that were so badly damaged they could not be reopened immediately. Seven of them were burned—two to the ground. Giant Foods, a locally based chain of supermarkets and a major Safeway competitor in the Washington area, suffered minimal damage to four stores—and no burning.

Before the riots, a Congressional committee, studying charges of discrimination against the poor in the sale of food in Washington and other cities, had concluded that the quality of food was lower and prices sometimes higher in ghetto stores. Although the chains denied following discriminatory pricing and distribution policies, it was disclosed that managers had leeway to adjust prices to compensate for lower volume and higher rates of spoilage, thus enabling them to maintain profit margins in their smaller, less efficient stores.

A black domestic worker who shopped in the bigger and pleasanter store near her white employer's residence might readily spot differences between that store and the one close to her home and feel that she was the victim of a discriminatory policy. Whether this was by accident or design made little difference.

Basil M. Winstead, Washington division manager of Safeway, insisted that the only reason his chain was hit was "because we had so many stores in the area."

Winstead had a point. The Safeway had been heavily engaged in doing business in the ghetto for many years, with forty of its 141 stores located in predominantly black areas. The Giant, a younger chain, had just four of its sixty-nine supermarkets on the fringes of the inner city. Safeway's program of replacing its more numerous, smaller, older, and less efficient stores with modern supermarkets was just reaching the inner city at the time of the riot. Its replacement stores fared better than the others.

A similar situation apparently applied to the city's chain drugstores. Peoples, Washington's largest drug chain, had seventeen stores that were damaged, including one totally burned. That outlet and one other, where vandalism was very heavy, did not reopen. Peoples, founded in 1905, had many of its forty-seven Washington stores in areas where severe rioting occurred. Drug Fair, a major competitor operating in Washington since 1938, suffered no damage except for one broken window. None of its stores was located in a major riot area.

Studies by the National Advisory Commission on Civil Disorders, covering Washington and fourteen other cities after the 1967 disorders but before the April, 1968, riots following the death of Dr. King, indicate that there has for some time been reciprocal distrust between the merchant doing business in the ghetto and his customers. One of these studies noted that "there is a great deal of complaint by Negroes concerning the prices they pay in their neighborhood stores and the quality of goods they buy."*

A companion study reported:

The retail merchant in the ghetto apparently saw himself as surrounded by untrustworthy and sometimes hostile customers, neighbors, and even employees. A majority of the merchant complaints involved people around him and their propensity to be criminal, violent, lazy, and rude.

The merchants in our sample were among the most unsympathetic to the plight of the ghetto Negro of any occupational group. Along with this lack of sympathy, they showed a series of beliefs from which one can infer that some merchants engaged in unethical practices. Further, the merchants endorsed attitudes toward Negroes that would lead us to believe that they are apt to treat Negro customers considerably less well than white customers.

This is not to say that all, or even a majority of the retail merchants in the ghetto deserve all of the criticism they receive. But a sizable percentage, from 25 to 50 percent, seem to do business in a way that leaves many improvements to be desired. As long as these improvements are not made, the retail merchant in our urban ghettoes will continue to be one of the primary targets of Negro antagonism.

The same study suggested that the "typical" merchant was a man of about fifty years of age, with a high school education, who has lived in the city a long time. In the fifteen cities studied, he was most likely to be Jewish, to own his own home, and to vote Democratic. Relatively few of the merchants lived in the neighborhood where they worked, but many lived within 2 miles and virtually all within 8 miles. Their clientele was largely black, as were half their employees.**

---

* Angus Campbell and Howard Schuman, "Racial Attitudes in Fifteen American Cities," in *Supplemental Studies for the National Advisory Commission on Civil Disorders* (New York: Frederick A. Praeger, 1968).

** Peter H. Rossi *et al.*, "Between White and Black: The Faces of American Institutions in the Ghetto," in *Supplemental Studies for the National Advisory Commission on Civil Disorders* (New York: Frederick A. Praeger, 1968).

After the Washington riot, attention was drawn to the extent of Jewish ownership in the inner-city areas, both by the merchants themselves, who enlisted the help of the Jewish Community Council to call their plight to the attention of the city government, and by the blacks on the street.

Build Black, Incorporated, held a series of neighborhood meetings about rebuilding the devastated areas. At these meetings individuals in the neighborhood were encouraged to tell what was on their minds. Complaints about the practices of some, ghetto businessmen were voiced with considerable heat. Those who were Jewish were generally described as "jew-merchant" or "jew-dealer" or "that Jew."

"I am sure glad that damn Jew got burned out," was one ghetto comment.

Some Jews felt that these were pejorative references. But thoughtful analysts, both black and white, have pointed out that the Jew was often singled out simply because of his presence in the ghetto—and that many blacks used "Jew" as a synonym for "whitey." There was a complete absence of swastika painting and other overt manifestations of anti-Semitism.

A young representative of Social Relations Organized Enterprise (SOLE), a group that wanted to set up wholesale cooperative clearing houses, was one of those who equated Jew and whitey. "We are saying to the Jew cat, 'In one night, we brothers hit you with what you've been doing for years, and now you're scared,'" he said.

Laurence Sigler, past president of the Metropolitan Washington Federation of Business Associations, was one of those who insisted that anti-Semitism was not involved in the rioting. "They would have looted a Greek as soon as they would a Jew (and did)—they would have looted anybody."

In his questioning of businessmen, Senator Byrd wanted to know whether any of them thought they had been victimized because they were Jewish. A few thought that anti-Jewish feeling entered into the rioting, but most did not.

One merchant gave this analysis:

"I don't think that anti-Semitism was at all the cause of the riots. I think that, after the fact, people reach for reasons why things are done. The fact is that historically the Negro has had a large exposure to the Jewish businessman, and just as the Negro feels a resentment against the larger society because of a history of ill-treatment, and I agree that the Negro has been treated badly, he finds the outpost of that white society in his own community in the guise of the Jewish merchant. His resentment against society as a whole is expressed where he can express it, against the local Jewish merchant."

One prominent Washington Jewish leader flatly stated that the "riot was no pogrom."

"There is no evidence that the rioters picked out Jewish stores or took actions that could be considered anti-Jewish in nature," he said. "However, a great many Jewish merchants were hit and the Jewish community feels picked on."

The extent of that feeling was revealed at a postriot meeting of Jewish businessmen in the suburban Montgomery County (Maryland) Jewish Community Center.

Morton Lebowitz, the owner of Morton's Stores, appealed for an end to hatred. He was roundly booed by many of the nearly 1,000 businessmen in the audience.

"Don't generalize," he appealed. "Don't generalize in your feeling. I have always identified the problems of the Negro with the problems of the Jew. I have always believed these were the problems of all of us. I had so many calls from Negroes to say how sorry they are that our stores were burned." Catcalls and boos drowned out his voice. Then a man in the audience mounted a chair and shouted, "Maybe you don't agree, but this is a democracy. Give him a chance to talk."

"I've been thinking of retiring," Lebowitz said. "But I'll never retire now. I've been hurt and I know it. But the hatred is unreasonable. If we continue to hate and hate and hate, the city will wind up in cinders. This thing was done by a handful of people."

Almost immediately after the riots, Washington businessmen faced an insurance crisis. Businesses in Washington had long enjoyed low fire- and riot-insurance rates, due primarily to the good record of the city's fire department. After the April riots, the city's superintendent of insurance estimated that the insurance policies of 2,900 merchants were canceled. And about 500 others were compelled to buy insurance at inflated rates. Legislation adopted in midsummer to pool insurance risks was expected to relieve this problem.

Instances of postriot harassment of inner-city merchants added to the troubles of Washington's business community.

Two women who ran a clothing store on 14th Street were visited by a group of about ten teenagers shortly after the troops departed. Once inside, an older boy snapped his fingers, and the others fanned out through the store. A second snap and the youths began plowing through clothes, knocking them on the floor. Two more quick snaps and the youngsters scooped up the goods and walked out.

The black youth of Washington had played a major role in the riot, and some of those who took part were emboldened by the experience—at least temporarily.

A liquor-store owner reported that some customers would enter his shop after the riot, take a bottle of liquor off the shelves, and toss a dollar bill on the counter, saying, "That's all it's worth."

Grumblings about "a complete breakdown in law and order" began to be heard.

April and May saw outbreaks of late-night fires, which were readily extinguished but added to the general uneasiness. Suspects arrested by police included some twelve- and thirteen-year-old children. One businessman said he had heard militant blacks use the slogan "Only burn one a day to keep the troops away." Merchants carried complaints to congressmen, to the city's newspapers, and to anyone else who would listen. But rarely did they report incidents of harassment to police, asserting they were afraid to do so.

Several merchants said they had received threatening calls at home. Two got calls at their business places from "a cultured voice, male, seemed educated," who told them to close their establishments or be prepared for their destruction. The voice identified himself as one of "Rap Brown's boys," the merchants said.

Some of the threats were sheer bravado. One liquor-store owner, for instance, said a customer demanded a free half-pint of whisky or he would "burn you down." The proprietor refused. The store was not burned.

The tension that continued to grip the city after the riot was aggravated by a series of five murders in late April and early May. Four merchants and a bus driver were shot and killed during that brief period, including two merchants whose stores had been damaged in the riot. Three of the five were killed after they had pulled guns on armed robbers; only two were shot in cold blood. This distinction made no impact at the time, however; nor did the fact that police closed all five cases with quick arrests allay the fear in the community.

The decision in late April to go ahead with the Poor People's Campaign, and the subsequent presence of the campaigners in Resurrection City, contributed to the city's uneasiness. Businessmen who depended on the tourist trade said the Campaign harmed them much more in May and June than did the public's memory of the April riot. The chanting, sometimes threatening demonstrators of the Campaign were regular features of the Huntley-Brinkley and Walter Cronkite television news shows, from Miami to Seattle, and during this period tourist business fell off 30 to 50 per cent. Many downtown restaurants were almost empty at night.

In early May, the city assigned extra police patrols on overtime to the neighborhoods where merchants said they were being harassed. Late in May, President Johnson signed a bill increasing the starting salary of Washington's policemen to $8,000 a year and proposed that the 3,100-man force be enlarged with 1,000 additional patrolmen, a suggestion that was enacted into law in August.

But some congressmen had bitterly criticized Public Safety Director Patrick V. Murphy for not enforcing "law and order," and said more policemen were not the answer. They wanted tougher policemen. In that vein, Senator Byrd, in June, highlighted for the Washington Board of Realtors the testimony of his riot witnesses. "Almost uniformly," he said, "these people told a story of a situation that one can hardly believe could exist in any supposedly civilized urban community and especially in the federal city. It is a story of a breakdown in police protection, a breakdown in court responsibility, and a giving way to gang rule by street hoodlums and thugs."

Earlier, in a hearing before the critical House Committee on the District of Columbia, Pat Murphy, an affable, gentle man in private, had withstood harsh criticism. At one point, he had had this exchange about police restraint during the riots with Representative Thomas G. Abernethy, a Mississippi Democrat:

ABERNETHY: Your position is a rather soft one, isn't it?
MURPHY: No, it is not.
ABERNETHY: Do you think all that was done was all that could have been done?
MURPHY: I'm generally satisfied with the response.
ABERNETHY: Are you satisfied with the destruction?
MURPHY: I'm terribly dissatisfied with the destruction. I am satisfied with the police response.

The policy of restraint that directed policemen to avoid using their weapons was the real target of attack by some businessmen, but few of them were ready to come right out and advocate the shooting of looters, as Chicago's Mayor Richard J. Daley did in mid-April when he ordered police in his city to "shoot to kill" arsonists and "maim or cripple" looters in future riots. Murphy said publicly at that time that he would resign if he were ever told to give such an order to his policemen in the District of Columbia. Mayor Washington backed him up.

"Violence only begets violence," Murphy told a reporter later. "That's why the FBI's own riot-control manual contains admonition after admonition not to use firearms."

Among businessmen who supported city officials were William Calomiris, President of the Metropolitan Washington Board of Trade, who testified before a Congressional committee that "this could have been a sea of blood" if police had failed to use restraint in the riot, and Joseph B. Danzansky, of Giant Foods. Danzansky said: "We are heading for apartheid if we don't do something. There is a need for better communication between the races, a need to keep talking while we develop means for coping with the problem. We need something in the nature of a New Deal—a new approach to the problem. The New Deal was a bloodless revolution, and that's what we're looking for here."

As the Washington summer of 1968 wore on, stores in the riot areas that had not been too severely damaged were able to reopen, to report that business had returned to "normal." Many merchants who had been forced to close were holding back. They were waiting for the general atmosphere to cool down, for insurance settlements to be made, for insurance renewals to be promised, for arguments over who should pay for bulldozing the ruins to be resolved. Most chain stores were doing their ordinary late summer business. No attempt had been made to rebuild two Peoples drugstores destroyed in the riot. But according to George Burrus, the chain's president, the other outlets in the inner city reported "normal operations" four months after the events of April, with only "the usual problems."

Seymour Rosenberg of the National Liquor Store at 14th and U streets, N.W., one of the first stores looted after Dr. King was assassinated, said that business was about the same in August as it had been before the riot, although he was closing his store at 7 P.M. instead of at 9 P.M.

He spoke approvingly of the restrained way in which the police had approached problems in the 14th and U riot hub:

"The police have been handling it pretty good around here. They haven't been rushing fifty of 'em in to create an incident. That's been the biggest factor, leaving the cops out of here and not bothering people for little misdemeanors, being drunk, double parking and like that."

XII

Resurrection City, May-June

"It seemed like April 5 all over again, except we were finding out about it at the beginning this time," Mayor Walter E. Washington said. He was speaking of Monday, June 24, 1968, when the permit for Resurrection City expired. The shantytown built near the Lincoln Memorial for the Poor People's Campaign had meant many different things to its residents, to the late Dr. Martin Luther King's successor, the Reverend Ralph Abernathy, to the poor of the country, and to the citizens of Washington, still edgy from the April riots. As the moment of its closing approached, D.C. officials feared a new wave of rioting.

The marks on the map at the month-old Executive Communications Center in police headquarters "showed trouble starting all over town," the Mayor said later. Police and fire department radio-bands, commercial radio and television, and special telephones were all connected to the new Center, which was created after the April riot. Through it, the Mayor and top city officials were able to keep in direct touch with other city offices, the Pentagon, and the White House, while monitoring the condition of the city's streets. On June 24, two dozen people were busy keeping track of reports of crowds forming, windows breaking, looting, and fires.

The Mayor remembered that failure to see and read the early signs of trouble in April had delayed police and military response to the riots following Dr. King's death. This time, armed with up-to-the-minute intelligence about the condition of the streets, Mayor Washington was able to respond quickly and decisively.

D.C. guardsmen, already in uniform and at police precinct station houses for the closing of Resurrection City, were put on the streets, and a curfew was imposed. Washington police, out in force and equipped with gas masks and tear gas in case of trouble at Resurrection City, quickly filled 14th Street, where windows had been broken and crowds were massing along a twenty-block area.

The records of the Executive Communications Center showed later that, when the police moved in and began firing tear gas in all directions, the crowds and the window breaking were limited to 14th Street. In fact, the crowd was initially limited to 200 people, at 14th and U, who broke the window of the same Peoples Drug Store that had been one of the first places hit in April. Trouble along the rest of 14th Street came after the first barrages of tear gas were fired in the U Street area. Crowds began forming on other thoroughfares such as H Street, N.E., after radio stations began broadcasting reports of what was happening on 14th Street.

Did the police overreact on June 24? If they did, they had plenty of impetus to do so.

The short, sad life of Resurrection City, with its mud, its confusion, and its noisy demonstrators, had kept Washingtonians tense and fearful from early May. Every day, there had seemed to be some possibility that a Poor People's Campaign demonstration or a confrontation between police and rowdies at the shanty-town site would ignite new rioting in the city. When the day came to close down the encampment, under a federal order, the police were anticipating trouble.

The closing of Resurrection City itself and the symbolic, invited arrest at the Capitol of hundreds of members of the Poor People's Campaign were peaceful enough. The expected trouble erupted at 14th and U, where campaigners who did not want to be arrested had converged on the office of the Southern Christian Leadership Conference (SCLC). A disorder arising out of a gathering of campaigners was the last thing that the SCLC wanted. But it was ironically consistent with the daily crises that had confronted the organization's ill-fated campaign and Resurrection City.

The Poor People's Campaign had been the last grand dream of the Reverend Dr. Martin Luther King. Using a great march on Washington of poor people—black, white, and Indian—and a makeshift shantytown to symbolize the plight of poor America, he had hoped to stage demonstrations—acts of civil disobedience if necessary—to pressure Congress into listening to and acting on the poor people's demands. A small group of key federal officials had been negotiating with SCLC leaders to iron out plans for the Campaign and its Resurrection City when the talks, begun in late March, were interrupted by Dr. King's death. They were resumed in mid-April, when National Park Service, Justice Department, and other federal officials began to meet with several SCLC leaders, including the Reverend Walter E. Fauntroy, Vice Chairman of the new City Council and SCLC's Washington representative.

Fauntroy became a key figure in the talks, mediating disputes and encouraging practical discussion rather than rhetoric. In the end, he suggested the compromise site for Resurrection City: 15 acres of West Potomac Park, alongside the tree-lined Reflecting Pool at the foot of the Lincoln Memorial, off the Mall but in view of tourists and commuters. A six-page permit for the use of the parkland was signed, with the federal government making one concession that later caused much official regret. The U.S. Park Police, who have jurisdiction in all federal parkland, were not to enter Resurrection City unless invited. The permit prohibited firearms, liquor, or open fires in the encampment and required removal of garbage, provision of sewage and bathing facilities, and adherence to local safety regulations.

Nearly every provision was destined to be violated, as Resurrection City became engulfed in dissension and torrential rains.

Resurrection City, U.S.A., had a lifespan of six weeks and a peak population of 2,600. It was an encampment of plywood and plastic-sheeting huts, built under the direction of a professor of architecture. Snow fencing surrounded it. It had a city hall, a dispensary, a dining tent, and a psychiatrist. Its residents came mostly in huge bus caravans from the South, a few large northern states, and California. There were family groups, but a disproportionate number were teenagers and young adults, mostly young men. Two of every three residents were black. The rest included Indians and young white college students from the North. A Mexican-American entourage stayed in separate quarters at a private school in Washington.

Almost from the first day that people moved into Resurrection City in mid-May, it rained. Rain fell on the shantytown twenty-eight of the forty-two days it existed. An inch or more fell on half a dozen days and more than two inches on a single day, June 12. The grassy parkland turned to trampled mud, ankle-deep, with some puddles of water hip-deep. The plywood houses were soaked. Washed clothes would not dry. Dampness and surprisingly low temperatures for May and June chilled the nights. Mud seeped in everywhere. Moving from place to place meant sloshing around in water and mud. Trash, rotting food, discarded clothing, packing boxes, cans, and liquor bottles slowly sank into the mud throughout the encampment. Huge oil drums, crammed with refuse, burned day and night. Their smoky stench carried all the way downtown and through the surrounding parkland and Mall area.

At the beginning, Resurrection City's older people—parents and grandparents, mostly blacks—whiled away their time by sitting, chatting, keeping up their small plywood houses, watching other people, and talking with the hordes of newsmen. The white residents, largely college boys and girls, were in and out of the camp, disproportionately active in its administration, helping to pass out clothing and meals donated by Washington businessmen and the federal government. Apart from the others stood the big-city black youths. Street-wise, spirited, these young men from New York, Chicago, and elsewhere ultimately came nearest to running the camp, in one way or another.

Many of these youths had been deliberately recruited by the SCLC from city streets, to include the toughest street gangs of the nation in a bold experiment. They were made marshals, in charge of maintaining order and security in the encampment, under the supervision of the Reverend James Orange, an enormous bearded Negro who always wore bib overalls, and Alfred Spencer, a muscular black man with a swift military stride, who wore dark glasses rain or shine. The marshals were as loosely organized as the settlement itself, however, and sometimes disturbed as well as kept order.

"These gang members—like the Blackstone Rangers in Chicago and the Invaders in Memphis—have always lived ouside the system," SCLC staff official Albert R. Sampson explained. "Our idea was to bring them into the system, let them have a role in the functioning of Resurrection City. It was the first time for a lot of them to be somebody, to be a man."

Their behavior was erratic. At the gate of the fenced-in encampment, they would let anyone in to visit one day and no one but newsmen the next. For residents, such trifling things as entering their city hall at the wrong time could bring a sharp reprimand from marshals, while heavy drinking, fist fights, and thefts of valuables from shanties might be ignored. Many of the marshals and other young residents went into Washington at night, up the 14th Street, N.W., strip and elsewhere, to relieve the boredom of the encampment. Often they returned drunk, with more whisky in hand, and staged wild all-night parties inside the fence. On different occasions, they assaulted four newsmen, two of them black. Some marshals told outsiders that guns, knives, explosives, and a lot of liquor were stashed away inside various shanties. The Park Police were never allowed to come into the city and were seldom notified even when someone inside was hurt.

To try to maintain better order, Reverend Orange organized a group of men in their late twenties as the "Tent City Rangers," with distinctive Australian-style campaign hats and uniforms of blue denim or khaki. They were supposed to oversee the marshals, and more than once they were instrumental in restraining overzealous demonstrators outside the encampment and quelling serious disturbances inside it. But often the regular marshals and other residents ignored them. However, continuing confrontations enabled the participants to push the goals of the Campaign and direct national attention to claimed inequities in the federal handling of such matters as public welfare and surplus food distribution.

The Reverend Ralph Abernathy, now the top SCLC leader, grew testy with the press over criticisms of the conditions inside Resurrection City and the state of the campaign as a whole. He had been criticized even from within the SCLC leadership cadre for spending most of his nights away from Resurrection City and not exerting firm enough leadership over its activities. He admitted there were difficulties in running the encampment, and added:

"The chaos and violence are part of the American sickness. The American system has created a monster in the ghetto. The people of the ghetto are not the cause of the violence. It is the exploiters and the leaders of Congress who do not see the need for every American to have a full belly and an equal opportunity who have caused the violence."

Top marshals Orange and Spencer met repeatedly with National Park Service Director Nash Castro, who pleaded with them to restore order. The youths in Resurrection City had become increasingly bored and troublesome as protest activity carried on by the residents outside the campsite became sporadic and disorganized.

"They claimed they had removed 1,000 undesirables from Resurrection City," Castro said. "They did the very best they could. I really felt sorry for them. They were extremely conscientious, but the job was too much for them."

By early June, the boredom, rowdyism, and rains had cut the encampment's population to about 700 on some nights.

Because delays in the start of the Poor People's Campaign had made impossible a planned Memorial Day massing of thousands of demonstrators and sympathizers at the Washington Monument and Lincoln Memorial, the government allowed the permit for the encampment to be extended from June 16 to June 23. A "Solidarity Day" demonstration was planned for June 19, "Juneteenth," the day Negroes traditionally celebrate the freeing of slaves in Texas.

About 50,000 people in all, many from the Washington area and others who came by bus- and car-caravans from much of the eastern part of the country, participated. Solidarity Day was smaller in scale than the 1963 March on Washington led by Dr. King, and it lacked the drama of the earlier gathering. But SCLC organizers were pleased that the attendance was so good and that the demonstration went off without any trouble. About 300 participants stayed behind during the night of June 19 to spend a day or two in Resurrection City.

Then, late Thursday night, June 20, as 300 Resurrection City demonstrators crossed the Washington Monument grounds returning to the eastern end of the encampment, a few youths began arguing with Washington policemen, who were following them. Some of them picked up stones and threw them at the police. Led by Assistant Chief Jerry Wilson, who towered above the others, the police responded with tear gas. Wilson threw the first grenade. The confrontation was brief as tent city rangers intervened and pushed the youths through the fence into Resurrection City.

After that, conditions inside the encampment began to deteriorate quickly. There were more and more reports of fights, thefts, even attacks on women residents. From behind the snow fence, black youths began stoning cars that passed the settlement along Independence Avenue and other nearby streets.

Three nights later, in the early morning hours of Sunday, June 23, much more tear gas was used, this time by Park Police. After a few youths threw missiles over the fence at passing cars and police, the Park Police fired shotgun-like launchers and tossed baseball grenades, in a bombardment of the encampment. As thick clouds of tears gas rolled through the shantytown, hundreds of residents were shocked from their sleep and ran choking, vomiting, and screaming out the east gate toward the Washington Monument grounds.

One of the Justice Department officials charged with trouble-shooting at Resurrection City, Nathaniel "Tully" Kossack, drove quickly to the area, put on a gas mask, and ran into the encampment. He located several people overcome by gas and got them out to ambulances.

The Reverend Andrew Young, a SCLC official, called the gassing "worse than anything I ever saw in Mississippi or Alabama. You don't shoot tear gas into an entire city because two or three hoodlums are throwing rocks."

It was against these confrontations, climaxing weeks of tension, that the city government decided to be ready for the worst. SCLC leaders had agreed with federal officials to allow Resurrection City to be closed down by the police and to have the residents who remained, as well as others who would march to Capitol Hill with Reverend Abernathy, arrested as a symbol of their protest. But the Executive Communications Center, which had been keeping track daily of Resurrection City events, was fully manned and kept the Mayor informed about every move the police and the campaigners were making. Seven hundred members of the D.C. National Guard were on duty to help the police and to be on hand if trouble occurred.

On the morning of June 24, while 200 guardsmen performed station-house duties normally handled by the police, 1,000 policemen arrived at the gates of Resurrection City. With 750 of them held in reserve outside, 250 policemen, all Civil Disturbance Unit (CDU) members, moved into the encampment. They wore military flak jackets and riot helmets and were armed with riot sticks, tear-gas canisters and launchers, revolvers, and shotguns.

They found 115 people singing freedom songs just outside the city-hall shack. These residents were arrested, and the rest of the deserted camp searched. By afternoon, National Park Service workers were preparing for the bulldozing of the site. With just as little trouble, police arrested 200 more campaigners, including Reverend Abernathy, on Capitol Hill. Most were charged with minor technical offenses and jailed briefly or fined.

The situation reports coming out of the Executive Communications Center described a calm city until 1:15 P.M., when the police reported a crowd of people at the intersection of 14th and U. The group included about 100 people from the Poor People's Campaign who evidently had not understood the agreement about the closing of Resurrection City and the mass arrests. They were angry about the arrests and anxious to leave the city. They had come to the SCLC office to see what would happen next. Watched closely by tent city rangers and a few policemen, the campaigners and a crowd of curious youth from the neighborhood filled the sidewalk and overflowed into the street. It was necessary to reroute traffic around the intersection, the police reported, "but there are no other problems at this time."

During the next three hours, there were a few anxious moments. The window of a jewelry store on U Street near the intersection was smashed and some jewelry taken. A busload of CDU policemen, who had been at Resurrection City, raced to the scene, and youths in the crowd at 14th and U reacted angrily. Public Safety Director Pat Murphy and Inspector Robert Hough, a black policeman, arrived soon afterward and directed that only black policemen be kept in the area.

A block away, employees of a storage company warehouse reported that one of a group of five youths had thrown a fire bomb into the building. As firemen fought and put out the blaze, the crowd in the area grew larger and traffic became more snarled. At 16th and U streets, the window of a liquor store was broken, but nothing was taken from inside. People in the crowd at 14th and U became embroiled in an argument with the management of the Peoples Drug Store next to SCLC headquarters when several persons refused to pay for lunches at the soda fountain. The store was shut briefly, then reopened with guards at the doors and a private guard, armed with a shotgun, stationed on the roof.

At 3:45 P.M., it appeared that the tension would ease because SCLC officials were busing most of the Poor People's campaigners in the crowd to a downtown church to be fed and housed temporarily. But the remaining neighborhood youths stayed on the corner and were joined periodically by others passing by. They continued to argue with the Peoples Drug guards and began breaking bottles on the sidewalk outside the store. Then, at 5:30 P.M., some older youths in the crowd loudly and grinningly decided to have a contest to see who could first break the store's plate-glass window. First they threw bottles, then stones. A piece of brick shattered the glass first.

The police, with the aid of tent city rangers, rushed into the crowd, pushed it back from the store, and pulled out the missile throwers. The rangers thought they were gaining control of the crowd, which now numbered nearly 500. But Assistant Chief Jerry Wilson, who had arrived at the intersection, was worried by what he saw. He called for the CDU again. Two busloads of policemen arrived, armed with tear gas.

The rangers were enraged. One ran up to Inspector Hough and yelled: "What the hell is going on? We had them quiet and on the sidewalk and you bring in the fucking troops. If you want trouble, you're damn sure going to get it now. I'm finished."

He and most of the rangers left.

The CDU police massed in the middle of 14th Street between U and V streets, just north of the crowd. Standing shoulder to shoulder, they began moving toward the crowd. Some stones and bottles were thrown into the phalanx of police. Tear gas was shot back at the crowd, and a melee began.

Still firing tear gas, the police pushed into the intersection and began to break up the crowd. A group of about seventy-five youths starting running south on 14th Street, yelling and singing. They threw stones through two store windows as they moved quickly along a dozen blocks.

Police in patrol cars headed off the youths at K Street, just north of downtown, arresting a handful of them. The rest turned around and began running north again. Other youths and adults noticed them and congregated on the sidewalk to see what was happening. The sound of exploding tear-gas canisters and the white smoke of the gas itself could be heard and seen coming from 14th and U. Crowds began forming along the sidewalks of 14th Street and moving north toward U.

Assistant Chief Wilson drove up and down the street and ordered his men to disperse the growing crowds. When police in cars and buses arrived at intersections between N and U streets on 14th, youths on the sidewalk jeered them, and a few more bottles, cans, and stones were thrown. Each time, the police quickly answered taunts and missiles with clusters of tear-gas grenades. As the street began to fill up with tear gas, policemen drove by in cars and used bullhorns to tell everyone to get off the street. Other policemen following them then threw tear gas at persons who did not move. Even small clusters of as few as half a dozen onlookers, black and white, were gassed.

Crowds began forming farther on up the 14th Street hill, at Euclid Street and Park Road, and almost identical skirmishes between them and the police took place. Some youths stoned passenger cars, as well as police cars, until routed by tear gas.

At 7 P.M., Wilson asked for and got the Mayor and federal officials to authorize guardsmen to move onto 14th Street. They moved in quickly in jeeps and dismounted at intersections to block them off and protect storefronts. They were armed with empty rifles and tear gas, some of which they used on unruly crowds.

Reports of the confrontation on 14th Street had already been flashed on several Washington radio stations, and crowds began gathering elsewhere in the city. The largest were on H Street, N.E., where clusters of from twenty to 100 people suddenly mushroomed on each street corner along a ten-block stretch, filled with the hulks of stores burned in the April rioting. Police at the scene reported that the H Street crowds were calm and quiet.

A message came to Mayor Washington at the Executive Command Center that "Wilson wants to know about a curfew. . . . he wants to get the people off the street."

At 8:45 P.M., Mayor Washington read a statement on radio and television imposing a 9 P.M. to 5:30 A.M. curfew and calling for the restoration of order. As police and guardsmen moved to enforce the curfew and send people home, looting occurred at a few scattered locations just outside the areas hit hardest by the April rioting: off H Street, N.E., Florida Avenue east and west of 7th Street, N.W., Columbia Road west of 14th Street, N.W., and the Mount Pleasant neighborhood around 18th and 19th streets, N.W.

The police made 175 arrests, among them 81 for curfew violations, 60 for disorderly conduct or drunkenness, 10 for looting, and 3 for assaulting a policeman. One man looting a liquor store was shot, but not killed, by the police when he began throwing things at them as he emerged from the store.

Newsmen who covered both the April riot and the June 24 affair noticed a change in police demeanor. Police were more brusque and displayed a generally tougher attitude. Some black reporters who attempted to cover the police action said they were warned to leave the area after the curfew was imposed and they were jostled on their way.

Only twenty windows were broken and only three fires started throughout the city during the brief disturbance. All was quiet before midnight, and there was no further trouble during the days that followed. The National Guard was withdrawn from the city the next day.

Senator Byrd of West Virginia praised the Mayor and the police. "Had the same firm and prompt action been manifested in the April riot," he said, "the city and Washington's business community would have been spared the looting, the arson, and the destruction it suffered."

Within twenty-four hours, the Mayor, the police, and the rest of the city government were deluged with praise from the same businessmen and congressmen who had assailed them with criticism after the April riot. Businessman Abe Liss, who had led a group of complaining white merchants in April, said, "The response Monday showed you can do a beautiful job without shooting but with enough other force."

But in black Washington, along 14th Street and in other areas, the swift response left much bitterness. Oppressive tear gas, aggravated by the hot, humid weather, hung over the streets and pushed through open windows into crowded buildings, where residents were confined after the curfew went into effect. The police had detonated 1,000 tear-gas grenades, mostly during a two-hour period, to break up crowds and answer youths tossing stones, bottles, and cans.

There were also complaints about unequal enforcement of the curfew. The lid had evidently been clamped down tighter on inner-city neighborhoods than in the predominantly white sections, but police pointed out that they concentrated their enforcement efforts where the disturbance was. A performance of the Supremes was allowed to run its scheduled course that night at the Carter-Barron Amphitheater because the authorities decided it would be better to do so than to turn loose the audience, which included many thousands of youths of both races, while the disorder was in progress.

The City Council investigated citizen complaints about the amount of tear gas used and asked for an explanation. The Mayor sent the Council a report from Pat Murphy,* saying:

> The use of tear gas was determined to be the most humane method of dispersing the crowds, protecting innocent citizens, avoiding bloodshed and protecting property.
>
> Generally, the amount of gas used was deemed proper to meet the needs of the situation. Its impact was aggravated by the prevailing weather conditions which extended the effect of the fumes for a prolonged period.
>
> However, a few reports of isolated incidents of excessive use were received and investigated. These reports formed the basis for supplementary instruction by the Department in the use of tear gas.

This supplementary instruction placed restrictions on when and how much tear gas should be used by the police. Privately, one police official said, "We overdid it at times June 24 and we don't want it to happen again."

---

* In mid-September, President Johnson announced that he was nominating Washington's Public Safety Director Patrick V. Murphy as administrator of the new National Safe Streets Act. The appointment, subject to Senate confirmation, will enable Murphy to make grants to police departments across the country to improve law enforcement techniques.

Epilogue in August: The City's Voices

"There is a voice coming from this city's ghetto neighborhoods," Mayor Washington said late in August. "That voice says, 'We would like to be relevant to what happens in our communities. We would like to have entrepreneurship. We would like to be part of the American dream.'"

In the months after April's riots, many voices spoke out in Washington. They were the voices of disputing citizens and bankrupt merchants, of a beleaguered city government and worried officials, of a shaken school system and bewildered pupils.

"Do not fail them by lecturing them when they need to talk," Assistant Superintendent of Schools Norman Nickens told teachers in the inner city on Monday, April 7, after the weekend of looting and burning.

"Unusual events have occurred and your children are preoccupied with them," Nickens said in a circular to teachers in the Cardozo area, which comprises much of the 14th Street and 7th Street riot areas. "They are desperately in need of your support."

With the help of federal troops, the city had set up machinery to stop the rioting and restore order, but at best that was a short-run solution to the problems, a way of keeping the lid on temporarily. Nickens saw the need to let the children talk out their troubles. Others set out to give older persons a similar outlet, although that was not as easy.

Children returning to school that Monday "were very con-

77

The Reverend Ralph Abernathy, who took over the Southern Christian Leadership Conference after the death of Dr. Martin Luther King, Jr., carries out his slain leader's plan for a massive spring protest in Washington. On the Mall, an encampment is set up and called Resurrection City *(below)*. One of the protest's toughest enemies turns out to be the weather: Dr. Abernathy and his group suffer rain for twenty-eight of the forty-two days of the camp's existence. The Weather Bureau reports a total of 9.53 inches in the May 13 to June 24 period, and the camp becomes a sea of mud and misery.

78

79

80

On June 19, the Poor People's Campaign draws 50,000 persons from around the nation and the city to observe Solidarity Day along the Mall. At the Lincoln Memorial, Mrs. Martin Luther King, Jr. *(left)*, addresses the crowds and reminds Congress of the immediate needs of the millions of poor people.

81

Twenty-four hours after the peaceful Solidarity Day crowd has dispersed, a group of Resurrection City demonstrators leave the Agriculture Department building, where they have been sitting down outside, in order to sit down on 17th Street, N.W., the east boundary of their encampment. Police move in quickly, opening up with tear gas *(below)*. Assistant Chief of Police Jerry V. Wilson *(above)*, tear-gas grenade in hand, tells a group of Resurrection City marshals to move into their city; they tell him they will get their people inside when his police pull back to the curb. Both sides comply.

On June 24, a line of policemen *(above)* moves through the nearly deserted Resurrection City, which had been ordered vacated when the permit expired the day before. The residents who chose to remain are arrested peacefully. Meanwhile, the Reverend Dr. Abernathy leads a group past the Agriculture Department and then on to the Capitol where, by prearrangement, they are arrested *(right)*.

Later, the Reverend Jesse Jackson addresses a crowd at 14th and U.

Clouds of tear gas are everywhere as police swarm into the street.

There is a report that a shot has been fired; a busload of Civil Disturbance Unit police sweeps 14th Street and saturates the area with tear gas.

At the Monarch Novelty Shop on 14th Street, Mr. and Mrs. Jack Robinson, expecting repetition of the April rioting, stand with three sons, guns ready.

Rubble has been bulldozed out of sight at 7th and O streets, N.W., but telltale marks of burning remain outlined on an adjacent structure. The capital prepares to tackle the problem of rebuilding the ruined sections of the city.

fused," a white teacher in an inner-city school said. "They had been excited. In retrospect, to the children themselves, it was a thrilling time—bringing to life what they see on television."

Some children arrived in school wearing clothes acquired in the looting, "but conscience hit them at the front door," the teacher said. "I had children who looked at me and said, 'I just can't keep these clothes on; I have to go home and put on my own things.'"

At one elementary school, a sixth-grade teacher asked her pupils why they thought it was all right to loot stores.

"They cheat people all the time—especially, they cheat children," a girl replied. "If you go in, they'll give you less change than you got coming, if they think they can get away with it."

The teacher asked if the merchants in all the burned-out stores cheated their customers.

"No," was the reply. "The man at the grocery store on the corner was real nice to everyone, and I'm sorry he got burned."

The students were able to make a distinction between looting and burning. To many of them, looting was all right, but burning was too destructive.

"It's okay to loot white people's stores, but not to burn," said one fourth-grader, "because they could put the clothes back, but they couldn't build the stores back once they were burned."

As part of the effort to help children to get their bearings, some Cardozo area teachers asked the elementary school students to write short essays, completing the sentence, "Right now, I feel . . ."

A desire to erase the weekend was shown through much of the writing.

"Right now, I want to be in another place and forget about all this rioting," was one comment.

Another child wrote:

Right now I want to be American, not a black and not a white man, but a American boy. To do the right things because now I go to school and want to go to U.C.L.E. [sic] college when I grow up. To have a wife and have a family a house with a big yard for my children. To change the war between races so there will not be a black man and a white man but an American man. To remember

that you can not judge a man from a color. Right now I would like
to forget about Black Power, Soul, and all the burning of stores.
I would like to forget about 14th street.

To some, the white man still remained the villain.

A fourth-grader wrote, "If I were a white person this weekend, I would put tar all over me or go to a place and hide."

The adult concern of putting the city back together again
also challenged the children. One wrote:

> The stores in my neighborhood should not have been burned be-
> cause a lot of people were put out of jobs. The people who burned
> down the grocery stores had no where to get food. The people who
> didn't take a part in the riots had to go to Maryland to shop or they
> suffered with the other people. Burning down these stores caused
> million [sic] of dollars damage. A lot of people will never get their
> businesses put up again.

Another child put it very simply: "Washington wasn't Washington last week."

These reactions of school children were collected over the
Easter holiday by members of the Cardozo "Innovation Team,"
and were published in a booklet entitled "Children of Cardozo
Tell It Like It Is."*

While teachers in the riot areas were encouraging school children to express themselves, adult community leaders were also
focusing on the problem of reducing tensions and dealing with
such problems as immediate relief, longer-term rebuilding, and
relations between the races. They, too, were trying hard to tell it
like it is.

From the start of the April riot, community leaders were walking the streets, acting as "counterrioters" to cool things. Typical
was City Councilman Stanley Anderson, who had directed the
Recreation Department's Roving Leader program before President Johnson named him a councilman. On the streets Thursday night in southeast Washington, Anderson told threatening
crowds, "Martin Luther King did not stand for violence, so
cool it."

Sterling Tucker, then Director of the Urban League's Wash-

---

* Copyright by the Education Development Center., Inc., Cambridge,
Mass. (Princeton, N.J.: D. Van Nostrand Co., 1968).

ington office, reached 14th Street at about 11 P.M., Thursday night, after cutting short an out-of-town trip. He was surprised at the number of black pastors he saw working to bring things under control.

"I doubt that anyone called them, but they were there," he said.

Tucker also saw workers from neighborhood organizations and some young men who had worked for the Urban League in Washington's ghettos during the summer of 1967 trying to control troublemakers. He saw members of a youth group, which was once called the "Losers" but had recently and optimistically become the "Winners," trying to calm rioters. And he saw the familiar, round figure of Father Geno Baroni on the street Thursday night. "Some of the rioters did not want any white people around, but they did not ask Father Baroni to leave."

Father Baroni was one of those white persons working in the inner city who had acquired unwritten passports of acceptance enabling them to move about freely at all times. He was head of the office of Urban Affairs of the Catholic Archdiocese of Washington.

With the Reverend Philip Newell, head of the Urban Institute of the Protestant Washington Council of Churches, he had made preliminary plans to deal with emergency human needs in the immediate aftermath of a possible riot in Washington.

As soon as they heard of the trouble on Thursday night, the two white clergymen were on the telephone to each other.

"It took us ten to twelve minutes to figure out what to do," Newell later told a newsman. "You've got to give people something to do. We had to get hold of the right people right away. I took the Protestants. He took the Catholics."

The Friday noon service at the National Cathedral, which the President and the Mayor attended, was soon arranged. It was a way to show those in the riot areas of Washington and other cities that important persons in the capital cared about Dr. King. More than 2,600 persons attended the service.

The team of Newell and Baroni then went on to other things. They sent out advice that only those white clergymen who were "known in the neighborhood" should be on the streets. They had worked out detailed plans for a church-coordinated emergency relief program to provide food, clothing, and shelter for riot victims until public services could take over. The plan was put into effect.

"We knew that even people with money would not be able to buy food," Father Baroni said. "We were talking about a large number of people who were in trouble."

Compassion, not anger, was the initial reaction of many of the city's residents, and members of both races—2,000 in all, including many white suburbanites— volunteered to help. By Saturday, they had operating thirty-eight collection points at suburban churches and forty-two distribution centers at inner-city churches, It was a remarkable performance.

Father Baroni was not bemused by the outpouring, however.

"Ideologically, that was okay, but a few days later some of the same people had tremendous feelings about how we should shoot looters, some of the same people who had been giving food."

Unlike some other cities, Washington, D.C., does not have a highly organized leadership structure among blacks or whites. There is no one to call who can press buttons to mobilize the city. But leaders were needed in this crisis to get certain things done —and to look ahead.

A month before the riot, a group of eighty persons had gotten together somewhat tentatively and formed a Washington offshoot of the national Urban Coalition to attack the "state of profound crisis" in the city. Representatives of rich and poor, business and labor, government and private enterprise attended. When the riot struck, Mayor Washington asked the group's head, Walter McArdle, a printing industry executive and leading Catholic layman, to call his people together. Although barely organized, they met in the Mayor's office Saturday afternoon. First, some of the businessmen present needed to tell the Mayor that they were unhappy with the city's handling of the riot—the police policy of restraint and the failure to summon troops until Friday. But, with that out of the way, they turned vigorously to the task of setting up programs to handle the riot-created emergency needs for food, shelter, jobs, and ready cash.

Providing food proved to be the critical need. Spurred by the feeling of urgency that the riot created, the Washington area also produced more housing, more jobs, and more money than the needy victims could use.

Baroni's and Newell's food distribution machinery was turned over to the city's Welfare Department, which wanted to "professionalize" it. As the professionals moved in and the amateurs moved out, it soon became clear that the welfare workers were not as well prepared as the volunteers. It took a couple of days and the technical guidance of Joseph Danzansky, president of Giant Foods, and his industry committee to work out the kinks. To some welfare workers, "professionalizing" meant making sure that only "deserving" persons received food, a cautious attitude that has often frustrated the department's work in the ghettos, and one curiously out of keeping with the purposes of the emergency program. Department of Agriculture surplus foods, donations by individuals and the food chains, and stocks purchased by the Welfare Department were pooled to provide food for nearly 2 million meals. There was no evidence that any riot victims went hungry.

Housing was handled as a joint effort by historical antagonists: the Washington Urban League and the Washington Board of Realtors, with the assistance of the Redevelopment Land Agency, the city's urban renewal agency. A total of 888 dwelling units were found from public and private sources in a city that has had notorious housing shortages for the poor. Only 169 units were used. An estimated 600 dwelling units had been destroyed or damaged in the disorders, but many of the displaced families apparently melted into their neighborhoods, getting lodgings from friends or relatives or in churches, while seeking new places in which to live. It was the inner city's own informal shelter program.

Perhaps 2,500 jobs vanished because of the looting and burning. During the first few days, the Washington branch of the National Association for the Advancement of Colored People had a key role in the Urban Coalition's Emergency Employment Committee. Then the Job Development Center, a Coalition-sponsored agency with five centers, took over. There were more than twice as many jobs listed (3,100) as applications for employment

(1,460), and fewer than half the applicants were riot victims. The centers placed a total of 455 by the last week of April. Some of the "burn-outs" found jobs on their own; chain stores absorbed many displaced employees by transferring them to other branches.

The city's Health and Welfare Council had the job of raising and distributing money for basic needs. The money poured in at about nine times the rate that it was disbursed. By June, collections reached close to $148,000, while slightly under $16,000 had been spent. There was some feeling that the intentions of the donors had been ignored, as strict standards of assistance were applied. Most of the money went for rent payments for hardship cases who were not eligible for public welfare assistance. It turned out that many families seeking help had been eligible for welfare aid all along, "but didn't even know it," Flaxie Pinkett, chairman of the Emergency Fund Committee, said.

These emergency tasks of feeding, housing, and finding jobs for the riot-afflicted were met with energy and good will. And they were quickly done. But rebuilding the riot-torn areas, the big task facing the city, was another matter. Private initiative was required in the commercial areas, but there was also an inescapable public responsibility.

Wrecking cranes began knocking down the walls of unsafe buildings soon after the fire engines left the riot-ravaged areas. But the resulting piles of rubble and the shells of scores of burned-out buildings remained for months. The city asked Congress for money to clear the remains of devastated structures, but Congress refused. Eventually, the city got a grant from the Department of Housing and Urban Renewal to clear the rubble. The grant was not a gift: The city was required to demand payment for cleaning up from the owners of the property involved. But this was enough to bring the bulldozers onto 7th, 14th, and H streets. By midsummer, much of the cleaning-up was under way.

At the end of June, after the threat of the Poor People's Campaign had dissipated, Senator Robert C. Byrd of West Virginia told the Board of Realtors, with a rhetorical flourish, that the "city of fear" should be remade into something better.

"Let each of us," he said, "strive within his own means and

in his own way to emulate Caesar Augustus, who . . . found a city of brick; he left it built of marble."

Senator Byrd failed to explain that Augustus did not build marble buildings. Like other Roman emperors, he merely covered brick and stone with white marble facades. Eventually, the marble was looted by the conquerors of Rome; the ruins of Rome are ruins of brick and stone.

In midsummer, there was a specter still hovering over the burned-out areas of Washington—the possibility that some bulldozed and cleared sites might stay that way indefinitely, as many of them have in Watts since 1965. The city was confronted with this dilemma: Blacks without capital said they wanted to rebuild; whites with capital were afraid to do so.

The Jewish Community Council, speaking for many of the burned-out white businessmen, accepted the principle of neighborhood participation in the reconstruction of the devastated areas, but asked that businessmen in the affected areas be included in "representative neighborhood planning groups."

The Council advised Mayor Washington that they favored helping black businessmen establish themselves in the devastated areas, but opposed the "black only" type of agitation.

A key section of their statement developed this point:

> Both Negro and white racists have been trying to use the current ferment as a device to institute an apartheid system in our community. This must be opposed on moral grounds and because such a system would wreck the economic structure of the Nation's Capital. The Jewish Community Council will align itself now, as it always has in the past, with integrationist forces, Negro and white, rather than acquiesce in or accept the false, simplistic solutions of racists and segregationists. One application of this principle is that we emphatically believe that, in a democratic society, no location of residence or business should be proscribed on racial grounds.

The Jewish group also proposed the establishment of a "businessman's task force" to provide needed economic aid to the inner-city areas affected, "including jobs, credit unions, consumer protection, a Better Business Bureau for the ghetto, and intensified assistance to black entrepreneurs." At least one firm took action along these lines during the summer. Three brothers who owned an H Street menswear store burned out in the riot gave shares of the company to three Negro employees.

An early interest in rebuilding parts of upper 14th Street was voiced by Build Black, Incorporated, an outfit set up for this purpose but with no resources other than the energy of its sponsors. They hoped that white merchants would be willing to turn over to them existing business sites on the shopping strip for modest fees, arguing that only by doing so could the white man hope to salvage his investment. The militant antiwhite tone of the neighborhood meetings Build Black held was set by the organization's circulars.

"Stop shufflin' and beggin' whitey. Build Black," one was headed.

"No more mom and pop stores, slumlords and other exploiters of black people allowed in black communities. No more honkie unions—without black members—and no more honkie owners and contractors without black participation—allowed in black neighborhoods."

The circular ended in blank verse:

> this land is your land
> you have the right
> and the power
> to say who uses it for what

The polarization of black Washington and white Washington was beginning to show.

Other Negro groups also said that the riot should mark the end of white dominance of inner-city commerce. Marion Barry, a one-time Washington representative of SNCC who became director of operations of Pride, Incorporated, a bootstrap black enterprise organized in 1967 with governmental assistance, laid down this policy in an interview:

"White people should be allowed to come back only if the majority of the ownership is in the hands of the blacks. That is, they could come back and give their experience and give their expertise—and then they should leave."

The Black United Front (BUF), a coalition of Negro action groups, declared early in May: "We wish to emphasize very strongly that black people are going to rebuild this black community."

Many Negro organizations and self-appointed spokesmen repeated the same message: Black citizens demanded a significant voice in community planning. They were not going to be planned for any longer, just as they would not accept a preponderance of white merchants doing business on the same old basis any longer.

The City Council held a series of hearings to give everyone a chance to have his say on rebuilding. Some of the testimony was presented by persons who were appearing before a public body for the first time. Many of them wanted assurances that blacks would have an important role in planning, rebuilding, and operating the new facilities.

In May, the Mayor had announced a hundred-day program to prepare rebuilding plans and "start actual rebuilding before the end of this summer." Although a few businessmen did rebuild their stores during the summer, the Mayor found that his timetable was too optimistic. The first job was to "rebuild confidence." "As long as the city was covered with an umbrella of apprehension and fear," the Mayor said in an interview, "we could not get businessmen to talk about planning for rehabilitation."

The unsettled business climate created by the Poor People's Campaign, the insurance crisis, and the lack of an effective dialogue between blacks and whites all combined to slow the planning work. However, the principle of encouraging black entrepreneurship in the inner city was accepted by the City Council, and the Mayor, in setting up machinery to speed the rebuilding of the riot-torn areas, moved to encourage it.

On the hundredth day, August 28, with legislation for the pooling of insurance risks enacted and with business—including tourism—picking up again, the Mayor called a press conference to announce what progress had been made. Before a cross section of citizens—including white businessmen from the riot-torn areas

and both militant and moderate blacks—the Mayor unveiled preliminary plans prepared by civic groups, architects, and community organizations.

A Community Reconstruction and Development Corporation
was set up on a non-profit basis with a $600,000 grant from the
Ford Foundation to "provide the initial thrust to our rebuilding
efforts," the Mayor announced. The Ford-sponsored corporation
was to be directed by the membership of the previously appointed
Community Development Committee, a group that had a black
majority and was headed by Dean C. Clyde Ferguson of Howard
University Law School. The Corporation was given, as a principal
task, the development of black businesses. Ford participation
was conditioned on the city undertaking a special effort to involve
both blacks and whites in the rebuilding work.

"Meaningful city involvement," Mayor Washington said,
"would be the central aspect of rebuilding. Such involvement is
not easy, but whether it is easy or not it must be done."

Also established by the city in August was a new Economic
Development Committee, which was asked to find venture capital
for black-owned businesses in and out of the riot areas and to
channel federal development funds into the city. The Committee
was headed by Joseph B. Danzansky, who had emerged as a white
businessman who could work effectively with black citizens, after
his successful untangling of the emergency food distribution problem during the riot period and later at Resurrection City. An
activist black minister who worked with Danzansky has described
him as a man who "knows how to listen to an idea and carry
it to the next practicable step."

Another issue dividing black and white that continued to
occupy the attention of the city government in August was the
demand of the Black United Front for black citizen control of
the police department at the precinct level. An original demand
of the BUF when it was founded early in 1968 as a coalition of
militant and moderate blacks, it was pushed to the fore after
Resurrection City was closed and the incipient riot on 14th Street
checked with massive applications of tear gas. After the April
riot, some white businessmen had indicated their displeasure

with the policy of restraint exercised by the police department. At the end of June, it was the turn of some black militants to be unhappy with the way the police department had acted.

A series of incidents involving the use of police weapons focused the issue more sharply in July. When a white policeman was killed with his own gun while attempting to arrest a robbery suspect, the BUF declared that "the alleged slaying of the honkie cop is justifiable in the same sense that police are allowed to kill black people and call it justifiable homicide." BUF used the opportunity to renew its demand for black control of the police department.

Mayor Washington immediately attacked the statement as "inflammatory and irresponsible," and Reverend Walter Fauntroy, a member of the BUF, said he thought it wrong to suggest that homicide was justifiable under any circumstances. Although Fauntroy was one of the few black leaders other than the Mayor to speak out against the statement, some members of Congress demanded that he leave the BUF or the City Council, while the predominantly white Policeman's Association called for his resignation from the City Council.

The BUF had been the creation of revolutionary activist Stokely Carmichael, who had summoned most of the city's Negro leadership to a meeting in January to set it up. Although some black leaders felt "put on the spot" by the call, few dared to refuse the bid. As the summer wore on, other difficulties arose. For example, a demand from BUF militants that all whites leave a meeting called to discuss the police control issue resulted in the protest and departure of the Urban League's Sterling Tucker and others.

The Reverend Channing E. Phillips, a black activist minister who was elected Democratic National Committeeman one month after the riot, defended the statement of the BUF on the police as designed to provoke a "constructive dialogue on the system which invites such violence." (In August, Phillips was nominated as Washington's favorite-son candidate for President at the convention in Chicago. His name was proposed to call national attention to the plight of black people in Washington and throughout the country. He won 67½ delegate votes.)

The police issue produced an interesting reaction at a Group Relations workshop in August, which Phillips and thirty city officials of both races attended.

"Why don't blacks get together with whites to present their problems and discuss them fraternally?" a white man asked Phillips.

"Blacks have sought a dialogue with whites for years without effect," Phillips replied.

One white questioner suggested that blacks were taking "the easy way" by setting up all-black groups such as the BUF instead of sitting down and talking with whites, "eyeball to eyeball."

Remaining cool and good-humored throughout the intense questioning, Phillips said that there was no real evidence that whites wanted more than a "token" dialogue with blacks. "There can be no true dialogue, except between peers," he said.

Phillips referred to the government of the city of Washington as a "colonial" regime, run by "outsiders," namely, the members of the District of Columbia committees of the Congress.

Several black leaders have said since the riot that they see the resolution of the question of the role of whites in the Negro community, whether they be store owners, policemen, organizers or economic developers, as the big hurdle that has to be surmounted in Washington's postriot period.

"Look," said one, "I guess if we want to have a black community with no whites in it at all, we probably could. But that would mean we had decided to completely isolate ourselves, with damn few resources. I don't think that's what the black community of Washington wants."

At the root of questions on rebuilding, the police, and home rule, is the basic question in a city two-thirds black: Just how much self-determination can its citizens achieve?

The Reverend E. Franklin Jackson, the black incumbent national committeeman whom Phillips defeated, told the City Council hearings on rebuilding that he believed interracial cooperation was both morally right and financially mandatory. He was applauded for saying so. However, another activist minister said privately said that if he had "made Jackson's speech before the Council, I would have been denounced as a sell-out by the movement."

A National Advisory Commission on Civil Disorders study of civil-rights attitudes made before the death of Dr. King indicated that black residents of Washington and fourteen other cities overwhelmingly preferred the stands of moderates over extremists. Dr. King was approved by nearly three out of every four blacks questioned, while Roy Wilkins of the NAACP held the approval of one out of every two. Only one out of every seven approved the stands of Carmichael and H. Rap Brown of SNCC. There was no way of telling how the death of Dr. King might have influenced the results. The University of Michigan group that made the study for the riot commission asked this question: "Now I want to read you a list of people active in civil rights. For each one, please tell me whether you approve or disapprove of what the person stands for, or don't know enough about him to say." The following replies were given:

| | (In per cent) | | | |
	Carmichael	Dr. King	Wilkins	Brown
Approve	14	72	50	14
Partly approve, partly disapprove	21	19	12	13
Disapprove	35	5	3	45
Don't know	30	4	35	28

Many of Dr. King's Washington followers were ready to turn to such extremists as Stokely Carmichael.* Undoubtedly, much would depend on the city's ability to respond to the messages conveyed by the riot.

The issues were complex—city planning and economic development questions were involved in the rebuilding issue; the ulti-

---

* Stokely Carmichael, who coined the term "black power," has swung from believing in nonviolent action for integration to suggesting that guerrilla warfare may be needed to achieve a black revolution in America. In August, 1966, Carmichael was named national chairman of the Student Nonviolent Coordinating Committee. As former chairman in 1967, he maintained his SNCC connection and began using Washington as a base. In August, 1968, SNCC announced his ouster. He promptly emerged as "prime minister" of the Black Panther Party, based in Oakland, California, a group created to arm Negroes for defense against whites, particularly police, which was now, according to Carmichael, on the brink of a "period of armed struggle."

mate question of who runs the town is implicit in the police control issue. Other issues that had faded into the background during the riot were sure to emerge again—the question of community control of schools would heat up when the school board electoral campaign got under way.

For the black Mayor of Washington, Walter Washington, the problem was a fantastic one of communication. He knew that he had to maintain communication between the races in the city to get anything done. But, because of the peculiar structure of the government of Washington, he had to work out ways of communicating with Capitol Hill, where Congressmen often were unwilling to hear rather simple messages from the city such as the need to provide adequate funds for city services. Not unimportant in the mix was the need to communicate with the White House, to convey the urgency of the city's problems and get the attention of the busy Chief Executive.

The city's five-month attempt at a dialogue—in the schools, in public meetings on rebuilding burned-out streets, in angry statements from black activists about the police—has brought out some of the problems and alienation that lay behind the rioting.

But, in August, the question remained whether the nation's capital would be able to do an effective job of coping with the conditions that caused the riots to occur.

Last March, the National Advisory Commission on Civil Disorders concluded its summary with this simple statement:

"It is time now to end the destruction and the violence, not only in the streets of the ghetto, but in the lives of people."

The sense of that inner violence leapt out of the notes of a white newspaperwoman, Carolyn Lewis, who talked to blacks on the street that wild weekend in April.

A woman from 7th Street: "Some blacks feel others are wrong to do these things, but you can only take it so long. When the white man wants something, he starts a war and gets it, so why not us?"

A youth in the same vicinity: "Now they'll have to sit up and notice us."

A youth who was asked why he had just fired a 7th Street

store: "I got mad, that's why. But, don't you cry, lady, we're burning the rats and roaches along with everything else."

For Washington, the message of April seemed clear: The capital of the nation had to rebuild in a hundred important ways to become a better place to live for all its residents.

Meanwhile, to the city's distress, a generation of children will grow up in Washington remembering the searing picture of the riot. One of them wrote:

"I saw a house burn down. I felt sad. . . . I hope I won't never see it again."

Appendix I

How Many Rioted

It is probable that the number of rioters in Washington in April was in the 17,600–22,800 range—roughly 20,000, or about one out of eight residents of the affected area. Experienced newsmen on the staff of *The Washington Post* who covered the riot intensively are prepared to accept this figure. Mayor Walter E. Washington believes the range accords with his personal observations, sharpened by several visits a day to the areas of rioting.

Not much scientific work has been done on the question of measuring riot participation, but some yardsticks were offered in a supplementary report of the National Advisory Commission on Civil Disorders, issued in July, 1968. These guidelines were developed by Dr. Robert M. Fogelson of the Massachusetts Institute of Technology and Dr. Robert B. Hill of Columbia University.

To produce comparable information on the Washington riot of April, 1968, the Fogelson-Hill work on the Detroit riot of 1967 was used as a base. Although there were significant differences between the riots in Detroit and Washington, application of the Detroit data to the Washington riot can be defended on the ground that the two disorders were of the same general order of magnitude.

In Detroit, postriot studies indicated that about 11 per cent of the riot-area residents in the ten-to-fifty-nine age group actually participated in the riot. The demographic analysis unit of the Washington Management Office estimated that there were 250,000 black persons living in the four precincts principally affected by the rioting, namely, the Second, Ninth, Tenth, and Thirteenth. In these four precincts, an estimated 160,000 persons of both sexes are in the ten-to-fifty-nine age group. Taking 11 per cent of this number would yield a figure of 17,600 as the number of rioters in Washington.

Another method used in the supplemental riot report was to multiply the total number of arrested persons (adults and juveniles) by a fixed multiplier—3, in the case of Detroit. Using the multiplier 3 for Washington, which had a total of 7,600 adults and juveniles arrested for a variety of riot-connected offenses, yielded a riot-participation figure of 22,800, compared to Detroit's 16,900. The multiplier was derived by dividing the potential nonwhite riot participants in a particular age category by the number of blacks arrested in that age category. Similar computations made with available Washington demographic data suggested that the multiplier 3 was not too far out of line for Washington, although the total probably was inflated somewhat by the fact that Washington police made an intensive effort to round up curfew violators to clear the streets.

The 20,000 rough estimate is approximately the average of the two figures (22,800 and 17,600). It has the virtue of occupying the middle ground that statisticians reserve for averages when they are in doubt.

The figure may be tested in another way. Police officials believe that they may have arrested about one in ten of the looters—those charged with actual stealing (a felony) as distinguished from those merely charged with violating the curfew (a misdemeanor). About 1,660 individuals, including juveniles, were charged with felonies when first arrested. Multiplying this figure by 10 would yield a riot participation total of 16,600, a figure not too far from the lower estimate.

Appendix II

Who Riots

Detailed statistics on D.C. rioters were gathered from reports of the D.C. Bail Agency, which customarily interviews persons charged with felonies in order to assist the court in determining whether bail should be required. The files on 856 cases out of a total of 1,468 were made available to *The Washington Post,* on the condition that personal information about individuals would not be disclosed.

The statistics gathered included race, sex, age, place of birth, charge, marital status, education, occupation, income, criminal record, place of residence, and length of residence in the District of Columbia. In the figures shown, the totals varied, because every case involving individuals about whom information was unknown was eliminated. The total number in the group was 856.

For the purpose of simplifying tabulation of the data, some of the more complex categories were grouped. For instance, income was split at the approximate median of the data—less than $4,000 per year and $4,000 or more per year. The income data is not completely reliable, since many of those arrested were part-time workers, or had occupations in which employment is intermittant, and gave hourly or daily wages as an income figure. Care was taken in multiplying these to an annual income, but some income figures were undoubtedly on the high side. Any error was not large, however.

For tabulation purposes, occupation was defined as blue collar, white collar, government, housewife, unemployed, military, or student. Marital status was tabulated as single or married—the married category including those previously married (widowed, separated, divorced).

The bail agency data covered only persons over eighteen, who, in the vast majority of cases, were no longer in school.

Statisticians may challenge the study on the grounds that the arrest process itself distorted the results. That the figures are relevant, however, was suggested by comparing the rioter profile obtained from the bail agency data with the comprehensive study made of 1967 rioters around the nation by the National Advisory Commission on Civil Disorders. (*See* page 235, "Data Comparisons.")

Below are tables showing the composition of the group arrested. Not all totals are the same because the D.C. Bail Agency data was, in some cases, incomplete.

| | RACE | |
	Negro	*White*
Number	759	16
Per Cent	98	2

| | AGE | |
Bracket	*Number*	*Per Cent*
18–20	197	23
21–25	213	25
26–30	155	18
31–35	103	12
36–40	74	9
41–45	48	6
46–50	33	4
51–55	23	3
56–Over	9	–

AGE BY MAJOR GROUPINGS

Bracket	Number	Per Cent
18–25	410	48
26–40	332	39
41–Over	113	13

(The average age was 24.6)

SEX

	Male	Female
Number	772	71
Per Cent	91	9

SEX BY AGE GROUPINGS

	18–25	26–40	41–Over
Male			
Number	374	301	96
Per cent	48	39	12
Female			
Number	31	26	14
Per cent	44	37	19

SEX BREAKDOWN BY MARITAL STATUS

	Single	Married or previously married
Male		
Number	323	438
Per cent	42	58
Female		
Number	25	46
Per cent	35	65

SEX BREAKDOWN BY INCOME

	Under $4,000	Over $4,000
Male		
Number	312	368
Per cent	46	54
Female		
Number	43	15
Per cent	74	26

SEX BREAKDOWN BY PREVIOUS RECORD

	No Record	Record	Total
Male			
Number	418	354	772
Per cent	54	46	
Female			
Number	61	10	71
Per cent	86	14	

LENGTH OF RESIDENCE IN WASHINGTON

Years of residence	Number	Per cent
1–5	152	20
6–10	101	14
11–15	74	10
16–20	155	21
21–25	118	16
26–30	62	8
31–35	34	5
36–40	23	3
41–Over	22	3

LENGTH OF RESIDENCE IN WASHINGTON BY AGE GROUPINGS

	Less than 8 years	8 or more years	Total
Total			
Number	221	559	780
Per cent	28	72	
18–25			
Number	133	244	388
Per cent	35	65	
26–40			
Number	75	227	302
Per cent	25	75	
41–Over			
Number	13	88	101
Per cent	13	87	

PLACE OF BIRTH

	Number	Per cent
Washington, D.C.	285	36
Southern states: subtotal	420	53
Alabama	10	
Florida	8	
Georgia	24	
Louisiana	4	
Mississippi	4	
North Carolina	154	
South Carolina	110	
Tennessee	2	
Texas	3	
Virginia	101	
Border States: subtotal	27	3
Delaware	2	
Kentucky	2	
Maryland	19	
West Virginia	4	
Northern States: subtotal	66	8
Connecticut	4	
Illinois	6	
Indiana	2	
Kansas	1	
Massachusetts	1	
Michigan	5	
New Jersey	6	
New York	9	
Ohio	5	
Pennsylvania	14	
Rhode Island	1	
Washington	11	
Virgin Islands	1	

EDUCATION BY LEVELS COMPLETED

	Number	Per cent
Four years of college	6	1
High school or better	224	29
Junior high or better	599	79
Elementary or better	688	91

EDUCATION BY GRADES COMPLETED

	Years completed	Total
Elementary grades	0	1
	1	5
	2	8
	3	8
	4	11
	5	14
	6	23
Junior high school	7	37
	8	52
	9	100
High school	10	124
	11	151
	12	182
College	1	15
	2	14
	3	7
	4	6

INCOME BY AGE GROUPINGS

	Average Income
18–20	$2,800
21–25	3,952
26–30	4,326
31–35	4,760
36–40	4,250
41–45	4,475
46–50	5,067
51–55	3,348
56–Over	2,500
Median for whole group:	$3,999.50
Average for whole group:	$3,703.00

INCOME GROUPINGS BY AGE GROUPINGS

	Less than $4,000 yearly	$4,000 yearly or more
Total		
Number	355	384
Per cent	48	52
18–25		
Number	213	131
Per cent	66	34
26–40		
Number	100	195
Per cent	34	66
41–Over		
Number	42	58
Per cent	42	58

INCOME BY MARITAL STATUS

	Less than $4,000 yearly	$4,000 yearly or more	Total
Single			
Number	196	97	293
Per cent	67	33	
Married			
Number	155	284	439
Per cent	35	65	

INCOME BY EDUCATION

	Less than $4,000 yearly	$4,000 yearly or more	Total
No high school			
Number	114	115	229
Per cent	50	50	
High school or better			
Number	200	239	439
Per cent	46	54	

OCCUPATION BREAKDOWN

	Number	Per cent
Blue Collar	585	70
White Collar	108	12
Housewife	8	1
Military	6	1
Student	40	5
Unemployed	90	11

ARREST RECORD BY AGE

	No Record	Record of murder, rape, or robbery	Other record	Total
18–25				
Number	276	10	132	409
Per cent	65	2	33	
26–Over				
Number	217	25	201	443
Per cent	49	6	45	

Note: Proportionately more of the older rioters had previous records—and the previous charge was more likely to have been a serious one.

Profile of a Rioter

When the D.C. Bail Agency data was fed into a computer and analyzed to see if a profile of a "typical rioter" could be obtained, the ranges in age, income, and education proved so great that it was concluded there really was no typical rioter among those arrested. However, the statistical tree below, charted to provide a sketch of some representative types, made evident the general conclusions stated in Chapter VII. The largest group, Negro males, was broken into two subgroups, based on whether they were single or married. Each of these was then broken down into age categories, and the largest age category for each into other subgroups based on education. Still further breakdowns based on income and arrest records were made.

WHO WHERE THE RIOTERS?

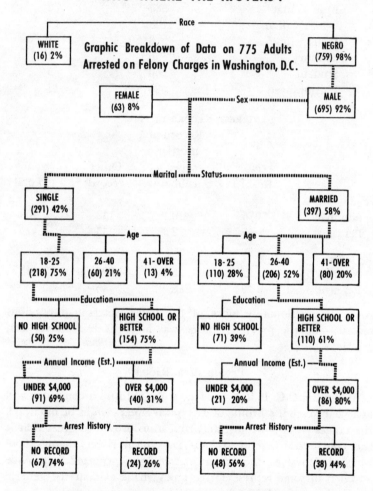

Records of the D.C. Bail Agency were analyzed for this statistical tree which shows the backgrounds of some married and unmarried Negro males who were arrested on felony charges during the riot. The two groups of Negro men were examined by categories, with the largest age group in each case subdivided on the basis of education and further subdivided on the basis of income and arrest history. Broken lines connect the related groups. Total number arrested in each category is shown in parentheses.

Data Comparisons

The table below compares the statistical information on rioters in U.S. cities in 1967, compiled by the National Advisory Commission on Civil Disorders, with the 1968 Washington data:

	(all figures in percentages)		
	Commis-sion Report		Wash-ington Data
Race			
Negro	83		98
Age			
15–24	52.5	(18–25)	48
25–35	28.3	(25–40)	39
Sex			
Male	89.3		91
Female	10.7		9
Marital Status			
Married			
(or previously married)	21		58
Single	79		42
Born in Riot City	59.4*		32
Charge Involving Weapon	4		6

* Detroit

Certain differences between the Commission report figures and the Washington data can be explained in part by the fact that the Washington figures did not include arrested persons under eighteen years of age whose cases were handled by the juvenile authorities. (More than 15 per cent of all persons arrested were juveniles, with an average age of sixteen.) Adding them to the total would markedly reduce the figures on marital status, of course.

Another factor affecting the marital status figures was the extent to which common-law relationships were counted. In compiling the Washington figures, the common-law relationship was treated as a valid marriage, as it is under local law. Those with prior marriages, although separated or divorced, also were counted as married in the Washington data.

Individual Case Files

The following are biographical notes on some of those arrested for participating in the rioting in Washington, D.C., in April, 1968. The facts have been extracted from D.C. Bail Agency records. Those cited are black persons, unless otherwise specified.

FILE CLERK, CIVIL SERVICE: A GS-2 ($4,231 a year), he is single and has completed high school. He is nineteen, was born in Atlanta, but moved to Washington after one year. On probation from an assault conviction, he was charged with destroying private property.

TRASH COLLECTOR: He earns $73 a week, is twenty-six, single, and has completed the sixth grade. Born in North Carolina, he has lived in Washington for one and a half years and has been arrested fourteen times for drunkenness. He was charged with attempted burglary.

UNEMPLOYED: Twenty years old, married with no children, he has finished the second grade. He was born in Pennsylvania and has lived in Washington for three years. He has no record and was charged with looting.

PIPELAYER: He earns $3.75 an hour, is nineteen years old, married, with one child, and has completed high school. He was born in North Carolina, and has lived in Washington for a year and a half. He has a record for drunkenness, and was charged with looting.

UNEMPLOYED: She is forty-one, married, and has four children. She has lived in Washington for thirty-nine years and has no record. She has completed the ninth grade and was charged with looting.

OFFSET DUPLICATOR: He is twenty-seven, married, and has three children. He earns $118 a week, has lived all his life in Washington, and has no record. He was charged with looting.

SHOE STORE MANAGER: He earns $75 a week, is separated from his wife, has two children, and has completed the ninth grade. He has a record for sale of narcotics, assault, possession of firearms, possession of number slips, and many disorderly charges. He was charged with looting.

CLERK, CIVIL SERVICE: He earns $109 a week, is married, with no children. He has lived all his life in Washington and has a record of disorderly conduct. He was charged with looting.

TRASH COLLECTOR: He is self-employed, estimates his income at $400 a month, is fifty-four, separated, and has eight children. Born in South Carolina, he has lived in Washington for twenty-three years. He was charged with robbery in 1955. The charge was looting.

ASSISTANT SOCIAL WORKER: She earns $103 a week, is divorced, and has two children. She graduated from high school, is thirty-seven, and has lived all her life in Washington. She has a disorderly-conduct record and was charged with looting.

LABORER: He makes $133 a week, is twenty-seven, separated, with two children. He completed high school. Born in South Carolina, he has lived in the District for six years. He has a record of charges of disorderly conduct and was charged with possession of stolen property.

STOCK CLERK: He earns $66 a week, is single and nineteen years old. He is a freshman in college, was born in the state of Washington, and has been in the city of Washington for seven months. He has no record and was charged with looting.

HOSPITAL ORDERLY: His annual income is $4,700. He is married, with one child, and has completed the tenth grade. He has lived all his life in Washington and has no record. He was charged with looting.

FREE-LANCE PHOTOGRAPHER: He makes from $75 to $100 a week, is separated, and has one child. He completed the ninth grade, was born in Chicago, is thirty-seven, and has lived in Washington for thirty-five years. He has a record in California for petty larceny, and was charged with carrying a dangerous weapon.

BARBER: He earns $40 a week, is nineteen, married, with one child. He completed the eleventh grade, was born in Washington, has no record. He was charged with looting.

DISHWASHER: He makes $50 a week, is sixty-eight, widowed, and had one child. Born in Virginia, he completed the second grade and has two drunk and disorderly counts. He was charged with looting.

GROCERY CLERK: He makes $1.40 an hour, is single and twenty-four years old. Born in Washington, he has a juvenile record of petty theft and disorderly conduct. Looting was the charge.

GARBAGE COLLECTOR: He makes $90 a week, is married, with no children. His age is unknown and he has no criminal record. He was charged with looting.

BRICKLAYER: He gets $90 a week, is married, with three children, and has completed the eleventh grade. He is twenty-five, was born in Washington, and has no record. He was charged with looting.

RESTAURANT OWNER: He has $100-a-month profits, is forty-six, married, with six children. He completed high school, is white, was born in Italy, and has been in Washington for twenty-seven years. He has no record and was charged with looting.

SECRETARY: Her income is $6,490 a year. She is twenty-seven, married, and has no children. Born in North Carolina, she has lived in Washington for twenty-five years. She completed high school and had some business college work. She has no record and was charged with looting.

GUARD: He makes $140 a week, is thirty-two, married, with one child. He completed the ninth grade, has lived in Washington for fifteen years, and has no record. Charged with looting.

BAKERY FOREMAN: He makes $150 a week, is twenty-nine, separated, with one child. He was born in North Carolina, graduated from high school, and has been in Washington for eight years. He has a 1967 record for carrying a concealed weapon. He was charged with looting.

CONSTRUCTION LABORER: He makes $130 a week, is twenty-four, married, and has four children. He completed the tenth grade, was born in North Carolina, and has been in Washington for seven years. He has no record and was charged with looting.

BRICKLAYER: He gets $197 a week, is twenty-nine, separated, and has four children. He was born in South Carolina and finished the seventh grade. He has lived in Washington for twenty-five years and has a juvenile record of housebreaking. He was charged with looting.

UNEMPLOYED: She is eighteen, single, and has completed the ninth grade. She is pregnant, has no record, and has lived all her life in the District. She was charged with carrying a dangerous weapon.

PORTER, DISHWASHER: He has two jobs, with a total income of $420 a month. He is thirty-two years old, married, and has three children. He finished the tenth grade and has lived in Washington for ten years. He has a record of five charges of disorderly conduct and was charged with looting.

Index